WORLD RELIGIONS

WORLD RELIGIONS

DR. IAN BARNES

Eagle Editions

A CARTOGRAPHICA BOOK

Published by Eagle Editions Ltd
11 Heathfield
Royston
Hertfordshire SG8 5BW

Copyright © 2007 Cartographica Press

This edition printed 2007

ISBN: 978-184573-356-8

QUMROTW

This book is produced by
Cartographica Press
6 Blundell Street
London N7 9BH

Printed in Singapore by
Star Standard Industries Pte Ltd

CONTENTS

INTRODUCTION

The religions of the world demonstrate the story of human thought and artistry whether it be the Palaeolithic bison painted in the caves of Lascaux in France or Michelangelo's fresco in the Sistine Chapel of the Papal Palace complex in Rome's Vatican City.

Defining religion is very difficult. From the very earliest times to the present day, humanity has shown its deepest beliefs about the universe, mortal life, death and morality through worship, symbol and ritual. Different faiths have utilised all manner of tools to embellish particular rituals: architecture, sculpture, writing, painting, music and priestly clothing.

Primitive belief systems, such as those in the Pacific and Africa, show a mixture of the spiritual, the dream world, reali-ty and the material world, where humanity and nature are blended together. Arguably, this 'spirit' world can also be found in Japanese Shintoism.

The contemporary world is moved by a variety of religions. Christianity and Islam have the most followers; approximately 29% of the world population are Christian and 26% are followers of Islam. However, if knowledge of ancient organised faiths is combined with an understanding of all other existing religions, including Hinduism, Buddhism, Taoism and Sikhism, in spite of utterly different cultures that are totally unconnected, we find an incredible number of similar beliefs.

Arguably, irrespective of any named doctrine, humanity has always been concerned with sacred, spiritual and mystical influences on life.

RELIGIOUS SYMBOLS
From left to right: the Latin Cross of Christianity; the Star of David of Judaism; the Omkar (Aum) of Hinduism, Buddhism, Sikhism and Jainism; the Star and Crescent of Islam; the Khanda of Sikhism; and the Ying-yang of Confucianism, Buddhism and Taoism.

EARLY ORGANISED RELIGIONS

The years 8000 BC to 6000 BC witnessed the growth of large communities in the river valleys of the Nile, Tigris, Euphrates, Indus and Huang Ho. The development of agriculture, together with irrigation systems and the use of flood plains next to rivers systems and deltas, facilitated cereal cultivation, which allowed small settlements to expand into sizeable urban communities. Millet and then rice were grown in China, while wheat and barley were cultivated extensively in Mesopotamia and India.

Around 3500 BC, cities spontaneously grew up first between the Tigris and the Euphrates, a little later in Egypt and then in the Indus valley. China enjoyed a parallel development at around about the same time.

THE GROWTH OF KNOWLEDGE

With agricultural improvements came improvements in transport. Improved sea communications allowed the spread of trade, ideas and knowledge. Records began to be kept using a variety of scripts. The Sumerians employed a cuneiform script that was used later by other Mesopotamian civilisations, as well as in Hittite Anatolia.

In China, pictograms have been discovered in the Shang sites at An-yang, a script that records the continuity of Chinese civilisation, despite long periods of war and political turmoil.

The commencement of the second millennium BC saw the Indus Valley being invaded by the Indo-Europeans who swamped and destroyed the Harappan culture, while spreading their faith by armed force and through Vedic texts written in their Sanskrit language.

As urban societies developed, supported by extensive agriculture, specialist occupations were created in metal-work, ceramics, textiles, and religion. Priesthoods, temples, rituals, faiths, and sacred texts emerged together with divine kingship as evidenced by the pharaohs of Egypt. Early Neolithic concerns about the relationship between humans, nature and gods gave way to more philosophical questions of immortality, life in the hereafter, suffering and pain.

THE RISE OF GOD KINGS

Over a considerable period of time Mesopotamia saw a sequence of civilizations: Sumerians, Akkadians, Babylonians, Assyrians, Hurrians, Hittites and Semitic groups. These all developed state religions, temple complexes, mythologies and creation stories, many of the values of society being contained in works such as the Sumerian *Epic of Gilgamesh*.

Organised religions spread beliefs and values through society, while providing temple administrations through a priesthood. Such activities necessitated food redistribution during poor harvests. The Ziggurats at Uruk demonstrated the bond between heaven and earth in a culture that regarded kings as having divine right. By 2000 BC Hittite kings were serving as supreme high priests.

THE EGYPTIANS

In the Nile Valley, the annual river floods that re-fertilised the soil brought agricultural stability, which generated a food surplus, which in turn could support a highly developed society. Local and state gods were often worshipped in magnificent, ornate temples. The pharaoh was depicted and believed to be an incarnation of the god Horus and was responsible for a cult that included all the other gods.

Egyptian concern about the afterlife is demonstrated by the importance that was given to mummification and the elaborate burials in the pyramids. This led to the growth of a major industry centred around death, body preservation and the afterlife.

Interestingly in a multi-god society, Pharaoh Akhenaten (1353 to 1336 BC) and his wife, Nefertiti, briefly made the sun god Aton, the sole national god. Aton was represented by a sun-disk whose rays ended in human hands. This early approach to monotheism did not last.

CHINA

In Shang China, the nobility ran the bureaucratic state and officiated in the rituals of ancestor worship together with a diverse set of fertility and nature cults. No priest caste emerged to combat the growth of a Taoist belief system that advocated complete withdrawal from worldly affairs into contemplation.

THE INDUS VALLEY

The Indus Valley civilisation was very sophisticated. Cities had drainage systems and some houses even had bathrooms and toilets linked to this. These people seemed to worship mother-goddesses, but their religion was swept away by the Indo-Europeans, the Aryans, who were the ancestors of the Hindus.

EUROPE

Elsewhere, western Europe witnessed megalith-building cultures, exemplified by stone circles, henges, menhirs, and megaliths (standing stones). Examples can be found in France, Malta, and throughout the British Isles with the Ring of Brogar in the Orkneys and Stonehenge. However, in terms of size and extent, these are totally overshadowed by the spectacular temples at Carnac in Brittany, France. Whether these megaliths were ritual gathering places, astronomical observatories or burial sites, the culture soon vanished leaving no records except its stone heritage.

HOUSES OF ETERNITY
The pyramids at Giza were built, like all Egyptian pyramids, as halfway houses between this world and the afterlife. The Ancient Egyptians' belief in life after death meant that they prepared their Pharaohs for the life to come with immense care. They believed that by carefully preserving a dead body, they would also preserve its spirit and give it everlasting life. A tomb was, therefore, a 'house of eternity'.

SPREAD OF RELIGIONS IN THE CLASSICAL WORLD

C. 600 *BC* – *AD* 600

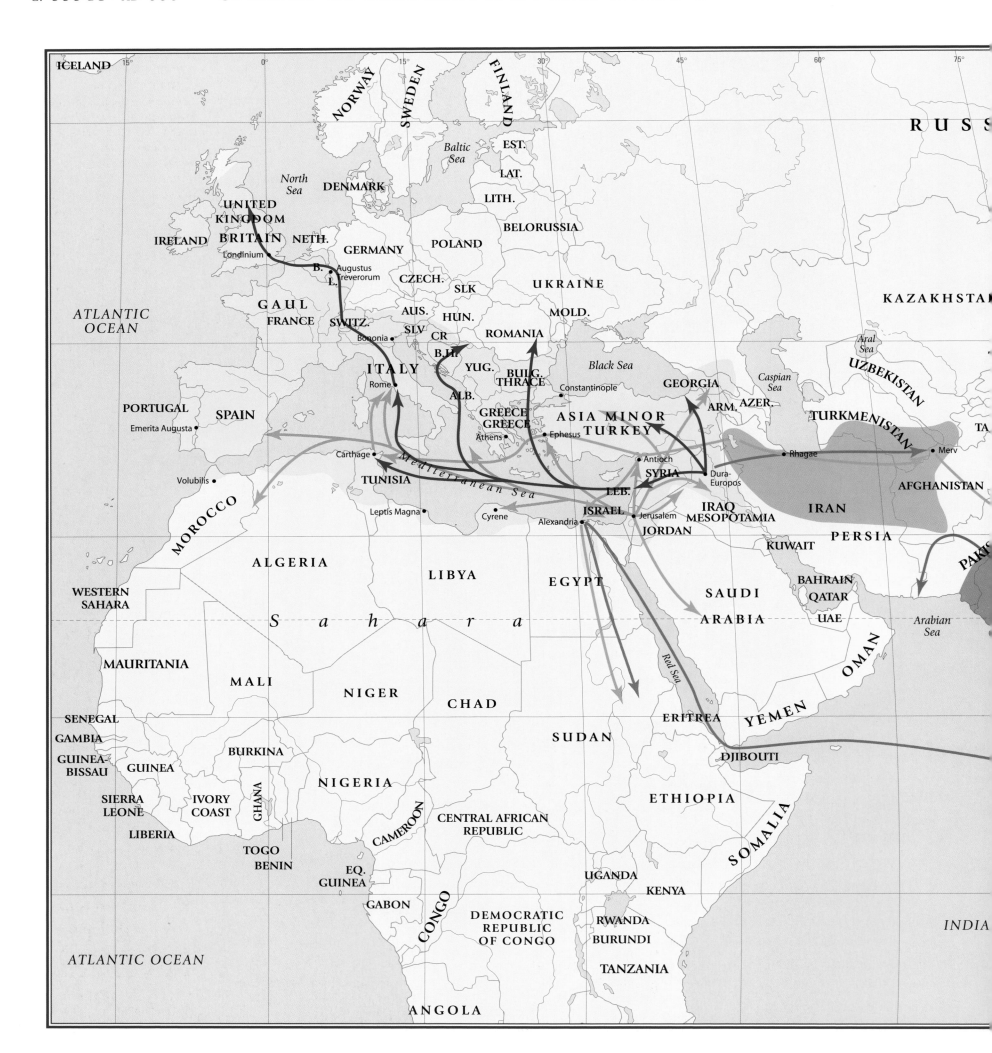

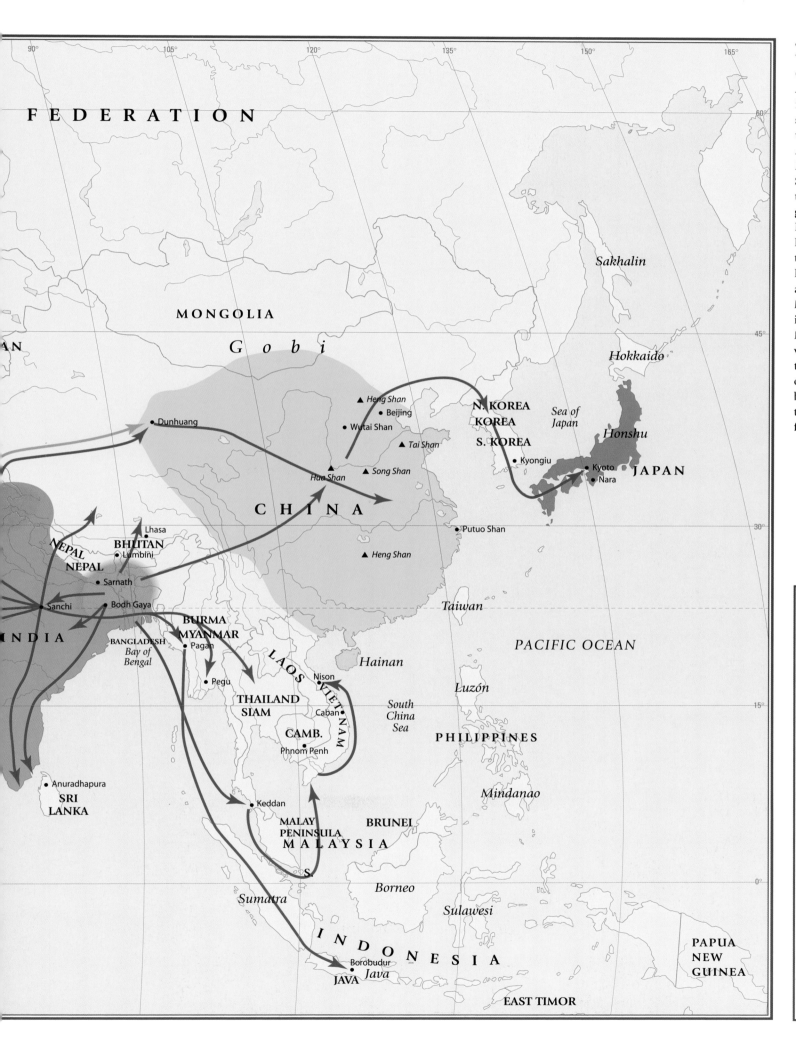

As different religions developed it was natural for them to spread. This often happened as trade routes developed. The Mahayana Buddhists from Northern India followed the Silk Route through Central Asia to China and took their religion with them. Similarly Hindu merchants from the Eastern Region of India took their religion to the Malay Peninsula, the South China Sea and on to Indo China. Meanwhile Judaism was spreading throughout the Mediterranean region through voluntary settlement or deportation. The most successful export was Christianity. Once it became the official religion of the Roman Empire, it faced no further rivals in that region.

SPREAD OF RELIGIONS
IN THE CLASSICAL
WORLD
c. 600 BC–AD 600

- Christianity by 600 AD
- Buddhism heartland
- Mahayana Buddhism
- Hinduism
- Confucianism/Daoism
- Shintoism
- Zoroastrianism
- → Dispersion of the Jews to 500 AD
- → Spread of Christianity
- → Spread of Buddhism
- → Spread of Hinduism
- → Spread of Mithraism
- → Spread of Manichaeism
- ▲ Mountains sacred to Daoism

9

PREDOMINANT RELIGIONS 2000

THE WORLD'S PREDOMINANT RELIGIONS

Christianity is by far the most predominant religion in the world accounting for around 2.1 billion, or 33 per cent of the world's population. There are around 1.3 billion Muslims in the world, accounting for around 21 per cent of the population. The majority of these are Sunni Muslims, but in Iran and Iraq the Shi'ite Muslims are in the majority. The third most popular religion is Hinduism with around a billion adherents, of whom about 905 million live in India and Nepal. Buddhists and Chinese Traditionalists both have just under 400 million and each accounts for around 6 per cent of the world's population.

PREDOMINANT RELIGIONS

- Catholic Christianity
- Orthodox Christianity
- Protestant Christianity
- Sunni Islam
- Shi'ite Islam
- Other Islamic groups
- Hinduism
- Judaism
- Chinese Religion
- Theravada Buddhism
- Mahayana Buddhism
- Vajrayana Buddhism
- Nature Religions
- Other Religions

ARCTIC OCEAN

NORWAY
SWEDEN
FINLAND
EST.
LAT.
LITH.
UNITED KINGDOM
DENMARK
NETH.
GERMANY
POLAND
BELORUSSIA
FRANCE
B.L.
CZECH
SLK.
UKRAINE
SWIZ.
AUS.
HUN.
MOLD.
SLO.
ROMANIA
ITALY
CRO.
YUG.
BULG.
Black Sea
GEORGIA
ALB.
GREECE
ARM.
AZER.
Caspian Sea
SPAIN
TURKEY
SYRIA
LEB.
TUNISIA
Mediterranean Sea
ISRAEL
JORDAN
IRAQ
MOROCCO
ALGERIA
LIBYA
EGYPT
KUWAIT
BAHRAIN
QATAR
UAE
SAUDI ARABIA
Sahara Desert
Arabian Peninsula
MALI
NIGER
CHAD
SUDAN
DJIBOUTI
ERITREA
YEMEN
OMAN
BURKINA
NIGERIA
IVORY COAST
GHANA
TOGO
BENIN
CENTRAL AFRICAN REPUBLIC
ETHIOPIA
SOMALIA
CAMEROON
EQ. GUINEA
GABON
R. CONGO
UGANDA
KENYA
RWANDA
BURUNDI
DEMOCRATIC REPUBLIC OF CONGO
TANZANIA
ANGOLA
MALAWI
ZAMBIA
ZIMBABWE
MOZAMBIQUE
MADAGASCAR
NAMIBIA
BOTSWANA
SWAZILAND
SOUTH AFRICA
LESOTHO
Cape of Good Hope

RUSSIAN FEDERATION
Siberia
KAZAKHSTAN
MONGOLIA
UZBEKISTAN
KYRGYZ.
TURKMENISTAN
TAJIK.
IRAN
AFGHANISTAN
PAKISTAN
Himalayas
NEPAL
BHUTAN
INDIA
BANGLADESH
MYANMAR
CHINA
N. KOREA
S. KOREA
JAPAN
Arabian Sea
Bay of Bengal
SRI LANKA
LAOS
THAILAND
VIETNAM
CAMB.
PHILIPPINES
MALAYSIA
BRUNEI
Sumatra
Borneo
INDONESIA
EAST TIMOR
PAPUA NEW GUINEA
SOLOMON ISLANDS

PACIFIC OCEAN

INDIAN OCEAN

AUSTRALIA

NEW ZEALAND

SOUTHERN OCEAN

0° 15° 30° 45° 60° 75° 90° 105° 120° 135° 150° 165° 180° 165° 150°

75°
60°
45°
30°
15°
0°
15°
30°
45°

HINDUISM

By 1700 BC the Indus Valley civilisation was disintegrating. This might have been as a result of climatic change, or the destruction of the irrigation systems caused by rivers re-routing themselves. Whatever the case, there was ineffectual resistance to the Indo-European Aryans who arrived over the course of several hundred years. Some came as invaders and some came as migrants, but the end result was the spread of Aryan culture throughout northern India, with influence in central India and maybe even the south. The incomers spread their language and culture together with their Vedic religion, which absorbed local traditions to create proto-Hinduism.

The Indo-Europeans were probably related to nomadic tribes that originally roamed the steppes west of the Ural Mountains. Venturing into Eastern Europe and northern Iran, they advanced into India. The Sanskrit hymns of India's oldest document, the Rig Veda, provide evidence of the settlement movement. No mention is made of the people of the Aryan migration, but there are several references to battles with the

INDIAN TEMPLES
The Hindu temples at Khajuraho in the heart of central India were constructed between 950 and 1050 AD during the reign of the Chandel Empire. The exteriors of the temples are decorated by highly erotic figures. Some say that these figures symbolise the emptiness of human desires, while others argue that they were to prepare the boys, who lived in hermitages, for their later role as 'householder'. Whatever the explanation, the difference between these temples and the sober and sometimes austere religious buildings of the Western religions is obvious.

inhabitants of what remained of the old Indus Valley civilisation. These victims were designated as dasa, a word eventually coming to mean 'slaves'. The Aryans regarded them as inferior on account of their darker colour and less angular features. They became untouchables, symbolising the beginnings of the caste system. A Vedic hymn to Agni, the fire-god, mentions: 'Through fear of you the dark people went away, not giving battle, leaving behind their possessions, when O Vaisvanara burning brightly for Puru and destroying cities, you did shine.'

Vedic civilisation consolidated itself until it came into contact with Buddhism. Between 321 and 297 BC, the Mauryan Empire, the first Indian Empire, was established by Chandragupta. Chandragupta was a Buddhist, although he later converted to Jainism and starved himself to death. His grandson, Asoka, was also very interested in religion and enlarged the empire's territories into southern India. This was at the cost of much suffering and death and Asoka was so disgusted by all the cruelty that he renounced armed force and adopted Buddhist principles which he then spread throughout his realm. Buddhism was given official recognition, but Hinduism was still permitted. Soon after Asoka's death the Mauryan Empire disintegrated.

Eventually, a new empire grew up, founded by Chandra Gupta. This became known as the Gupta Empire and lasted from AD 320 to 480. Regarded as the high point of Hindu culture, the Gupta era brought the development of the decimal system of notation, much Sanskrit and Hindu art and exported the Hindu faith along the trade routes into south-east Asia. Brahmin writers, such as Yanjavalkya, defined social and legal relationships, advocating the admission of documentary evidence into legal proceedings. Hindu philosophers flourished and advocated Yoga to concentrate the mind and body until spiritual release was obtained. Books were written including the Kamasutra, the Sakuntala, and Vikramorvasi. The Gupta period established the supremacy of the Brahmin priest who kept pre-eminence by absorbing popular beliefs into Hinduism. Sanskrit literature and the caste system reinforced this power.

From early times, Hinduism spread to Siam, Burma, the Malayan peninsula, the Indonesian islands, Cambodia and central Vietnam. In Bali, Hindus now comprise ninety-five per cent of the population and have developed their own particular variant of Hinduism. During the nineteenth century Hindus migrated to Indian Ocean islands and built up a significant presence in Natal in South Africa, Surinam, British Guiana, Trinidad and Fiji, where the majority of the population is Indian.

The 2001 population census in the United Kingdom showed 558,342 Hindus living in England and Wales, most living in the Midlands and London. About 2 million have reached North America, with about 1.5 million living in the United States. The Hindus and other Indians who migrated to East Africa suffered particularly badly, especially in 1972 when Idi Amin gave all Asians 90 days to leave Uganda. Most of them found refuge and new lives in England.

The early Vedic principle of animal sacrifice was abhorrent to many people and this led to the foundation of a new faith, Jainism that dates back to the sixth century BC. Although there are certain similarities with both Hinduism and Buddhism, Jainism attempts not to harm any living being and seeks the perfection of the soul. To kill any person is considered to be unimaginably abhorrent and it is the only religion that requires all of its members to be vegetarian. Jains have become important traders and business people. An important community lives in Leicester, England, where the first Jain temple in Europe was consecrated.

Hinduism has had a considerable impact on Indian politics. The first Indian Prime Minister, Jawaharlal Nehru, used Hinduism in political discourse, and Gandhi sought communal harmony by appealing to its beliefs. Gandhi was subsequently murdered by a member of Hindu Mahasabha, an extreme Hindu movement, that was bitterly opposed to Gandhi's advocacy of co-operation with India's Muslim inhabitants. Although it has subsequently changed its name, this organisation continues to attack mosques and to riot against Muslims to this day.

ZOROASTRIANISM

Zoroastrianism is an ancient faith that grew up in rural rather than urban areas and was the main faith of Persia prior to the spread of Islam. After the accession of Cyrus II the Great in 559 BC, Persia became a world power in the form of the Achaemenid Empire. The empire spread and this continued during the rule of Xerxes I who ruled from 519 to 465 BC. By this time the Empire ranged from Persia into Egypt, Anatolia and Thrace. The Empire was destroyed by Alexander the Great in 330 BC, but Zoroastrianism survived.

Over hundreds of years, the religion adapted and developed with the addition of immortals who followed Ahura Mazda and demons who followed evil. Zoroastrianism came to be symbolised by a struggle between good and evil, with prayer and meditation in front of fire. In AD 226, an ancient Iranian family, the Sassanids, overthrew the existing Parthian Empire in Persia. At their most powerful, the Sassanids controlled an empire from the Tigris and Euphrates

reaching to the Indus Valley and the River Oxus and from the Aral and Caspian Seas in the north to the Arabian Sea and Persian Gulf in the south. Under Shapur I from AD 240 to 271, Zoroastrianism became the official faith imposed upon the empire's subjects. Eventually, Shapur attacked other faiths, persecuting and massacring Jews, Buddhists, Hindus, Manichaeans and Christians.

Manichaeism was a religion that tried to include all known religious traditions in its faith. In spite of persecution it became widely popular throughout a huge area, between AD 300 and 500. Christians regarded Manichaeans as heretics. The religion spread as far as China. It became the official religion of the Uighurs in Sinkiang where it lasted for a century until the collapse of the Uighur state. It had percolated into China, where it was persecuted into the seventeenth century until it eventually died out.

Within the Sassanian Empire, Zoroastrianism spawned two spin-off groups: the Mazakdists, who maintained that the spirits of good and evil were entirely separate in origin; and the Zurvanists, who believed that the spirits of good and evil were essentially the same being. The Sassanid Empire collapsed under the impact of Islam, and eventually, after several revolts, many Zoroastrian refugees fled to India where they are known as Parsees, the Persians. These refugees have modified Zoroastrianism and no longer worship fire. Instead, they revere fire as a manifestation of the divinity of Ahura Mazda. The Zoroastrian community, some 90,000 to 150,000 strong is located mainly in Gujarat with a stronghold in Mumbai. It is a unified community whose wealthier members have established schools, making the Parsees one of the most educated groups in India. Under British imperial rule, the Parsees were renowned for their education and trading skills. Several families have achieved world renown in industry. The most noticeable is the Tata family, which owns the fifth largest steel industry in the world, has interests in the motor industry and founded Tata Airlines, which was eventually acquired by the Indian government as Air India.

Some five thousand Parsees live in Pakistan's Karachi, a few thousand have found homes in South Asia and North America and between 5,000 to 10,000 live in the UK, mainly in London. Remnants inhabit areas surrounding the old Zoroastrian heartland in eastern Iran, but the strength of Muslim influence in the country has made it almost extinct. One well-recorded aspect of Zoroastrianism is the belief that fire, earth and water should not be contaminated. Thus, Parsee dead are placed in towers of silence, which are circular buildings some six metres high where bodies are eaten by vultures.

JEWISH LAW AND CUSTOMS
The Talmud is a record of rabbinic discussions pertaining to Jewish law, ethics, customs and history. The Talmud has two components: the Mishnah (c. 200 AD), the first written compendium of Judaism's Oral Law; and the Gemara (c. 500 AD), a discussion of the Mishnah and related writings that often ventures onto other subjects and expounds broadly on the Tanakh, the Hebrew Bible. The terms Talmud and Gemara are often used interchangeably. The Gemara is the basis for all codes of rabbinic law and is much quoted in other rabbinic literature. The whole Talmud is also traditionally referred to as Shas (a Hebrew abbreviation of shisha sedarim, the 'six orders' of the Mishnah).

JUDAISM

The early history of Judaism and the Semitic Jews' relationship with God commenced when God called Abraham and his family to leave the city of Ur and journey into Canaan. Here his son Isaac was born and was circumcised after eight days; a ritual symbolising a covenant with God. Some Semitic tribes travelled to Egypt where they became state slaves, as described in Exodus. Pharaoah Rameses II, who ruled from 1290 to 1224 BC, used them to build a new capital and a store-city at Pithom. The prophet Moses guided the Jews to freedom in the deserts of Sinai. After wandering for many years, the Jews reached Mount Sinai where God gave Moses the Ten Commandments. These Commandments are the most famous of the 613 God-given laws. This extra covenant is the cornerstone of the Hebrew national identity and religious unity. In Jewish eyes, by accepting this bargain, the acquisition of Palestine was quite legitimate, despite the land already being settled.

The Hebrew migration into Canaan occurred at a time when the Near East was in ferment caused by weaknesses in the Egyptian and Hittite empires and the invasions of Sea Peoples, some of whom settled in southern Canaan. These Philistines giving the area its name of Palestine. A recurring theme in Biblical history shows that Canaan, situated as it was between different empires, could only develop its own interests in times of an international power vacuum. There was such a vacuum when Jacob led the tribes into Canaan and managed to crush any resistance from the indigenous people before apportioning the conquered lands amongst the twelve tribes of Israel. Once these nomadic groups had entered Canaan, they were exposed to the culture of settled farming communities, fortified towns, alternative modes of living and different gods.

The twelve tribes possessed no real political organisation and tended to fight the Philistines separately until Saul was chosen as king around 1030 BC. Judges recounts how various leaders sought to save the Hebrews from alien influences that were threatening them though trade, economic prosperity, inter-marriage with the Canaanites and the worship of fertility cults and the god Baal. The Bible records the changes of fortune of the Hebrews. When their mountain lands, corresponding to today's West Bank, were invaded and partially occupied, the Hebrew leadership realised that lack of tribal unity worked against Jewish political survival. The desire for a strong leader emerged and Saul was chosen because he was a notable warrior in campaigns against the Philistines. Samuel, who was the spiritual leader of the Jews, eventually anointed him king.

Saul defended the Israelites against all surrounding enemies including Moabites, Ammonites, Edomites and people from Philistia or Zobah. Saul's kingdom developed a measure of security but the king disobeyed God's will and Samuel began looking elsewhere for a replacement. David emerged as an alternative leader, which led to a power struggle for the monarchy. As a result the weakened Hebrews were attacked by the Philistines and Saul was killed.

David united the rival Hebrew tribes. His reign was marked by numerous wars and territorial gains. David nominated Solomon as his successor, who built a Temple in Jerusalem as a permanent home for the Ark of the Covenant. Up until then the Ark, containing all the holy scrolls, had moved around from place to place. This new Temple symbolised the transition from a nomadic to a settled style of Hebrew culture. The kingdom gained riches from the trade routes crossing its territory. Solomon was noted for his ability to mediate the divisive forces and tribal enmities within his country. When he died this unity collapsed.

The first three kings of Israel – Saul, David and Solomon – were southerners from Judah, a region often at loggerheads with the northern Hebrew tribes. After Solomon's death these northern tribes formed a separate kingdom of Israel. Israel later became larger, richer and militarily more powerful than Judah, but was more volatile politically.

The emergent kingdoms of Israel and Judah faced the Egyptian and Assyrian empires, each of which coveted the strategically important Palestinian lands. In 732 BC, Israel was destroyed by the Assyrians and its people exiled to other lands. Nevertheless, the loss of some tribes to exile has never diminished the belief that all Abraham's descendants will return to Jerusalem one day. Similarly, Judah was extinguished by 587 BC when the Babylonian King Nebuchadnezzar captured Jerusalem and deported thousands of important Hebrews, leaving only the poorest people behind.

The Babylonian Exile witnessed many Jews settling permanently in Mesopotamia. Later a new Persian Empire allowed some to return to Jerusalem under Nehemiah. The remaining Jews in Palestine were coerced back under the rule of God and the Temple rebuilt. However, the Promised Land became part of the domains of Alexander the Great's successors, the Ptolemaic and Seleucid dynasties. When the Greeks started to attack elements of the Jewish faith, and circumcision in particular, this triggered the Maccaabean revolt in 167 BC. The Jewish lands were freed and ruled by the Maccabee or Hasmonean dynasty until 39 BC, when the Judaean state became a target of Roman foreign policy.

Under the Roman Empire, Herod the Great became the king of Judaea. He was a much hated man. There were two Jewish revolts during the time of Roman rule. The first occurred in AD 66 when a Zealot uprising captured territories around Galilee and Caesarea, overthrowing the government in Jerusalem. Titus, the Roman Emperor's son, led a successful campaign against the insurgents, re-capturing Jerusalem and burning down the Temple, but leaving the Western Wall intact. This is now known as the Wailing Wall and is a sacred place to all Jews. The remaining Zealots retreated to Herod's palace at Masada where they were besieged. Ultimately, the rebels committed suicide rather than suffer capture, slavery or worse at Roman hands. Masada, excavated by Israeli General Yigael Yadin in the 1960s, remains an icon of Jewish resistance.

A second Jewish revolt occurred in AD 132, led by Simeon bar Kokhba, but was crushed by AD 135. The Babylonian Exile, the sale of Jewish prisoners after the two Jewish revolts, and the movement of Jewish traders created a spreading Jewish population throughout the known world. As the Roman Empire expanded, Jews were numerous in Mesopotamia, Egypt, especially Alexandria, Cyprus, Anatolia, Greece, Italy, Spain, Marseille in France, and north of the Alps in Germania. In all Jewish communities their particular rules made it easy to distinguish them from their host peoples. As minority groups, these strangers were sometimes victimised and attacked and discriminated against.

This geographic spread of Jewish people eventually led to them living in all lands ruled by Christians and Muslims. Islam spread rapidly after Muhammad moved to Yathrib in AD 622. By AD 750, Islam controlled Spain, North Africa, the Near East, Arabia and Persia. Jews had to pay an extra poll tax and wear designated clothing but were allowed judicial freedom and religious toleration. This stability allowed them to develop their culture while debating their newly written religious commentaries, the Mishnah and Talmud.

In Christian Europe, there is a long history of discrimination. Jews have been blamed for Christ's crucifixion, accused of using the blood of Christian children at the Feast of Passover and being responsible for the Black Death. Persecutions were common. Massacres occurred in the Rhineland as knights slaughtered fifty thousand during their travels on the First Crusade (1095). Jews were expelled from England in 1290 and from Spain in 1492. Some Jews in Europe were allowed to live in places where they could be controlled more readily, and these ghettos existed throughout Europe. Friendless, vast numbers fled to Poland in the thirteenth century where they were welcomed. European Jewry has witnessed the birth of a mystical movement in the Kabbalah and the creation of Hasidism whose radical ideas were opposed by conservative believers known as Mitnagdim. Other divisions appeared such as that between Ashklenazi and Sephardi. The former have European origins and speak Yiddish while the latter come from Spain, North Africa and Muslim lands and speak Ladino. These differences are characterised by different religious rituals.

The eighteenth and nineteenth centuries saw the emancipation of European Jewry starting with Holy Roman Emperor Joseph II's Edict of Toleration in 1781 and ending in England in 1890 with full freedom extended to the Jews. The Jewish Enlightenment followed with Reform Judaism being established. In Eastern Europe, however, the situation was parlous with substantial pogroms and even a state-sponsored anti-Semitism in Russia. France saw anti-Jewish hostility during and after the Dreyfus Affair. The east European violence resulted in some two million people emigrating to the USA. The French experience resulted in Theodore Herzl's Zionism and the desire to build a Jewish home in Turkish-controlled Palestine.

Jews in America have established themselves since the early nineteenth century, building a Reform community differing from the Orthodox one. Now successfully integrated, over six million Jews play a significant part in United States and are prominent in many industries. The number of Jews in New York State, for instance, makes them a powerful politically force. Major Jewish concerns are those of assimilation and inter-marriage and the diminution of the next Jewish generation; this is a concern also expressed in Britain.

The Zionist movement sought to buy land in Palestine for Jewish colonists who were determined to build an ideologically driven society. The use of Hebrew was demanded as an

KING DAVID
This image from Gentile da Fabriano's *Prophet David* depicts the second king of the united Kingdom of Israel. David is shown as a righteous king – although not without fault – as well as an acclaimed warrior, musician and poet (he is traditionally credited with the authorship of many of the Psalms). His life and reign, as recorded in the Hebrew Bible's books of Samuel (from I Samuel 16 onwards) and Chronicles, have been of central importance to Jewish and Western culture.

integrating tool and many East European Jews were prominent in the settlement of the Yishuv, the Jewish community that reached some 500,000 people by the outbreak of World War II. Britain responded to Arab resentment by restricting Jewish immigrants to this British League of Nations' mandate.

The Second World War witnessed the Holocaust, the attempt by the German Nazis to systematically eradicate the Jewish population of Europe. Following German conquests in Poland, Jews were forced into slave labour and concentration camps. In total there were some six million Jewish deaths as a result of: systematic gassing in death camps such as Auschwitz; murders by special Einsatzgruppen, paramilitary groups operated by the SS; as a result of disease; or simply by being worked to death.

By 1945, much of the European Jewish population and its communities had been destroyed. Those Jews living in Palestine attacked British authority, which had failed to deal with Arab-Jewish hostility. Britain responded by pulling out of the region, leaving the political mess to the United Nations, which devised a partition plan. The Jewish state of Israel, surrounded by antagonistic Arab states, was declared in 1947. The initial war of independence has been followed by other wars in 1956, 1967 and 1973, plus Israeli invasions of the Lebanon. Israel remains a state but is yet to sign peace with some of its neighbours. The entire region is bedevilled by mutual hostility.

Over thirteen million Jews live worldwide, with the largest community living in the United States wand sizeable groups outside Israel living in Canada, France, the UK, Argentina, South Africa and Australasia.

THE TEMPLE MOUNT
The Temple Mount, situated in the Old City of Jerusalem, is the holiest site for Judaism and is one of the most contested religious sites in the world. The Jewish Temple in Jerusalem stood there: the First Temple (built c. 967 BC, destroyed c. 586 BC by the Babylonians), and the Second Temple (rebuilt c. 516 BC, destroyed in the siege of Jerusalem by the Romans in 70 CE). According to a commonly held belief in Judaism, it is to be the site of the final Third Temple, to be rebuilt with the coming of the Jewish Messiah.

Known to Muslims as the Noble Sanctuary, it is also the site of two major Muslim religious shrines, the Dome of the Rock (built c. 690), shown in the top-left portion of the image, and the Al-Aqsa Mosque (built c. 710).

BUDDHISM

After the Buddha's death in around 483 BC, missionaries spread his word into the Greek-controlled kingdoms that had been established around Taxilia after Alexander the Great's death. This city became a Buddhist university and a jumping off point for missionaries penetrating Central Asia.

During the Mauryan Empire in India, King Asoka, 269 to 232 BC, converted to Buddhism, founding new monasteries and teaching the values of social welfare, tolerance, honesty, compassion, mercy, non-violence, non-extravagance, non-acquisitiveness and kindness to animals. He even built animal hospitals. He built the Great Stupa of Sanchi, a Buddhist monument, and begged people of all faiths to respect each other. Buddhist missionaries were despatched to Syria, Egypt, Greece, Macedonia and Epirus. Although these achieved little success, others who went to Burma and Ceylon fared better. Asoka's good works included the foundation of hospitals, supplying medicines, creating roadside shade by planting trees and groves and building rest houses. Buddhist precepts were engraved on rocks and pillars. Asoka's death in 232 BC led to his empire's division between his sons and Buddhism declined leading to the victory of Brahmin Hinduism in India. Meanwhile the invasions of the Yueqi and Sakas reduced northern India to chaos.

The Yueqi and Tocharians created the Kushan Empire during the first and second centuries AD and its power extended from northern India into Central Asia. The Kushans were key in diffusing Buddhism along the commercial Silk Road, converting the Central Asian oasis towns, and exporting Buddhism into China. The Kushans were very important in the development of Mahayana (Great Vehicle) Buddhism. This religious variant viewed the personal pursuit of nirvana as selfish and believed that one should become a bodhisavatta, an advanced spiritual being who would delay entry into nirvana in order to help others along their similar journey, thus allowing good karma to build up. Buddhism later travelled from China to Korea and Japan. A Tantric variant of Buddhism moved through Tibet to Chinese Xian and Therevada Buddhism reached China via Ceylon, Burma, and Vietnam, while Hinayana and Mahayana Buddhism entered Indonesia. Therevada or Hinayana (Small Vehicle) Buddhism was very conservative, adhering strictly to Buddha's word. Tantric Buddhism is renowned for its use of ritual and meditation, and known for the use of the mandala, the symbolic map of the spiritual world, and mantra, or sacred words used to focus meditation. Tibetan Buddhism, otherwise known as Vajrayans (Diamond Vehicle), developed the prayer wheel and entered Japan as the Shingon sect. Buddhism arrived in Cambodia, Siam and Laos much later, with the Khmers blending this faith with Hinduism.

The Khmer kings created a vast Cambodian state with its famous temple at Angkor Wat, the most illustrious of one thousand temples crammed into 200 square kilometres. Angkor Wat comprises a huge rectangle containing concentric walled courtyards surrounding five lotus-shaped towers, displaying a mixture of Hindu and Buddhist cultures. This temple symbolised Cambodia's vision of Hinduism but matters changed under King Jayavarman VII, 1181 to 1219, who favoured Buddhism and built many temples. The Thais founded the state of Sukhothai in the north in 1238, but only when their southern kingdom of Ayutthaya was founded did the Thais adopt Buddhism as a state religion.

AD 841 Chinese Emperor Wuzong began a programme of persecution against Buddhists, Nestorian Christians and Zoroastrians. Following his death in 846 the anti-Buddhist laws were repealed, but by then 250,000 monks and nuns had been forced into lay life, 150,000 slaves had been seized and some 4,600 monasteries and 40,000 small churches and shrines had been destroyed or re-utilised. Buddhism suffered immeasurably but the Chan School, later Zen in Japan, was best able to survive since its adherents relied on introspection and individual meditation rather than religious paraphernalia. Chan teaches that Buddha's enlightened nature is within all people and that inner calm and peace should be sought solely through meditation without the need for good works, prayer and asceticism. The importance of Chan Buddhism is the affirmation that enlightenment is a direct and personal experience. Chan Buddhists reject religious trappings such as religious texts, statues, and other images.

Another major Buddhist institution was the Tiantai school founded in the Zhejiang mountains by Zhiyi, who lived from around 531 to 597. His sermons were written down, becoming the Lotus Sutra. This school investigated the entire canon of Buddhist scriptures and sought to draw together the Ninanaya and Mahayana schools. This eclecticism was a sincere attempt to recognise all variants of Buddhism as part of a Chinese drive to obtain religious harmony. However, the creation of other schools and sects displays some failure in the Tiantai endeavour, but at least there was no apparent development of sectarian violence. Tiantai's great success was its emphasis on the universal accessibility of enlightenment. Tiantai also travelled to Japan, building a base on Mount Hiei near Kyoto. There, Tiantai digested some Shinto influences and Tantric Buddhist methods to become contemporary Tendai Buddhism.

In Japan, Buddhism attracted numerous adherents with monasteries and temples fighting each other and developing warrior monks noted for the use of the lethal weapon, the naginata. A renowned force was the fifteenth century Ikko-ikki, a Buddhist reform movement that drew its support from the masses. Warrior-monk armies were so large that feuding samurai families sought their alliance in war. In the sixteenth century, Odo Nobunaga (1534-1582) sought to unify Japan and fought lords and militant Buddhist communities, eradicating and massacring them, especially in the notorious destruction of the Tendai monastery of Enryakuji in 1571.

Since its formative years, Buddhism has existed in countries that faced the onslaught of western imperialism, Japanese invasion and the spread of communism. India, the home of Buddhism, saw the virtual disappearanace of the faith under Muslim invasions and the foundation of the Mughal Empire. Since World War II, Therevada Buddhism has returned to flourish in the Maharashtra region near Mumbai and in Madhya Pradesh and Karnatika. During his lifetime Bhimrao Ambedkar, 1891 to 1956, converted 3.5 million Hindu untouchables, and in so doing established a significant Buddhist group.

In the 1970s, Cambodia suffered the cruelties of Pol Pot's administration, during which the whole monastic population, along with many other elements of Cambodian society, was slaughtered in the Killing Fields. In Indonesia Therevada Buddhism is practised and the Mahayana variant is the preferred version of Chinese migrants. Elsewhere, communism has attempted to eradicate Buddhism. Tibet suffered a grievous blow when China invaded in 1950. Thousands of temples and monasteries were destroyed, with monks and nuns thrown out of their homes. Their spiritual leader, the Dalai Lama, was forced to flee to India. Since Buddhism is a constituent of the Tibetan identity, it continues to face constant harassment and suspicion.

In the West, people have toyed with many eastern faiths and Buddhism is one of the most popular. Tibetan refugees have established communities in the West and their Tantric form of Buddhism is followed by about half of western devotees. Other western groups follow various Buddhist forms such as Chinese Mahayana, Shingon, and Zen. Western countries have several hundred Buddhist monastic centres and meeting places. The Tara Buddhist Meditation Centre, at Ashe Hall in Derbyshire, England, practises Kadampa Buddhism, which aims to promote inner peace, love, and wisdom. Kadampa Buddhists have opened a World Peace Hotel in Malaga, Spain and another is due to open in Tuscany, Italy.

One enduring image of Buddha is Milofo, the Laughing Buddha, formerly Maitreya, the Future Buddha. This cheery, rotund figure is a common Chinese character, depicting prosperity, wealth, luck and plenteous food. He is a being content in his reclining position, often surrounded by happy children, and is taken to represent a large Chinese family.

BUDDHA
In Buddhism, a Buddha is any being who has become fully awakened (enlightened), and has experienced Nirvana, a state that is free from any negative desires and emotions such as lust, anger or craving. The founder of Buddhism, Siddhartha Gautama, was a spiritual teacher from ancient India. He is universally recognised by Buddhists as the Supreme Buddha of our age.

CONFUCIANISM

Confucius enjoyed a career as assistant minister of justice in the state of Lu but realised that his efforts bore no fruit in policy. He left Lu at the age of fifty-six and travelled to Wei, before visiting other feudal states. Frustrated at his advice being ignored, he returned to Wei in 489 BC and finally to Lu in 484 BC when he was sixty-eight. He then devoted his life to teaching and died in 479 BC. Apparently, his travels showed him the human condition of greed, dishonesty, irresponsibility, selfishness and social indifference. Thus, Confucius was driven to construct a utopian world where rituals and customs ordered society. Established hierarchies of rulers and ruled, men and women, aristocracy and common people and parents and children would ensure social harmony. Confucius revered filial piety and generational respect of youth to parents and the aged. "Being good as a son and obedient as a young man is, perhaps, the root of a man's character." (Analects 1:2)

The success of Confucianism can be attributed to its founder's successors, most noticeably Mencius, 370 to 300 BC and to Xunzi, 310 to 237 BC. Mencius travelled and taught like Confucius and even studied with the master's grandson. He developed the concept of the Mandate of Heaven and actually told rulers of its truth. Heaven conferred kingship on a virtuous ruler but could withdraw it from an evil, weak or corrupt king. In a version of early democracy, the will of Heaven was equated with the will of the people, who would live harmoniously under a beneficent ruler but would rebel and overthrow a tyrannical oppressor.

During the Han era, Confucianism became the state raison d'être, and was modified for utilisation under the Sung by Zhu Xi, AD 1130 to1200. His version of Confucianism became the state doctrine of Korea under the Yi dynasty from 1392 to 1910. Confucianism imbued Japanese feudalism but the occupying powers, after 1945, sought to eradicate its ethics from the educational system.

Confucian rituals exist within Chinese expatriate communities in East Asian countries. It coexists with other beliefs and is incorporated into the Vietnamese Cao Dai sect, which utilises Confucius along with Buddha, Jesus, Muhammad, Sun Yixian, and even Joan of Arc, who collectively preach that God will protect people from materialism.

CONFUCIAN TEACHINGS
Confucianism is an ancient Chinese ethical and philosophical system originally developed from the teachings of the early Chinese sage Confucius. Its focus is primarily on non-religious secular ethics, secular morality, as well as the cultivation of the civilised individual. Confucianism views the moral and cultural refinement of the individual as the best way to secure world peace. In addition to worshipping Confucius, Confucian temples also honoured the 'Four Correlates', the 'Twelve Philosophers' and other disciples and Confucian scholars throughout history.

TAOISM

Taoism emerged as a religion drawing inspiration from its meditative philosophy. Incorporated in it are strands of folk religion and techniques for increasing longevity and immortality; alchemy and magic combine in Taoism in the search for the elixir of life. Taoists thought that a red cinnabar tablet helped immortality and many Chinese emperors actually poisoned themselves with mercury-based concoctions. However, the search for immortality did create a health system that even today utilises a regular breathing and concentration programme. Taoism interacted with Buddhism after the fourth century AD and many Buddhist concepts were expressed in Taoist terms. The religion constructed a body of religious texts and a monastic-style organisation. The two faiths eventually competed for the support of the Chinese and between 842 and 845 one Taoist emperor of the Tang dynasty actually persecuted Buddhism for religious and economic reasons. Some romantic Taoists even claimed that Laozi, maybe a mythical Taoist teacher, had journeyed to India to become the Buddha. Later Buddhist teachings fused with Taoism to create Zen Buddhism and in around 1191 this export to Japan formed the Rinzai sect. Japanese Zen masters were also important in introducing Neo-Confucianism to the Tokugawa regime between 1603 and 1868.

Taoism has developed several schools of thought and allied itself with political movements such as the Yellow Turban peasant rebellion in the Shandong province of China and was instrumental in breaking the Han dynasty in AD 220. Chinese emigration has spread Taoism and its belief system, which has percolated into Korea as well as Japan. The religion was severely damaged during the Chinese Taiping rebellion between 1850 and 1864 and few Taoist monasteries existed when the Communists swept through China in 1949. The Cultural Revolution between 1966 and 1976 caused Taoism to vanish but the religion still exists in Hong Kong, Singapore, Malaysia, Indonesia, and Taiwan and is creeping back into China. The restoration and rebuilding of temples is prevalent and Taoists are lobbying for compensation for damages incurred under Mao Zedong's rule. Taijiquan is practised by many Chinese ensuring that Taoist breathing exercises, which cultivate energy (known as qi, or chi), still bring harmony with the Tao.

CHRISTIANITY

Jesus Christ was born in around 6 BC and was crucified some time around AD 30. He was about 30 when he began his religious ministry and this lasted for a mere three years. His teachings were legitimised by Old Testament prophecies of Isaiah and Jeremiah. His radical sermons to Jewish audiences angered conservative elements, which ultimately led to his subsequent crucifixion. A fundamental belief of Christianity is that Christ died for the sins of the people and that on the third day after his death he rose from the dead and subsequently ascended into Heaven. St. Peter and St. Paul were two leading early evangelists who spread Christian teaching amongst non-Jews.

At the time of Christ, Palestine was a province of the Roman Empire but was ruled by Herod the Great, followed by his sons. The Pax Romana, the 150-year period of relative peace in the Roman Empire, allowed Paul to undertake missionary journeys and these are recorded in his letters and in the Acts of the Apostles. He moved through Syria, Anatolia, and Greece, and maybe reached Spain. In spite of early persecution, Christianity gradually spread throughout the Roman Empire, making it largely Christian by the fourth century. In AD 313 Emperor Constantine decreed tolerance for the faith and gave his active support to Christianity, being baptised himself in AD 337. The first Christians were found amongst the expatriate Jewish population of the Mediterranean Region and early Christian communities mirrored their Jewish origins. During the expansion of Christianity, the strongest faith communities developed in Egypt, Cyrene, Carthage, Massilia (Marseille), Rome, Thrace, Anatolia, Cilicia, and Judaea.

In 331, in the hope that Christianity would unify the empire in a religious sense, Constantine moved his capital from Rome to Constantinople. This relocation caused a split between Greek-speaking Christians in the east and Latin-speakers in the west. The western empire was gradually disintegrating under attacks by migrating, Ostrogoths, Visigoths, Vandals and Franks. These peoples had established kingdoms throughout Western Europe and the bishop of Rome became instrumental in defending the interests of Christians in Italy against the controlling Ostrogothic kingdom. The Roman bishops became paramount among western bishops, enjoying the title of Pope. Eventually the Franks, established in France, befriended the Pope against the Visigoths and their king, Clovis, converted to Christianity in 496, thereby generating a link between the Frankish monarchy and a succession of Popes, culminating in the relationship with Frankish King Charlemagne in the 9th century.

Christianity spread throughout Western Europe, strengthened by the universal use of Latin in ecclesiastical and judicial matters. Thus, Latin Christianity moved even further from the Greek Orthodox Christianity and its Byzantine Empire. The two varieties of Christianity were completely separated by the Schism of 1054. Previously, in 800 the coronation of Charlemagne had tied the Pope to a Christian Emperor in the West, an ally who would protect the Church, the Vatican and the Papal States.

After Charlemagne's death, Western Europe disintegrated into a collection of new states, where local and feudal lords became virtually independent, constantly fighting each other in order to increase their landholdings and wealth. The Church wanted to pacify Christians and the Crusades provided an outlet for Christian idealism. The chief reason given was the liberation of Jerusalem, but it also provided an opportunity to acquire new lands and the riches of the east. Pope Urban II, 1088 to 1099, saw the Crusades as an opportunity to end private warfare between the feudal lords of Europe, by proclaiming peace in Western Christendom; by extending the Peace of God, which prohibited attacks on civilians; and the Truce of God, which outlawed war on holy days.

Another Christian institution was the Holy Roman Empire, a successor to Charlemagne's empire. It is generally accepted as commencing with Emperor Otto I, who ruled from 936 to 973.

CHRISTIAN SACRIFICE
This image of El Greco's *Christ Carrying the Cross* shows the Christian Messiah contemplating his fate on Earth. Central to the teachings of Christianty is the idea of sacrifice, that Jesus laid down his life so that his followers might be absolved of their sins. His subsequent ascendancy into the Kingdom of Heaven gives hope to Christians that eternal life will be theirs.

THE CHRISTIAN BIBLE
The Bible is the holy book of Christianity. Consisting of the Old Testament and the New Testament, the Bible is a collection of books written by Jewish prophets and early followers of Christ. The Guttenberg Bible, shown below, was the first book produced by a printing process, allowing for the first time the mass production of the Bible. This innovation was crucial in the development of Protestantism, with greater access to Christian teachings undermining the power of priests and introducing Christians to a more personal relationship with God.

Although the Pope crowned each emperor, this imperial status did not always generate authority over a group of largely independent states, especially after the Ottonians. When Otto I was crowned, he controlled the five traditional German duchies of east Francia, a collection of border states, or marches, and associated states like the kingdoms of Burgundy and eventually Italy. The Ottonian dynasty utilised the Christian Church by founding and endowing monasteries, which supported learning and provided administrators. Instead of relying on the nobility, the Ottonians granted lands to the Church. The bishops, abbots, and abbesses (capellani) were loyal servants rendering military service while acting as royal representatives of the Emperor. Although the Holy Roman Emperor claimed Italy, much remained under the control of the Popes, but Papal rule was generally more notional than real.

By the sixteenth century, the Roman Catholic Church required reform, especially after the Great Schism in the early fifteenth century when at one time there had been three rival Popes. Additionally, magnates in the Holy Roman Empire were consolidating their power and land holdings and exerting authority over the clergy. Although the growth of universities added prestige to a host prince, they also became the foci of critical thought. Scholars attacked the idea that man needed a priest to mediate between him and God, especially when the Church had grown so corrupt. This led to a protestant reformation under the leadership of Martin Luther, Huldrich Zwingli and John Calvin. Anti-clericalism was rife in Germany but the Reformation spread to France, England, Scandinavia and amongst the Hussites in Bohemia. France witnessed religious conflict between Protestant Huguenots and Roman Catholics that was only ended by the 1598 Edict of Nantes, which granted certain rights to Protestants. Enmity between Protestants and Roman Catholics caused the Thirty Years' War between 1618 and 1648, which engulfed the Holy Roman Empire. In some areas like Pomerania the population was reduced by over sixty per cent as a result. Religion permeated the English Civil war, which commenced in 1642 and ended with the execution of King Charles I in 1649. When the new French king, Protestant Henry IV of Navarre, converted to Catholicism this certainly aided a religious settlement that lasted until King Louis XIV pruned Nantes by the Edict of Fontainebleau.

When Christians entered the Americas, the Spanish and

Portuguese were exhorted by the Pope to freely convert the indigenous populations. However, disease and brutality severely reduced the native populations of the Caribbean, Central America and the Andes mountains. In Canada, Jesuit missionaries strove to convert Native Americans with little success. The Atlantic seaboard of English America witnessed a plethora of Protestant groups settling as colonists. The Pilgrim Fathers who arrived at Cape Cod in 1620 were Puritan separatists, mainly Congregationalists, and they comprised the dominant religious tradition for two centuries. English Roman Catholics went to Maryland in 1632 and William Penn founded Pennsylvania for the Quakers in 1681. These colonists simply wanted to establish townships where they could practise their faith; they were not interested in evangelising the Native Americans. Other groups entering North America were Dutch Calvinists, Baptists and the Anglican Church of England; Lutheranism was introduced by Swedish colonists.

The United States has given birth to one Christian Church, the Mormons, or Church of Jesus Christ of Latter-Day Saints. This was founded by Joseph Smith, who lived from 1805 to 1844. He gathered converts who built communities in Ohio and Missouri before being hounded out. After Smith was murdered, Brigham Young led the Mormons to Utah territory, where they founded Salt Lake City.

Christianity has more adherents than any other world religion and within the faith are many traditions and sects. Throughout history Christianity has been involved in politics. In more recent times churches played an important role in the 1960s Civil Rights campaigns in the USA and evangelical forces have linked up with Roman Catholicism on ethical issues such as abortion and stem-cell research. Also in recent times the collapse of communism in Eastern Europe and the Soviet Union has led to a revival of the Eastern churches. The re-opening of monasteries and the restoration of liturgical practices have revived the faith and helped rebuild a religious sense of identity. Religious pilgrimages also continue, with Lourdes in France and Fatima in Portugal being particularly popular.

ISLAM

Prior to Islam, people in the Arabian Peninsula had different religions and served several gods. For instance, the powerful Meccan Quraysh tribe had a religion with three goddesses, Al'Uzza, Manat, and Allat. The region had been subject to the influence of numerous outside forces over the years, but was gradually developing a linguistic unity and moving towards a system of family gods or one god that ruled supreme. There were, of course, other religions. Jewish tribes lived in Yathrib and in the Yemen and there were Christians in northern Arabia

and in Najran on the route from Yemenite Sana to Mecca.

The birth and spread of Islam not only changed Arabia, but changed the world. Islam was revealed through Muhammad's prophetic teachings, the verses now being contained in the Koran. Allah's, or God's, word demanded a return to morality, personal accountability and belief in one creator and one God. Muhammad wanted an Islamic community to unite the Arabian tribes. He generated hostility from conservative, pagan merchants and was forced to flee from Mecca to Yathrib (Medina). Here, he arbitrated local disputes, became a military commander and established Islam. Now that he was a man of some power, he used this to get his revenge on the pagan merchants of Mecca by cutting its trade routes. By 630 the Arabian tribes had converted to Islam and Mecca surrendered. Two years later Muhammad was dead, but he had laid the foundation of an Islamic empire.

Islamic expansion was aided by the military and religious enthusiasm of the caliphs, Muhammad's successors. The Byzantine and Persian empires were weak and readily succumbed to this new religious power, whose adherents demanded booty and land. Additionally, considerable

ISLAMIC PRAYERS
Prayer forms a crucial part of a Muslim's daily life. Followers of Islam pray at five set times every day. Muslim prayers all follow the same format, including set phrases and movements. A Muslim can pray anywhere, but most devout Muslims choose to pray with fellow believers in a mosque. Prayer is always directed in the direction of the Kaaba shrine in Mecca, the holiest place in the Islamic world.

population movements expelled the Persian ruling classes in Bahrain and Oman. Caliph Abu Bakr, 632 to 634, presided over the complete conquest of Arabia with advances into Iraq and Syria where Theodore, brother to the Byzantine emperor, suffered defeat at Ajnadain in 634. Omar, the second caliph, 634 to 644, made Arabia a theocratic state. His invasion of Syria saw the Byzantines totally defeated at Yarmuk in 636, followed by the capture of Damascus, Jerusalem and northern Syria. Next, the Persians were defeated at Qadisiya in 637, Ctesipon in 637, Jalula in 637 and finally at Nehavend in 642. Arab incursions into Egypt in 639 saw a further Byzantine defeat at Heliopolis in 640. Egypt surrendered in 642 through the mediation of Cyrus, the Alexandrine patriarch.

Despite disputes over the succession to the caliphate, imperial expansion continued under the Omayyids and their successors. Arab fleets fought at Cyprus and Rhodes while Arab troops, reinforced by subjugated peoples, acquired Kabul, Bukhara, and Samarkand, finally conquering Transoxiana and the Indus lands of Seistan and Makran by 711. North Africa witnessed the capture of Carthage in 698 with Tariq ibn Ziyad crossing the Strait of Gibraltar, defeating the Visigoths and

acquiring Spain. An invasion of France in 732 failed, with the Arabs being defeated at Poitiers by Charles Martel. An attack on Constantinople in 718 failed and the Islamic state was left to count its loot, turning Medina into a centre of Koranic learning and removing the capital to Damascus.

Harun-al Rashid's Abbasid caliphate from 764 to 809, saw the fullest extent of early Islamic expansion. His tolerance saw the spread of Islamic mysticism (Sufism). Meanwhile, Islam's adherents had split into two camps, the Sunnis and the Shiites, who fought over who should be caliph. Their enmity continues to this day.

The Islamic world suffered from internal divisions. Spain spawned an independent dynasty and independent polities emerged in Morocco and Ifriqiya. Successor regimes emerged: the Buyids in Mesopotamia; the Fatamids in Egypt; the Ghaznavids based in Aghanistan; and the Qaraqanids in Transoxiana.

Elsewhere, the Seljuqs, a nomadic Turkmeni tribe, migrating from central Asia and southeast Russia into the Near East, conquered Persia and established a military sultanate over the Caliphate by capturing Baghdad. The Seljuq Turks threatened Byzantium, conquering much of Anatolia. Their massive defeat of the Byzantine army at Manzikert in 1071 was a factor leading to the First Crusade in 1096. Seljuq military skill started to improve Turkish power in Asia Minor until internal bickering caused its collapse in 1200, except in Anatolia where Seljuq rule continued until the Mongols conquered them in the thirteenth century, after which Anatolia was made a Seljuq tributary.

One power confronting Seljuq expansion was the Fatamid Empire, 909 to 1171. Here a Shiite caliphate was established when the Kutama Berbers in Ifriqiya accepted a claim by Abdallah al-Mahdi to be a descendant of Ali, the original Shiite leader, and Fatima. The Berbers threw off Aghlabid rule in 909 and al-Mahdi inherited their fleets and Sicily. When his reign ended in 934, Fatamid rule ran from Algeria and Tunisia to Tripolitania. Caliph al-Muizz, 953 to 975, expanded the state into Egypt, Syria and Palestine. Fatamid authority penetrated the Hejaz and the emirate of Aleppo but the Seljuq Turks seized most Near Eastern Fatamid lands except for some coastal enclaves like Tyre, Acre and Ascalon. The latter was lost to crusading Franks, as was Sicily, while Salah al-Din (Saladin) finally eradicated Fatamid power in Egypt in 1171.

The sheer expanse of the Islamic world allowed an increase of internal trade, and merchants flourished, despite feuds between rival dynasties. Products from India and China reached Mesopotamia and moved up the Tigris and Euphrates and north into Eastern Europe via the Volga. Commerce moved south across the Sahara to Timbuktu and West Africa, while

PILGRIMAGE TO MECCA
Al-Masjid al-Haram is a large mosque in the city of Mecca and the largest in the world. It surrounds the Kaaba, the place which Muslims turn towards while offering daily prayer, and is considered to be the holiest place on Earth by Muslims. The current structure can accommodate up to 820,000 worshippers during the Hajj period, the annual pilgrimage to Mecca in Islam. Every able-bodied Muslim is expected to go on pilgrimage to Mecca at least once during their life.

traders travelled down the east African coast to Zanzibar and contemporary Mozambique. With goods went religion. For 400 years Muslim sailors and merchants monopolised Indian Ocean trade routes until the Portuguese, English and Dutch arrived in the sixteenth century.

The weakness of the Seljuqs and the internal territorial divisions made it possible for the Christian Crusades to make inroads into the Fatamid Near East. As well as gaining territories around Edessa, Antioch and Jerusalem, successive Crusades linked these territories into a series of petty coastal states while destroying Byzantine power along the way. Salah al-Din, the Muslim Sultan of Egypt, Syria, Yemen and Palestine, was founder of the Ayyubid dynasty. In 1187, a Crusader army was destroyed at Hattin and the Crusader states fell like ripe plums into his hands. Atrocious Christian behaviour during this period damaged Christian-Muslim relations and Byzantium was left incapable of confronting Islam.

The Ayyubid dynasty ended in 1250 when the last sultan was killed by his Turkish Mamluk soldiers. They elevated their own general to the sultanate and the skilful Sultan Baybars defeated Mongol invaders in a historical turning point battle at Ain Jalut in 1260. The Crusader remnants were expelled in 1291 before the Mamluks expanded into the upper Euphrates valley and Armenia. However, the Mamluks failed to produce long lasting dynasties.

In Spain, a Christian Reconquista commenced in the tiny northern Christian kingdoms of Leon, Aragon, Navarre and the county of Barcelona. By 1275, only Granada remained in Muslim hands. The Catholic monarchs, Isabella of Castile and Ferdinand II of Aragon captured Granada in 1492, and in a burst of intolerance expelled Jews and converted Muslims. Muslims had been living there for hundreds of years and although they had been expelled, their culture remained in the Alhambra palace, as well as in the architecture and garden design of the area.

In Africa, Arab influence and Islam moved down the east coast enriching the Swahii city states that were known for slave trading. Portugal seized control of the coast but Oman (Muscat) retained Zanzibar until Britain made it a protectorate and brought an end to slavery. Afterwards, minority Muslim groups (e.g. Ismaelis) from British India migrated to the island. Arab trade penetrated the Sahara, importing gold from the Akan goldfields along the Senegal river. Islamic rituals blended with African customs. The empire of Mali enjoyed an Islamic cultural centre at Taureg Timbuktu and scholars and teachers tweaked the Arabic script allowing teaching in languages like Hausa. West Africa witnessed several jihad movements from the seventh to the nineteenth century. Here, Islamic teachers sought to reform and attack notional Islamic rulers to remove pagan rituals from Islam. New states were created like Futa Jallon in 1725 and Futa Toro in 1776, but the most important was the Sultanate of Sokoto in current Nigeria, founded by Fulani nomads and led by Uthman dan Fodio.

The latest significant Islamic state was the Ottoman Empire. Built when Seljuq and Byzantine waned, the Ottomans entered Europe from Anatolia seizing Greece, Macedonia, Bulgaria and the western Balkans. By the seventh century the Ottomans took Hungary, modern Romania, areas of the southern Ukraine and the Crimea. Many Christian rulers welcomed Turkish suzerainty as a bastion against Habsburg encroachments. Elsewhere, the Ottomans controlled or made tributary the Caucasus, Anatolia, Mesopotamia, Palestine, Egypt and North Africa, and much of Arabia. Expansion continued until Christian powers united to defeat the Ottoman fleet at the Battle of Lepanto in 1571. After this a Mediterranean balance of power emerged.

Another Islamic achievement was the foundation of Timur's (Tamerlane, 1370 to 1405) empire, based upon Iran and Transoxiana. He and his descendants were instrumental in transforming the Central Asian cities such as Bukhara and Samarkand into sophisticated centres of trade and Islamic learning. In India, the Ghurids invaded, establishing Delhi sultanates which Timur's grandson, Babur, seized, founding the Mughal Empire. Aurungzeb, 1658 to 1707, witnessed the empire at its largest extent, an empire which had absorbed several independent dynasties, such as Bengal and Kashmir. Converting many lower caste Hindus, Indian Islam contained many variant cultures readily seen in architecture, literature, and language. The British terminated this empire in 1858.

In more recent times, the already weakened Ottoman Empire was torn apart after World War I. Central Asian oasis states and the Caucasus were swallowed by the Tsarist imperialists, although now all are freed following the collapse of the Soviet Union. Turkey has secularised and seeks entry into the European Union and many countries formerly controlled by western empires are now independent in Africa, Asia, and the Pacific. Several Islamic states possess oil riches, this being a factor in the Iran-Iraq War of 1980 to 1988 and the Gulf War of 1991.

SHINTOISM

Reverence for the spirits emanates from the Japanese people's awe of the wonders of nature created by super-natural powers. Based upon animism, the followers of Shinto believe the ghosts of gods dwell in objects. Even great warriors, leaders and scholars can be made divine. That the Imperial Family were declared divine is not surprising, but this notion was ended by the American occupation of Japan after World War II when church was separated from state. Shinto had been the state

SHINTO SPIRITS
Amaterasu is a sun goddess in Japanese mythology and is perhaps the most important Shinto deity. Shinto, the native religion of Japan, involves the worship of spirits, known as Kami. Some kami are local and can be regarded as the spirit of a particular place, but other ones, such as Amaterasu, represent natural objects and processes. As legend has it, Amaterasu had nothing better to do so she took a long stick and stirred up the Pacific Ocean. The mud that dripped from the wood fell to the earth and the islands of Japan were formed.

religion during the Meiji restoration commencing in 1868.

Shinto has evolved under the influence Confucianism and Taoism, but Buddhism has been its most significant influence. The outcome of this combination of religious beliefs was Shingon Buddhism which claimed that Shinto deities were manifestations of Buddha's divine aspects. The Sun Goddess was identified with Buddha. The Kamakura era, from 1185 to 1333 witnessed the freeing of Shinto from Buddhism when Shinto worshippers claimed that Buddha was a manifestation of Shinto deities. Now, Shinto remains the Imperial Family's faith and many Japanese national holidays originate in Shinto rituals. Shinto has no written literature and most shrines contain sacred objects such as mirrors, the symbol of Sun Goddess Amaterasu, as well as swords and jewels, these being objects of imperial regalia. These are placed on altars where the gods are said to reside.

There are various Shinto subgroups, each sect focusing on a different issue. Faith healing and folk Shinto worship at holy roadside or agricultural shrines is common. Each shrine is reached through the torii, a gateway into the sacred world. Shinto ceremonies can mark different stages in life. Babies and their families thank Shinto gods for the birth and the baby's health and happiness. A second visit occurs at different ages to pray for a good future. Weddings occur using Shinto priests with a sake drinking ritual.

Japan possesses some 80,000 shrines but the most important are Hachimangu, Tenjin, Inari and Jingu. The Jingu shrines are associated with the Imperial Family. Amongst these are Meiji Jingu in Tokyo, Ise Jingu, Heien Jingu in Kyoto, and Atsuta Jingu in Nagoya.

The Yasukuni Shrine in Tokyo commemorates Japan's 2.6 million war dead.

SIKHISM

Sikhism is the fifth largest religion in the world. It was founded in Northern India in the fifteenth century. It is a religious community that has changed in character when confronting the state. The reign of Mughal Emperor Akbar from 1556 to 1605 was marked by a period of religious tolerance. Akbar spoke to the leaders of all major faiths, including the incumbent Sikh guru, Arjan Dev, 1563 to 1606, the man who finished the Golden Temple. The emperor then selected aspects of different faiths to form his own.

During the leadership of gurus Tegh Bahadur, 1621 to 1675, otherwise known as 'Brave Sword' and Gobind Singh 1666 to 1708, conflict grew with the Mughal authorities. Gobind Singh created the Khalsa in 1699, a group of disciples with five religious symbols: kes, (uncut hair); kangha (comb); kara (steel bracelet); kirpan (sword); and kacch (loose trousers). This warrior class comprised an army that defended the faith by attacking the Mughal Empire. The khalsa are deeply religious and the men take the name Singh (lion) and women Kaur (princess).

When the Mughal Empire disintegrated after Emperor Aurangzeb's death in 1707, under attack by the Sikhs, Jats, Marathas and the British East India Company, a Sikh state in the Punjab arose, led by Maharaaja Ranjit Singh 1801 to 1839, with a capital at Lahore. After Ranjit Singh's death, the Sikh state fell into disarray providing the British with the opportunity to annex the Punjab after two hard fought wars in 1845 to 1846 and 1848 to 1849. When India was partitioned a hundred years later in 1949, millions of Sikhs fled from the West Punjab, which became part of Pakistan, into East Punjab in India rather than risk persecution by the new Muslim state. Thousands of the refugees died. Some Sikhs have sought independence from India and this led to violence, climaxing in an Indian army assault on the Golden Temple at Amritsar in June 1984 and the Sikh assassination of Prime Minister Indira Gandhi in October 1984.

Some of the twenty million Sikhs have left India to create communities in Canada, the Near East, East Africa, South-east Asia, the USA, Europe, and Australasia. In the United Kingdom, some 420,000 Sikhs worship at three hundred temples, with the largest communities being in London, Bradford, Leeds, Huddersfield, Birmingham, Coventry and Wolverhampton.

PART 1

HINDUISM AND SIKHISM

THE HISTORY OF HINDUISM stretches back to around 1500 BC, when charioteering Indo-Europeans, or Aryans, invaded northern India bringing their Vedic faith with them, which was superimposed upon the regional faith of the indigenous Harappan civilisation.

Hhinduism is not a polytheistic religion since it recognises only one God, Brahman, but it does involve the worship of numerous gods. The Hindu trio of major gods are Brahman, Vishnu and Shiva, and each of these has a partner. The trio with their partners possess many incarnations, resulting in the Hindu pantheon of an estimated 330 million gods. Hindus worship in temples and own many sacred texts.

Gurmat, or Sikhism as it is known in Western society, was a religion founded by Guru Nanak in the Punjab area of India, and unlike Hinduism is a relatively new religion, founded in the late 15th Century.

Sikhism is open to the adherents of any other faith but remains an admixture of Islam and Hinduism, expressed in the Punjabi language. Sikhs believe in one God who cannot be represented by idols or any other image. God (Waheguru) created the Universe and all its contents and is characterised by being immanent, omnipresent, transcendent and omnipotent. This shapeless, inscrutable God can only be reached by achieving divine self-expression and truth via meditation taught by a Guru.

6000 BC – AD 535 CIVILIZATION IN THE INDUS VALLEY; ARYAN INVASIONS

CIVILISATION IN THE INDUS VALLEY

The fertile lands of the Indus River and its tributaries was home to the earliest known civilisation in South Asia. Covering almost 500,000 square miles this sophisticated culture developed in parallel with Mesopotamia, Egypt and Crete. The region eventually became dominated by two major cities, Harappa and Mohenjo-daro, which seemed to have controlled the region politically. By 2000 BC the region was in decline perhaps driven by climatic change. About this time or shortly after Indo-European invaders or migrants arrived, the Aryans their Vedic texts describe the destruction of forts and cities.

Within these Vedic traditions are the deeply rooted origins of Hinduism. It has become a harmonious conglomeration of ancient traditions and beliefs. Considered by many the world's oldest existing religion, Hinduism has no known founder.

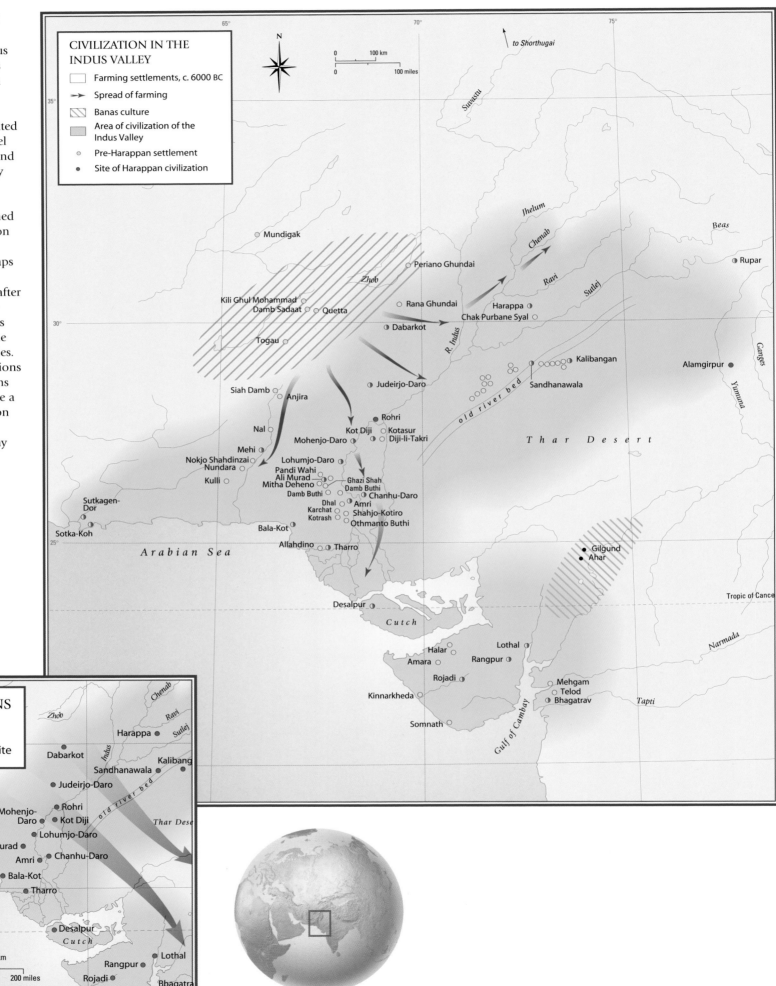

CIVILIZATION IN THE INDUS VALLEY
- Farming settlements, c. 6000 BC
- → Spread of farming
- Banas culture
- Area of civilization of the Indus Valley
- ○ Pre-Harappan settlement
- ● Site of Harappan civilization

AYRAN INVASIONS
- → Ayran Invasions
- ● Major Harappan site

THE GUPTA EMPIRE

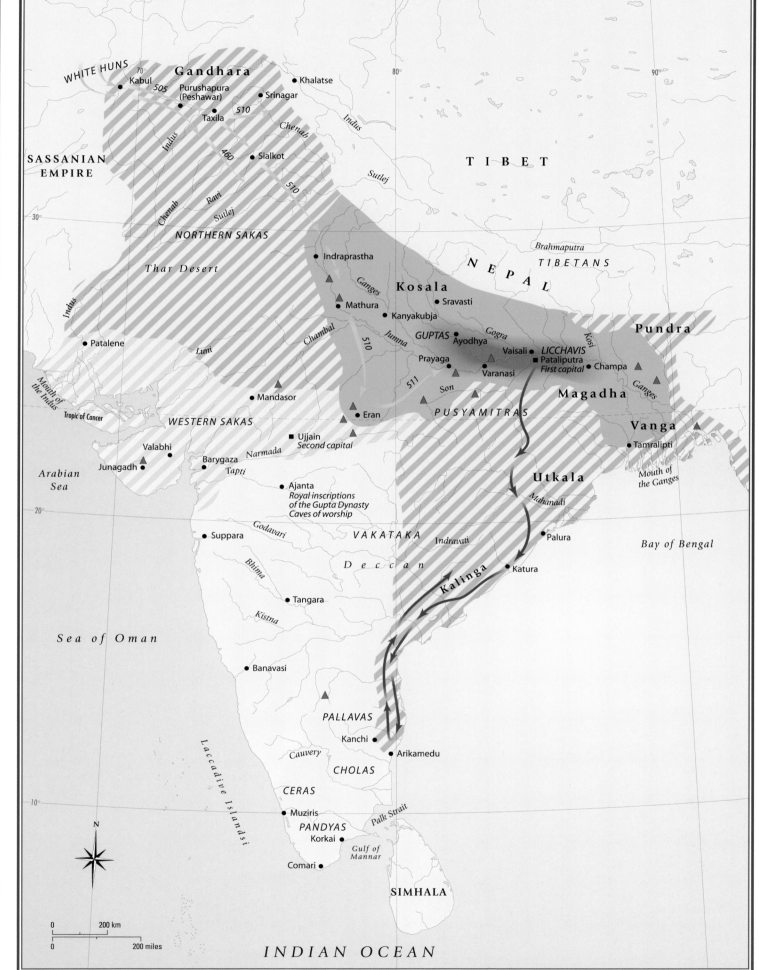

THE GUPTA EMPIRE
AD 320–535

- ▨ Gupta Kingdom of Chandra Gupta I, c. 320
- ▨ Gupta Empire of Samudra Gupta, c. 370 (under direct rule/ tributary)
- ➝ Expeditions of Samudra Gupta (335–375)
- ▨ Tributary territory added to the Gupta Empire by the death of Chandra Gupta II, 414
- ▲ Gupta inscription
- ➡ White Hun (Ephthalites) invasions, 480–511

THE GUPTA EMPIRE

The Gupta elite were religiously eclectic, though Hindu they also made gifts to non-Hindu institutions and may have contributed to the founding of the Buddhist university at Nalanda.

The wide pantheon of Hindu beliefs enabled the Guptas to embrace other religious beliefs whilst remaining Hindu. During the Gupta period, reforming priesthoods enjoyed the support of the ruling class by the direction of tax revenues called 'copperplates', or tamrasasana.

6000 BC – TODAY HINDU DEVOTIONAL SECTS

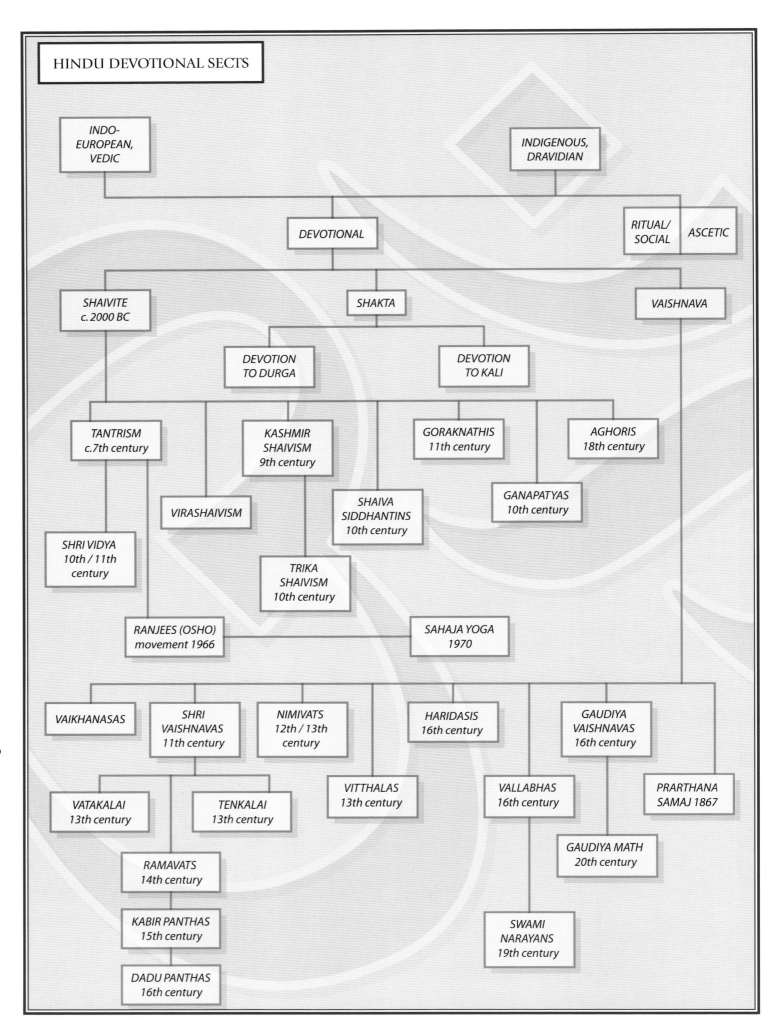

HINDU DEVOTIONAL SECTS

DYNASTY POLITICS AND HINDU TEMPLES

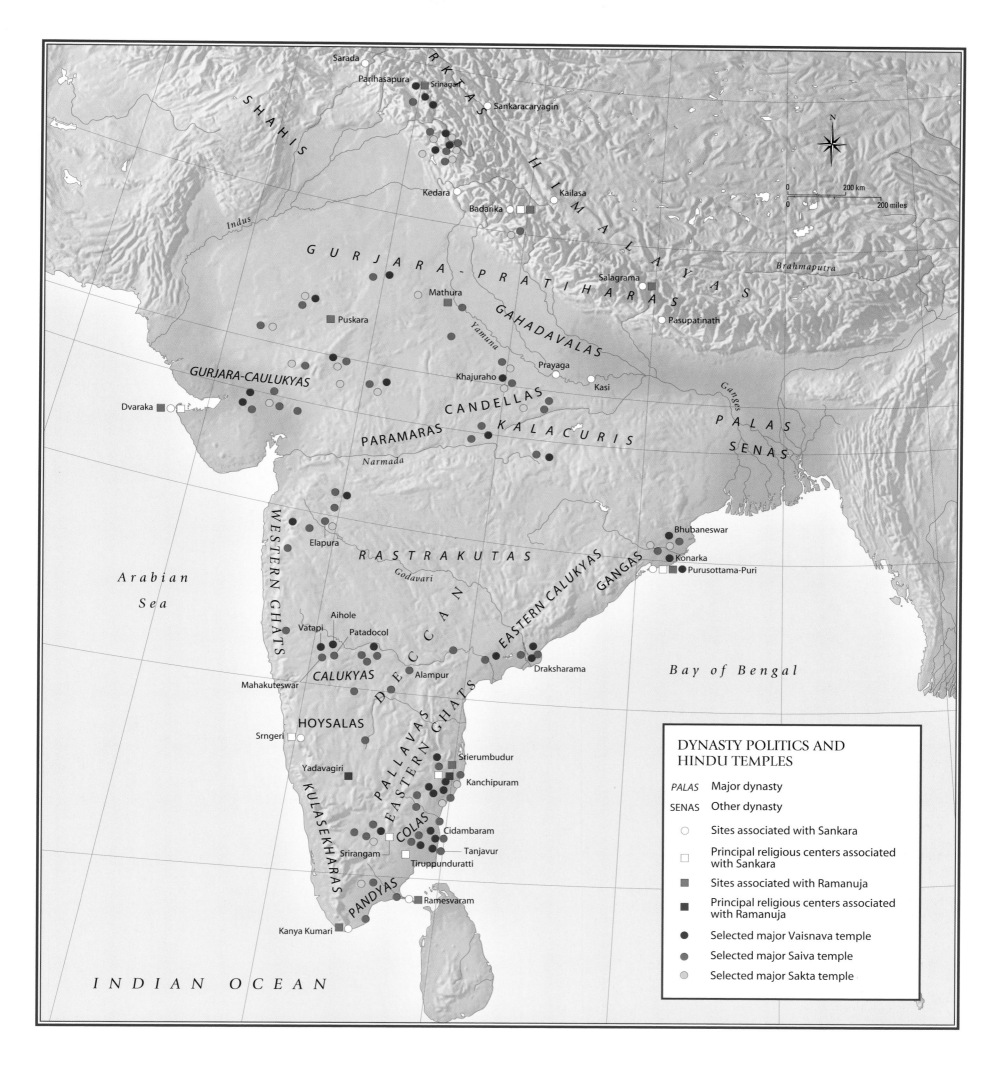

Sarada
Parihasapura
Srinagar
Sankaracaryagin

SHAHIS

HIMALAYAS

Kedara
Kailasa
Badarika

Indus

GURJARA-PRATIHARAS

Brahmaputra

Salagrama

Mathura
GAHADAVALAS
Pasupatinath

Puskara

Yamuna

Prayaga

GURJARA-CAULUKYAS
Khajuraho
Kasi

Dvaraka

CANDELLAS
PALAS

PARAMARAS KALACURIS
SENAS

Narmada

WESTERN GHATS
Elapura
RASTRAKUTAS
Bhubaneswar

Godavari
Konarka
Purusottama-Puri

Arabian Sea

EASTERN CALUKYAS GANGAS

Aihole
Vatapi
Patadocol
DECCAN

Mahakuteswar
CALUKYAS
Alampur
Draksharama
Bay of Bengal

HOYSALAS
Srngeri
PALLAVAS
EASTERN GHATS
Srierumbudur

Yadavagiri
Kanchipuram

KULASEKHARAS
COLAS
Cidambaram

Srirangam
Tanjavur
Tiruppunduratti

PANDYAS
Ramesvaram

Kanya Kumari

INDIAN OCEAN

0 200 km
0 200 miles

N

DYNASTY POLITICS AND HINDU TEMPLES

PALAS Major dynasty

SENAS Other dynasty

○ Sites associated with Sankara

□ Principal religious centers associated with Sankara

■ Sites associated with Ramanuja

■ Principal religious centers associated with Ramanuja

● Selected major Vaisnava temple

● Selected major Saiva temple

● Selected major Sakta temple

HINDUISM IN THE WORLD

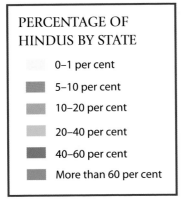

PERCENTAGE OF
HINDUS BY STATE

0–1 per cent

5–10 per cent

10–20 per cent

20–40 per cent

40–60 per cent

More than 60 per cent

HINDUISM IN THE WORLD

Hinduism is still largely concentrated in India though there are communities connected with the old British Empire in Guyana, the United Kingdom and growing communities in Canada and Australia. Indians have also migrated in more recent times to the United States founding Hindu temples across the country. Various Hindu missionaries have also travelled to the USA.

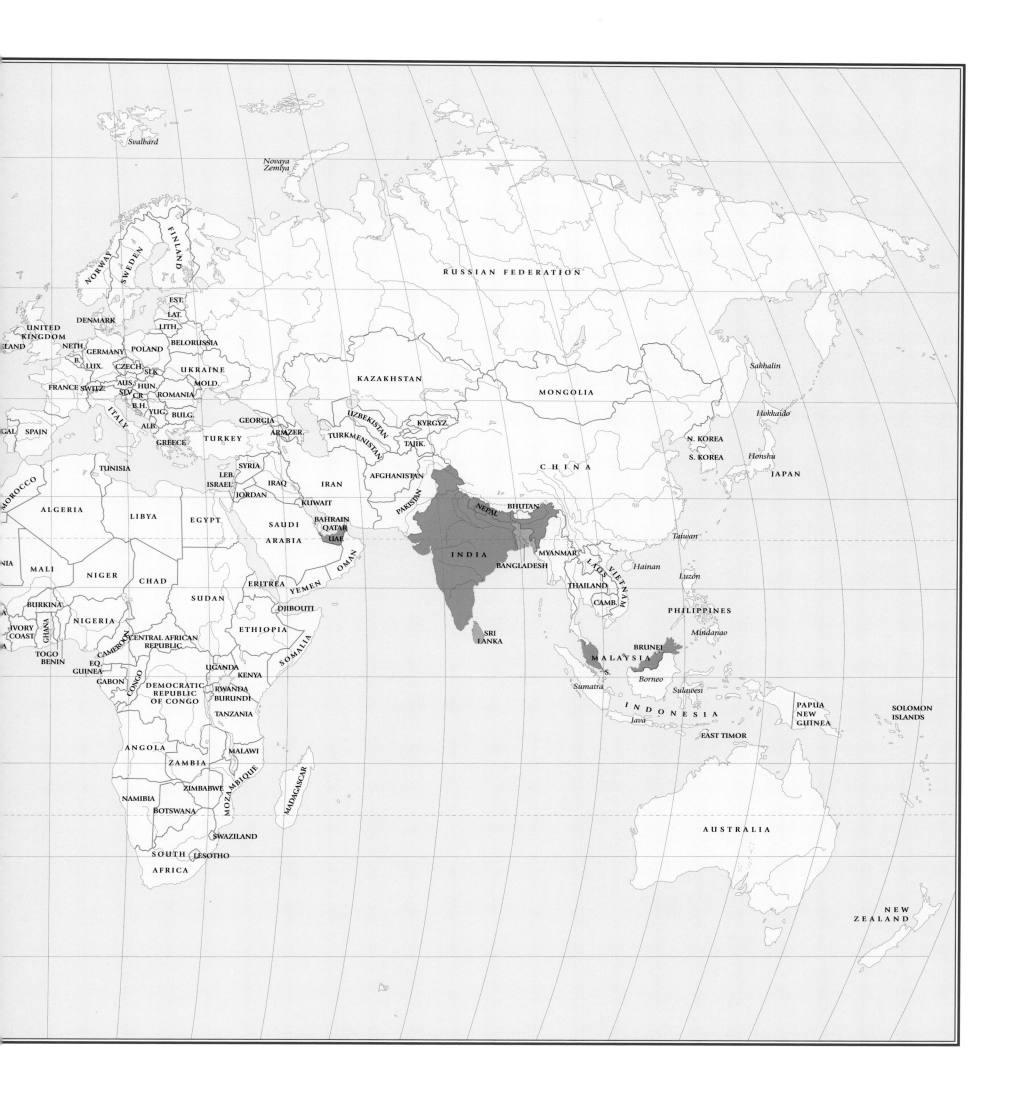

MIGRATIONS TO USA; THE SIKH GOLDEN TEMPLE IN AMRITSAR

MIGRATIONS

→ Hindus and Sikhs migration

→ missionary

THE SIKH GOLDEN TEMPLE IN AMRITSAR

Amritsar, which means 'Pool of the Nectar of Immortality', is situated in the Punjab Region of India and is Sikhism's holiest city. The city got its name from the fourth Guru of Sikhism, Guru Ram Das (1534-1581 AD), who excavated a pool here. Harimandir Sahib, popularly known as the Golden Temple, was completed in the middle of the pool in 1601 and the city of Amritsar developed around this. Following Sikh tradition, anyone may enter the temple provided they do not drink alcohol, eat meat or smoke while in the shrine.

THE SIKH GOLDEN TEMPLE IN AMRITSAR

This temple, situated in the Punjab, is the most sacred shrine of Sikhism. Its official name is Harmandir Sahib, which literally means 'the Temple of God'. The temple is surrounded by a small lake, which consists of holy water. Most Sikh people try to visit the Golden Temple at least once in their lifetime. There are four entrances to the temple, signifying the importance of acceptance and openness. Anyone who wishes may enter, regardless of religion, colour, creed or sex. The only stipulations are that the person must not drink alcohol, eat meat, or smoke cigarettes or other drugs while in the shrine.

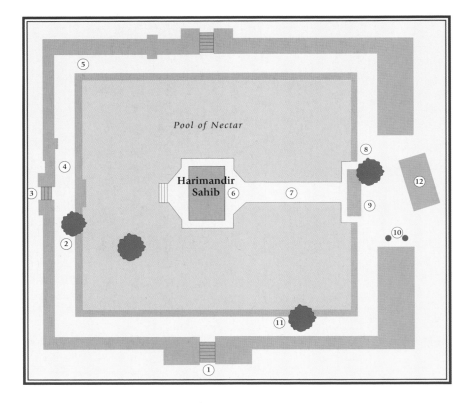

THE SIKH GOLDEN TEMPLE IN AMRITSAR

1. Main Entrance and Clock Tower
2. Dukh Bhanjani Ber
3. Entrance
4. Ath Sath Tirath (Shrine of the 68 Holy Places)
5. Shrine Baba Deep Singh
6. Entrances to the Golden Temple
7. Causeway
8. Lachi Ber (Guru Arjan Dev's Tree)
9. DarshaniDeori (Gateway to the Golden Temple)
10. Flagstaffs
11. Ber Baba Buddha (Three Shrine)
12. Akal Takhat

PART 2

ZOROASTRIANISM

THIS FAITH, NATIVE TO PERSIA, was founded by Zoroaster, or Zarathustra, allegedly around 1000 BC. Zoroastrianism was the official religion of the Persian Sassanid Dynasty between AD 224 and 636 following the defeat of Alexander the Great's successors. It currently has some 200,000 adherents, the majority living in India where they are known as Parsees.

Zoroastrianism is a monotheistic religion recognising a supreme god in Ahura Mazda, the Wise Lord. This deity had two children representing two opposing characters. Spenta Mainyu is the good spirit and Angra Mainyu, the evil spirit. These spirits took their persona from the constant choice between good and bad deeds, portraying the distinction between truth and lies, and light and dark. The religion requires ritual meditation before fire, the symbol of the faith. Zoroastrianism spread its influence outside Persia, being incorporated into the Roman cult of Mithras. A Zoroastrian heretic, Mani (216–c. 275) combined aspects of Christianity and Zoroastrianism to create a new religion known as Manichaenism. Despite Mani being executed by King Shapur I, Manichaenism transmuted itself and infused the Bogomils, Paulicians and Cathars in Christian Europe and travelled along the Silk Road into central Asia, where it became the official religion of the Uighur Empire, speading further into China.

THE HEARTLAND OF ZARATHUSTRA (ZOROASTER)

THE PERSIAN EMPIRE
The Achaemenid Persian empire under Cyrus II, 'the Great', emerged to become a world power. After conquering Babylon, Egypt and Anatolia Cyrus controlled most of the near east. With this political expansion so followed Zoroastrianism, which had developed over the centuries after originating in a remote area of eastern Persia. A monotheistic religion, it worshipped one supreme god, Ahura Mazda (wise lord), alongside the opposing spirits Angra Mainyu (evil) and Spenta Mainyu (good), the twin children of Ahura Mazda. The spirits of good and evil offer a guide to the choices faced by humans between good and bad acts and truth and untruth. Other spirits were added, such as immortal beings who followed the wise lord and demons who urged evil acts amongst humans.

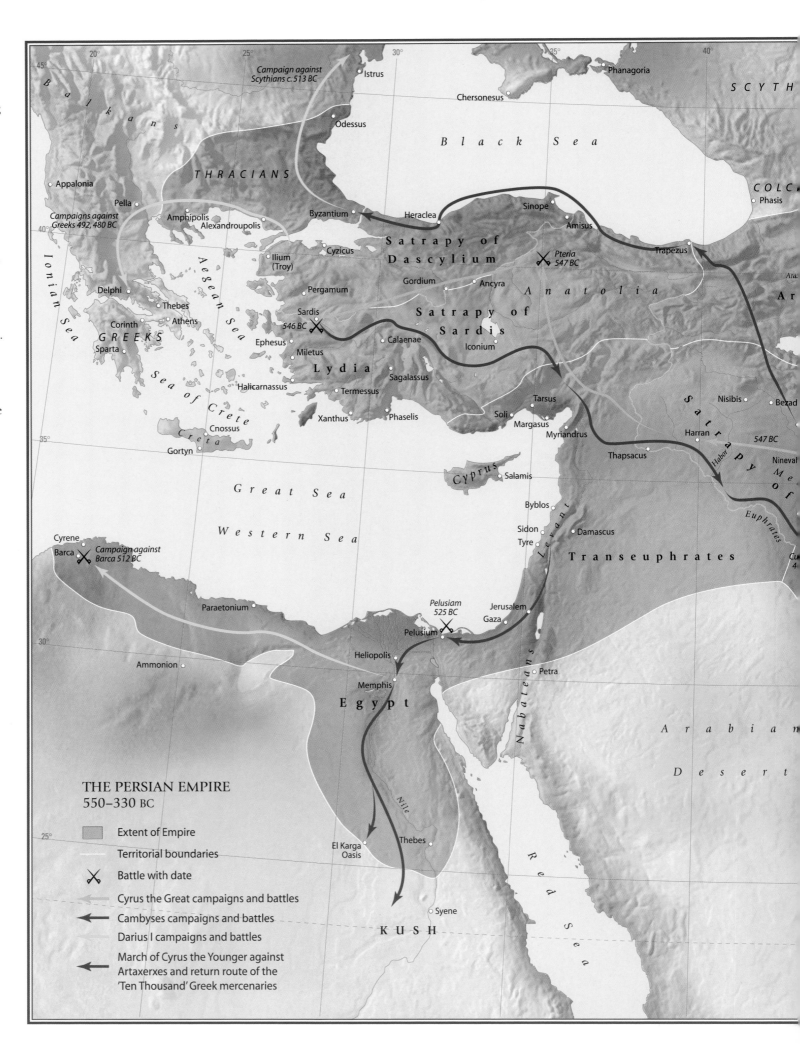

THE PERSIAN EMPIRE
550–330 BC

- Extent of Empire
- Territorial boundaries
- ✕ Battle with date
- Cyrus the Great campaigns and battles
- Cambyses campaigns and battles
- Darius I campaigns and battles
- March of Cyrus the Younger against Artaxerxes and return route of the 'Ten Thousand' Greek mercenaries

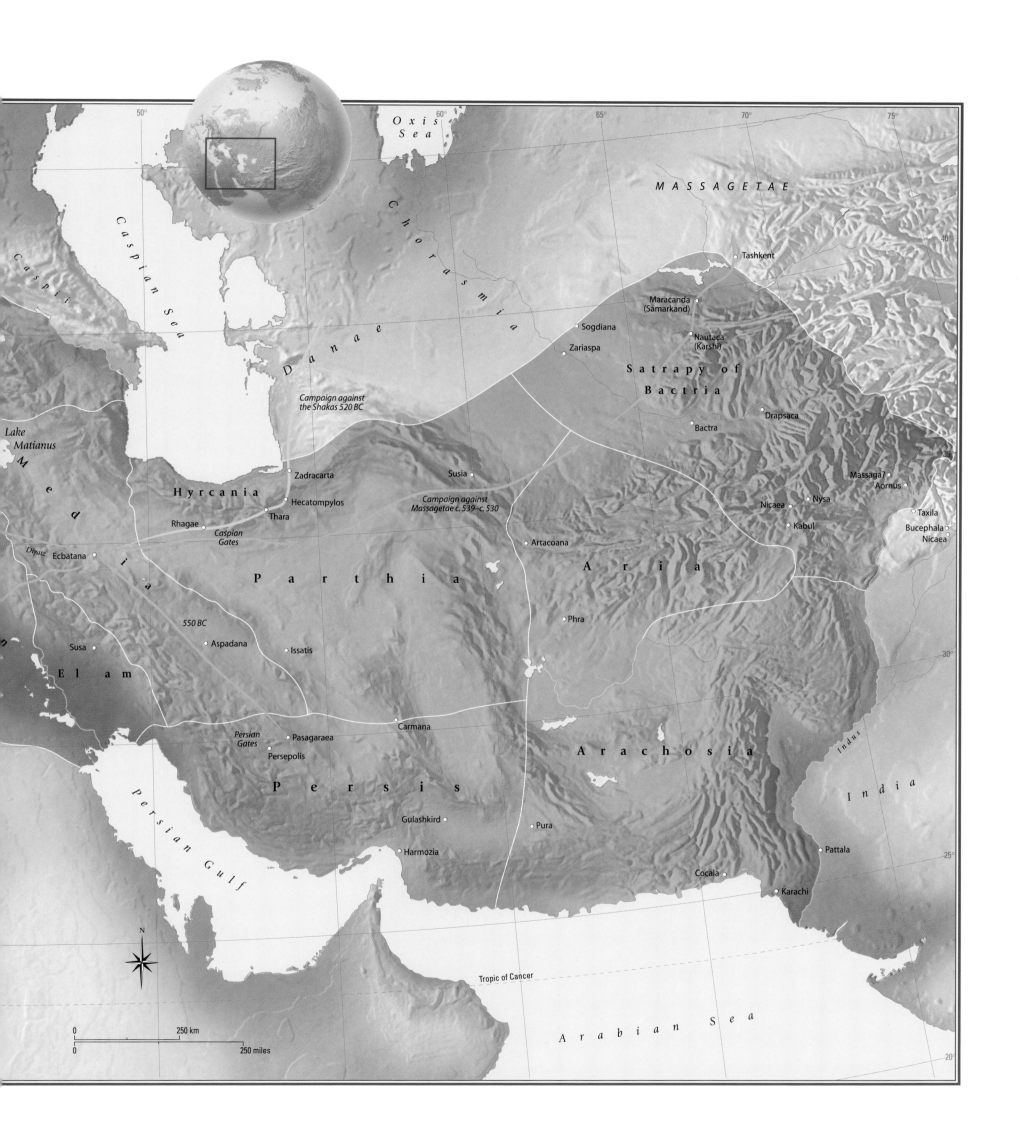

Oxus Sea

MASSAGETAE

Chorasmia

Tashkent

Maracanda
(Samarkand)

Sogdiana

Caspian Sea

Danae

Zariaspa

Nautaca
(Karshi)

Satrapy of
Bactria

Drapsaca

Campaign against
the Shakas 520 BC

Bactra

Caspi

*Lake
Matianus*

Med

Zadracarta

Susia

Massaga?

Aornus

Nysa

Hyrcania

Hecatompylos

Campaign against
Massagetae c. 539–c. 530

Nicaea

Taxila

Thara

Artacoana

Kabul

Bucephala

Nicaea

Rhagae

*Caspian
Gates*

Aria

Diyalz Ecbatana

Parthia

Phra

550 BC

Susa

Aspadana

Issatis

Pasagaraea

Carmana

El am

*Persian
Gates*

Arachosia

India

Persepolis

Indus

Persis

Gulashkird

Pura

Pattala

Harmozia

Cocala

Persian Gulf

Karachi

N

Arabian Sea

Tropic of Cancer

0   250 km

0   250 miles

112 BC – AD 270   THE SASSANIAN EMPIRE; THE SILK ROAD

THE SASSANIAN EMPIRE

The Sassanids, an ancient Persian dynasty, saw themselves as successors to the Achaemenids.

By AD 270 the Sassanian empire encompassed much of the near east and central Asia. Their ruler Shapur I saw himself as the inheritor of Cyrus the Great, imposing the dualist orthodox Zoroastrian faith upon his subjects as the official religion of state.

THE SILK ROAD

The Persian Empire and later the Sassanian Empire lay astride the Silk Road that led from China to Europe and vice-versa. Along this highway travelled religious ideas, beliefs and developments. From Persia westward spread the cult of Mithras and eastward spread a Zoroastrian development that became Manichaenism.

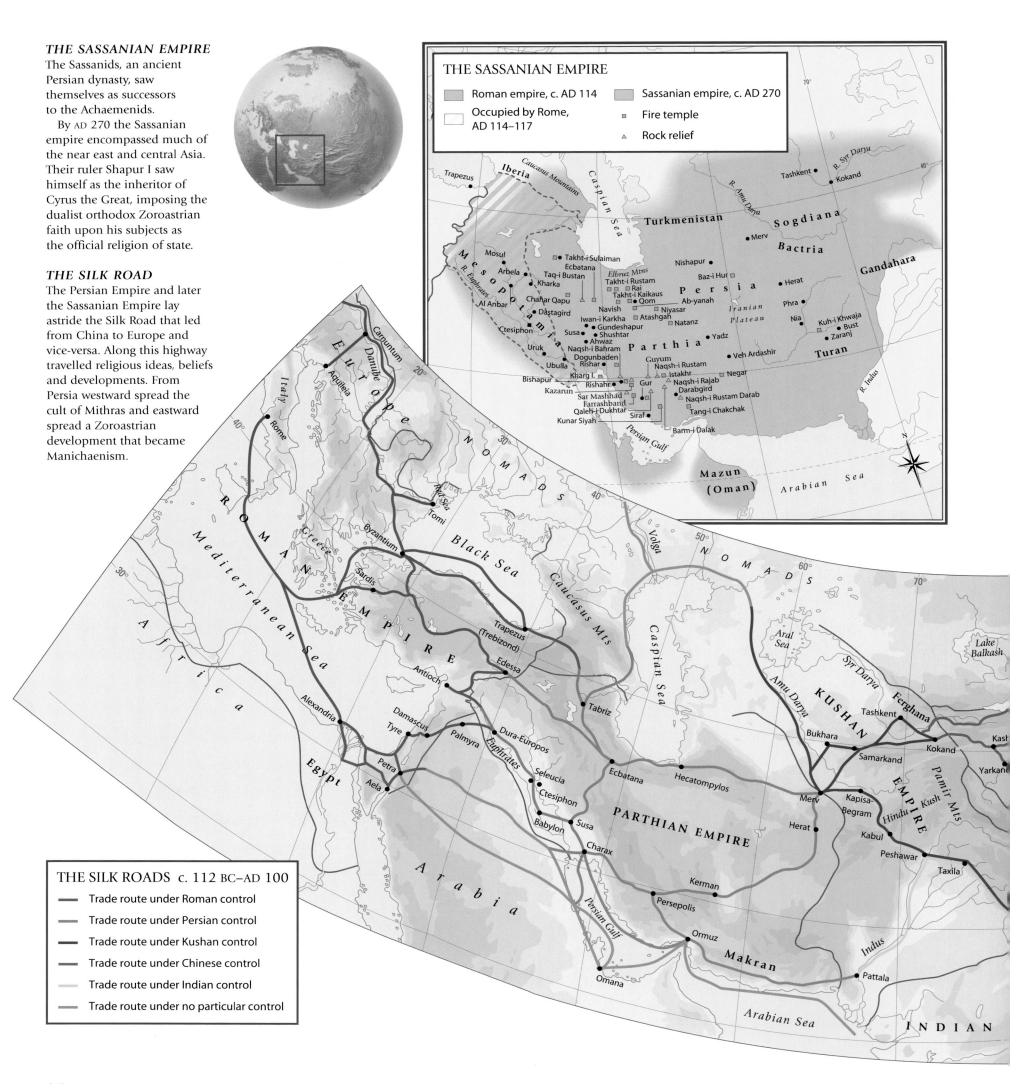

THE SASSANIAN EMPIRE

- Roman empire, c. AD 114
- Occupied by Rome, AD 114–117
- Sassanian empire, c. AD 270
- Fire temple
- Rock relief

THE SILK ROADS c. 112 BC–AD 100

- Trade route under Roman control
- Trade route under Persian control
- Trade route under Kushan control
- Trade route under Chinese control
- Trade route under Indian control
- Trade route under no particular control

THE OFFSHOOTS OF ZOROASTRIANISM

THE OFFSHOOTS OF ZOROASTRIANISM

- ▢ Heartland of Sassanian Empire
- → Spread of Mithraism
- ■ Mithraic sites
- → Spread of Manichaenism

North Sea

BRITAIN

London

Trier

GAUL

ATLANTIC

OCEAN

Alps

Albi

Pyrenees

ITALY

Split

Rome

SPAIN

Carthage

Mediterranean Sea

Amur

Laptis Magna

Alexandria

EGYPT

Thebes

AFRICA

Black Sea

Caucasus

BOGOMILS

THRACE

GREECE

ASIA MINOR

Trapezus

Edessa

MESOPOTAMIA

Rhagae

Sidon

Damascus

Jerusalem

Dura-Europos

Susa

ARABIA

OFFSHOOTS OF ZOROASTRIANISM
Zoroastrianism's first influence outside of its own homeland was the cult of Mithras. Mithras had long been worshipped as a major deity in the Persian empire and became the centre and supreme god of the cult of Mithraism that would spread westward throughout the Roman Empire.

Siberia

NOMADS

Mongolia

Lo-Lang

Urumchi

Kumul (Ha-mi)

Karashahr

Turfan

Lou-lan

Chinese Western Protectorate

Tun-huang

Miran

Cherchen

Kunlun Range

Chiu-Ch'uan

Chang-yeh

Wu-wei

Lanchow

Lo-yang

Kaifeng

Huang Ho

Lin-tzu

Yellow Sea

Yang-ti

East China Sea

HAN EMPIRE

Ch'eng-tu

Chian-ling

Ch'ang-sha

TIBET

Himalayas

Lhasa

Ganges

Pataliputra

TES

N

Tropic of Cancer

EASTERN INFLUENCE OF ZOROASTRIANISM

**EASTERN INFLUENCE
OF ZOROASTRIANISM**
The formal state religion
of Sassanid Persia was
Zoroastrianism. During the
rule of Shapur I the religion
became less tolerant of other
beliefs – Christians, Hindus,
Jews, Buddhists and others
were persecuted. Mani, 216–
c. 275, combined elements
of Christianity with
Zoroastrianism producing a
new offshoot, Manichaenism,
in which Mani himself was the
final revelation of God.

Cartir, the chief priest of
Shapur I had Mani executed
and made every effort to
suppress his new religion.
However, it had already spread
beyond the borders of the
Sassanid state eastward along
the Silk Road until it reached
the Uighur Empire, where it
became the state religion in
AD 762.

Manichaenism also spread
into China, where its followers
suffered persecution over
several centuries. It also spread
westward to Europe appearing
in various forms among the
Bogomils in Thrace and the
Cathars of southern France.

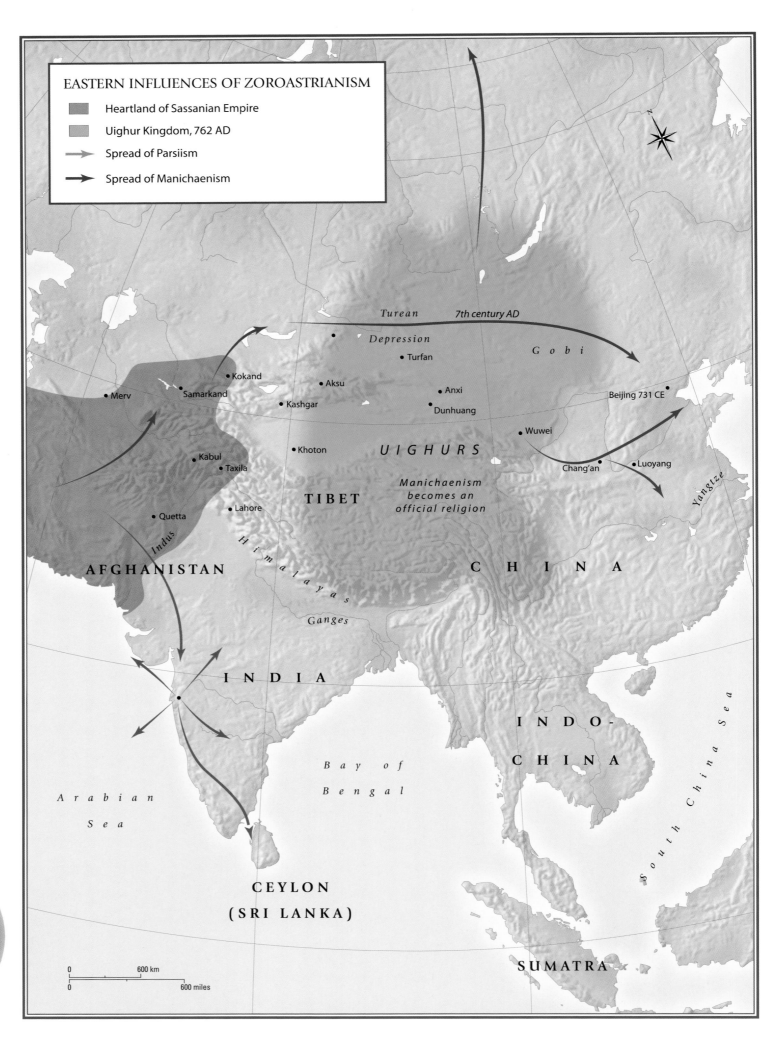

EASTERN INFLUENCES OF ZOROASTRIANISM

- Heartland of Sassanian Empire
- Uighur Kingdom, 762 AD
- Spread of Parsiism
- Spread of Manichaenism

PART 3

JUDAISM

JUDAISM IS THE RELIGION of the Jewish people, who believe that there is only one God, with whom they have a covenant. This covenant stretches back to the time of Abraham, some 3,500 years ago. Jews believe that they were chosen by God to provide an example of holiness and good behaviour in the world. Incorporated in the faith is divine revelation and a pledge to obey God's will. The strong link between religion and a people's religious personality provides Judaism with a unique character, reinforced by the impossibility of separating the histories of Judaism and the Jews. Over several thousand years, Judaism has witnessed reforms of its theology and practice but the constant theme in the religion is the guidance and divine inspiration given by the Old Testament of the Bible; hence, the Jews have been dubbed 'the People of the Book'. The Jewish Bible was written over some one thousand years, reaching its full canonical form toward the end of the 1st century AD. The most important part of this Bible is the Torah, or Pentateuch, which comprises the first five books of the old Testament – Genesis, Exodus, Leviticus, Numbers and Deuteronomy – all supposedly written by Moses after being inspired by God in the Sinai Desert. The rest of the Bible includes the books of the prophets and sundry other writings.

13TH CENTURY BC

EGYPT AT THE TIME OF EXODUS; THE ROUTE OF THE EXODUS

EGYPT AT THE TIME OF THE EXODUS

Abraham, regarded as the father of the Jewish people, was commanded by God to lead his people from their native country, Mesopotamia, toward a new land. This was dependent on his and his descendants' obedience to God, 'all the land of Canaan, for yours in everlasting possession'. Some Jews decided to continue the journey westward and eventually settled in Egypt. At that time the Egyptian Empire and its area of influence reached from Cush and Irem in Africa to the frontiers of Syria and the Hittite Empire in Asia.

THE ROUTE OF THE EXODUS (FACING PAGE)

Most probably the Hebrews crossed the marshy region to the east of the Nile delta where Moses' 'parting of the waters' would have occurred. They then journeyed to the sacred mountain, Sinai – its exact location is still open to conjecture – where God gave Moses the commandments that became the foundation of the Jewish nation's religion and identity.

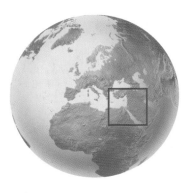

EGYPT AT THE TIME OF THE EXODUS

Maximum extent of Egypt and its Empire

✕ Battle

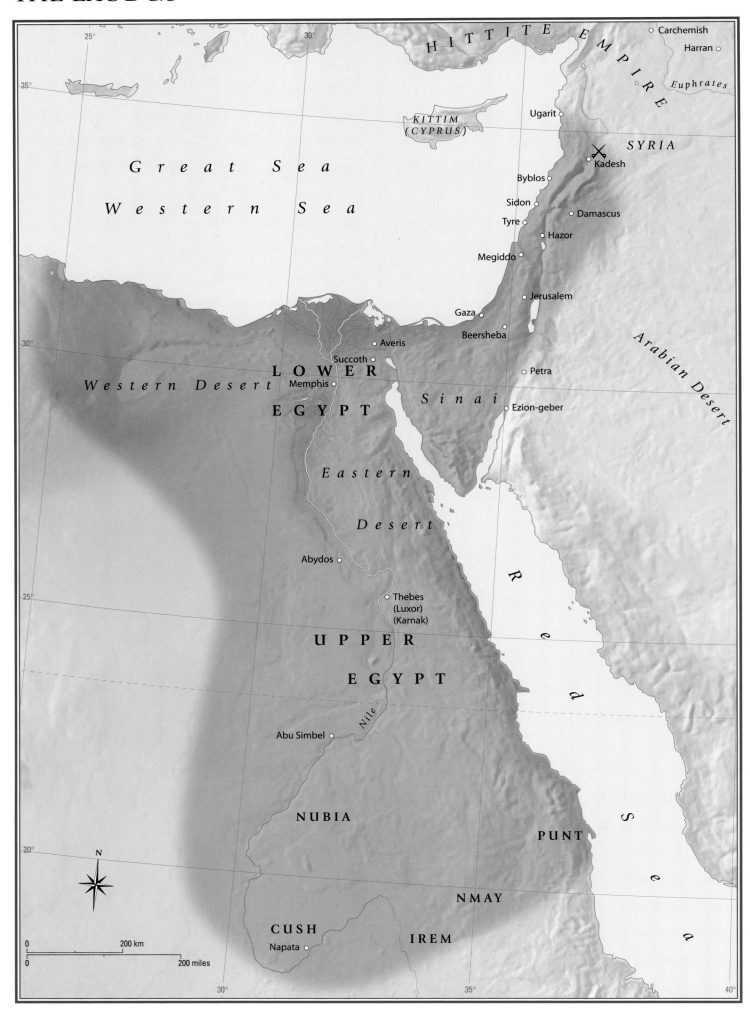

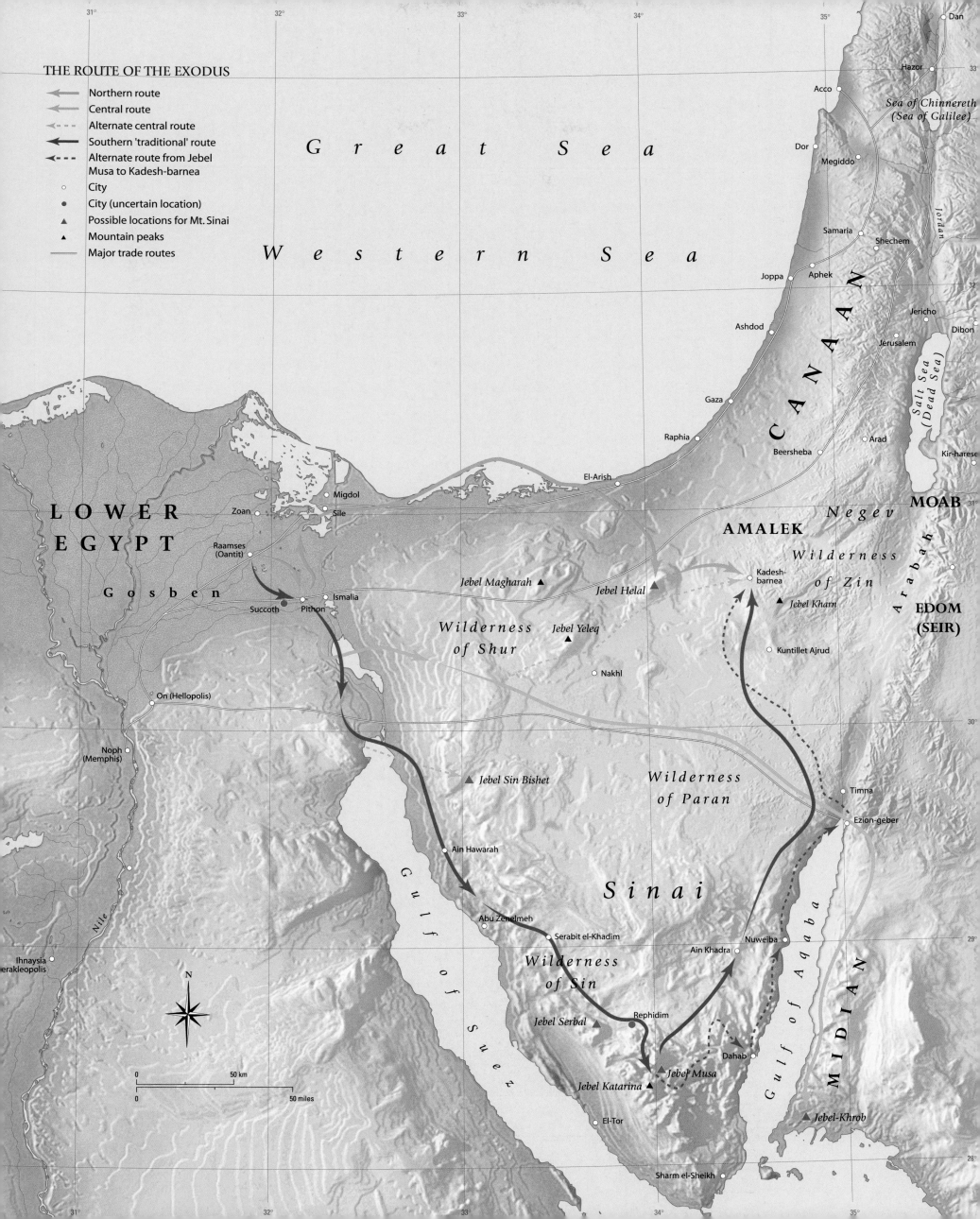

THE ROUTE OF THE EXODUS

→ Northern route
→ Central route
⇠ Alternate central route
➜ Southern 'traditional' route
⇠ Alternate route from Jebel
Musa to Kadesh-barnea
○ City
● City (uncertain location)
▲ Possible locations for Mt. Sinai
▲ Mountain peaks
— Major trade routes

Great Sea

Western Sea

LOWER EGYPT

Zoan
Migdol
Sile
Gosben
Raamses (Oantit)
Succoth Pithon
Ismalia
On (Heliopolis)
Noph (Memphis)
Ihnaysia erakleoplis
Nile

El-Arish

Jebel Magharah ▲
Jebel Helal ▲

AMALEK
Kadesh-barnea
Negev
Wilderness of Zin
▲ *Jebel Kharn*

Wilderness of Shur
Jebel Yeleq ▲
Nakhl
Kuntillet Ajrud

Dan
Hazor
Acco
Sea of Chinnereth (Sea of Galilee)
Dor
Megiddo
Jordan
Samaria Shechem
Joppa Aphek
Ashdod Jerusalem Jericho Dibon
Gaza
Raphia
Beersheba Arad
Kir-harese
Salt Sea (Dead Sea)
MOAB
CANAAN
Arabah
EDOM (SEIR)

Gulf of Suez

▲ *Jebel Sin Bishet*

Wilderness of Paran

Timna

Ezion-geber

Ain Hawarah

Sinai

Abu Zenelmeh
Serabit el-Khadim

Wilderness of Sin

Ain Khadra Nuweiba

Gulf of Aqaba

MIDIAN

Jebel Serbal ▲ Rephidim ●

Jebel Katarina ▲ *Jebel Musa* ▲

Dahab

El-Tor

Sharm el-Sheikh

Jebel-Khrob ▲

N

0   50 km
0   50 miles

INVASION AND CONQUEST OF CANAAN

**INVASION AND
CONQUEST OF CANAAN**
The invasion of Canaan began
by the crossing of the River
Jordan. Fortunately the river
was at a low level or almost
dry. The army crossed with
ease and began their campaign
of conquest. Forming a base at
Gilgal, Joshua attacked Jericho,
capturing the city. He then
moved into the central
highlands but the city of Ai
blocked his route. After an
unsuccessful first attack he
developed a strategem that
eventually captured the city.
His campaign continued
through the highlands and
towards Philistia.

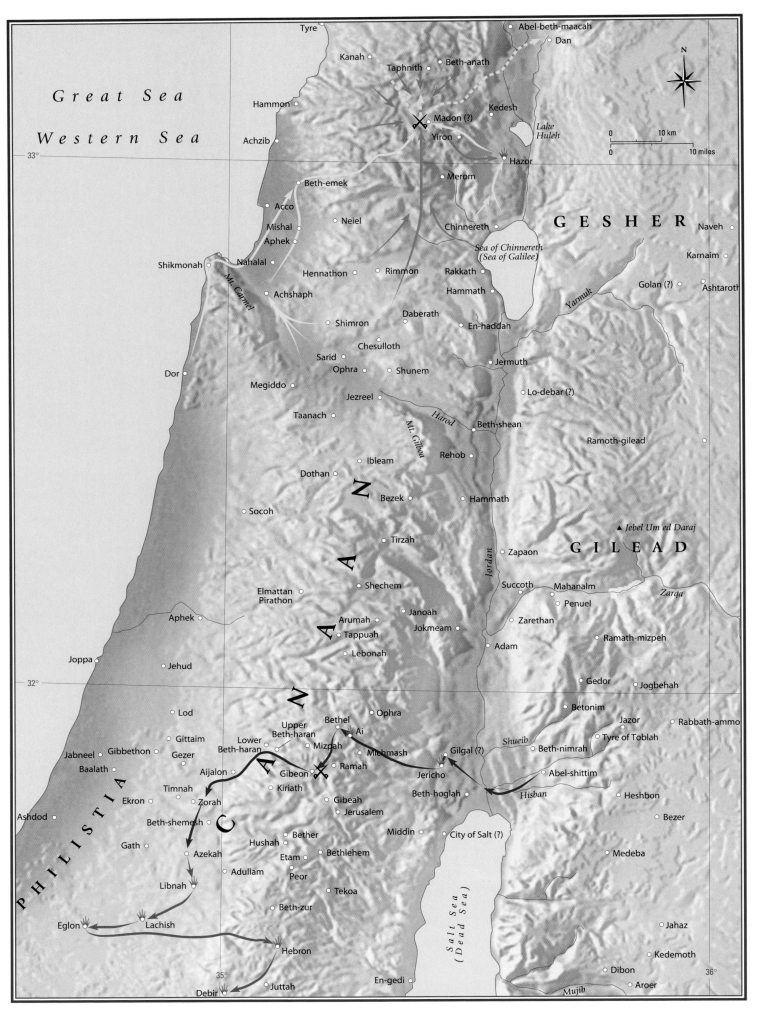

HEBREW SETTLEMENT AT THE BEGINNING OF THE PERIOD OF THE JUDGES

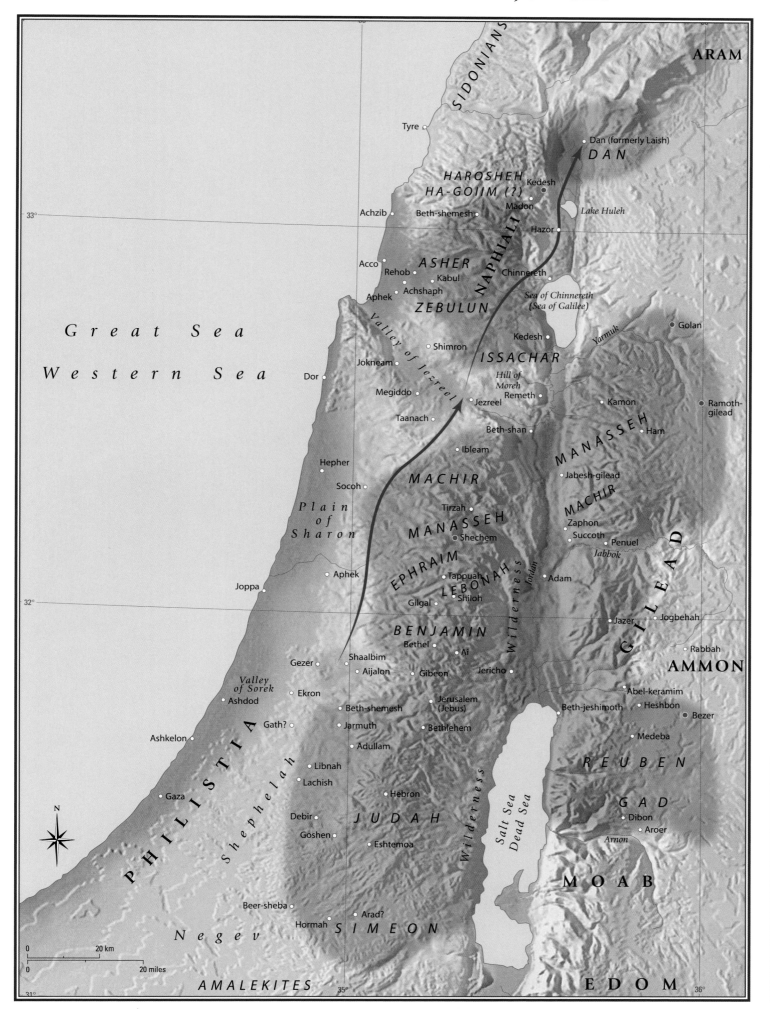

ARAM

SIDONIANS

Tyre

Dan (formerly Laish)

DAN

HAROSHEH HA-GOIIM (?)

Kedesh

Achzib

Beth-shemesh

Madon

Lake Huleh

Hazor

Acco

ASHER

Rehob

Kabul

Chinnereth

Aphek

Achshaph

NAPHTALI

ZEBULUN

Sea of Chinnereth (Sea of Galilee)

Great Sea

Western Sea

Valley of Jezreel

Kedesh

Golan

Dor

Shimron

ISSACHAR

Jokneam

Hill of Moreh

Yarmuk

Megiddo

Jezreel

Remeth

Kamon

Ramoth-gilead

Taanach

Beth-shan

Hepher

Ibleam

MANASSEH

Ham

Socoh

Jabesh-gilead

MACHIR

MACHIR

Plain of Sharon

Tirzah

Zaphon

MANASSEH

Succoth

Penuel

Shechem

Jabbok

GILEAD

EPHRAIM

Tappuah

LEBONAH

Wilderness

Adam

Aphek

Jordan

Joppa

Gilgal

Shiloh

Jazer

Jogbehah

BENJAMIN

Bethel

Rabbah

Gezer

Shaalbim

Ai

Jericho

AMMON

Aijalon

Gibeon

Valley of Sorek

Ekron

Jerusalem (Jebus)

Abel-keramim

Heshbon

Ashdod

Beth-shemesh

Beth-jeshimoth

Bezer

Gath?

Jarmuth

Bethlehem

Ashkelon

Adullam

Medeba

PHILISTIA

Libnah

REUBEN

Lachish

Shephelah

GAD

Gaza

Hebron

Dibon

Debir

Salt Sea

Dead Sea

Aroer

Goshen

JUDAH

Arnon

Eshtemoa

Wilderness

MOAB

Beer-sheba

Arad?

Hormah

SIMEON

Negev

0   20 km

0   20 miles

AMALEKITES

EDOM

HEBREW SETTLEMENT AT THE BEGINNING OF THE PERIOD OF THE JUDGES

The Hebrew settlement of Canaan probably took many years to complete. At first the Hebrews tended to occupy marginal land that had not been bought under cultivation by the Canaanites. Only later did they capture the cities. The Canaanites themselves were too disunited to be able to offer any coherent resistance. They would normally have appealed to Egypt for help, however, Egypt herself was beset by internal problems.

HEBREW SETTLEMENT AT THE BEGINNING OF THE PERIOD OF THE JUDGES

Occupation by the Hebrews

• City of refuge

→ The tribe of Dan unable to establish itself in its allotted area migrated to the north and seized the city of Laish, renaming it Dan

43

C. 1100 *BC*

TRIBAL AREAS ACCORDING TO JOSHUA

***TRIBAL AREAS ACCORD-
ING TO JOSHUA***

The Book of Judges begins
with an account of the
attempts of various tribes to
conquer their allotted
territories, some successful
and some total failures.
In Judges I the recorded
failures were more significant
for the subsequent history of
the region than the successes,
notably Canaanites remained
in several areas especially in
the north. Israel also faced
many invasions from the
Philistines in the west, to
Moabites, Edomites and
Amalekites in the south
and east.

Judges demonstrates that
the tribal league survived as
a loose governmental form
for a long time throughout
a series of defensive wars.
Possibly, the Israelites
controlled less land by
Samuel's time than at Joshua's
death. The tribe of Reuben
was virtually wiped out. The
tribe of Dan could not retain
control of the central
Shepheleh and moved north
to seize land around Laish,
north of the Sea of Galilee.
All tribes were bedevilled by
the Canaanite enclaves
remaining in their midst.

DAVID'S WAR OF CONQUEST

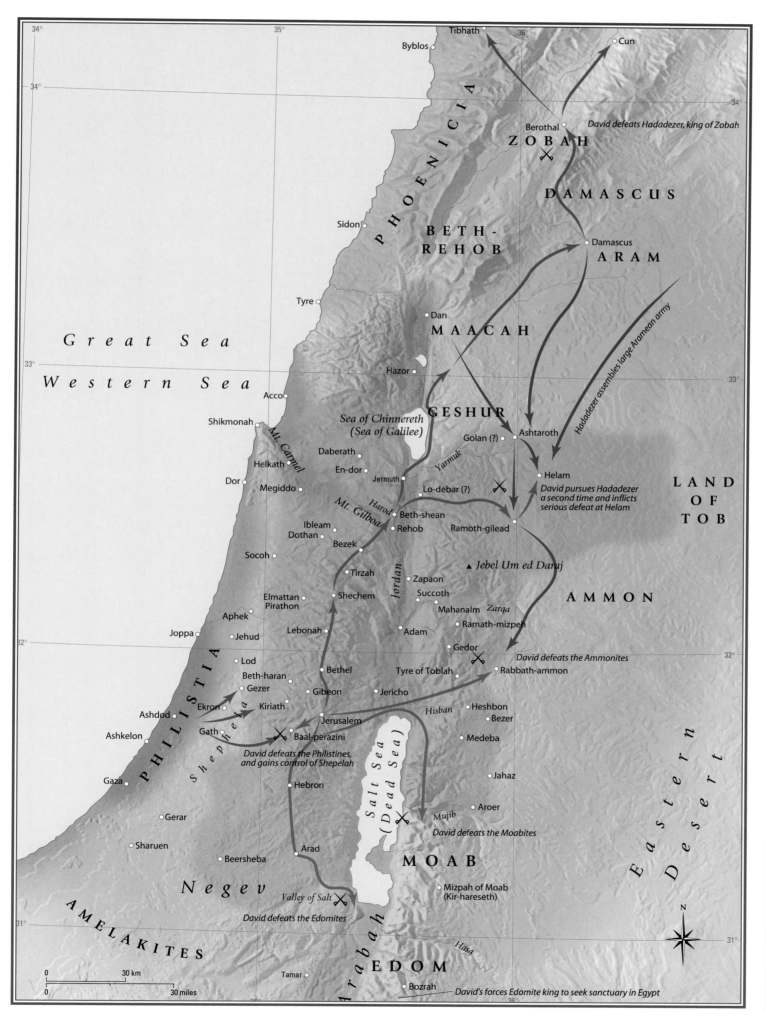

DAVID'S WAR OF CONQUEST
Defeating the Philistines, King David gave his people and their religion security in their homeland. His rule extended to the Syrian Desert in the north and the borders of the Egyptian Empire to the south, and from the coastline of the Mediterranean in the west to deep into the Syrian Desert in the east.

Tibhath

Cun

Byblos

David defeats Hadadezer, king of Zobah

Berothal

ZOBAH

DAMASCUS

Sidon

**BETH-
REHOB**

Damascus

ARAM

Tyre

Dan

MAACAH

Hadadezer assembles large Aramean army

Hazor

Great Sea

Western Sea

Acco

GESHUR

Shikmonah

*Sea of Chinnereth
(Sea of Galilee)*

Golan (?)

Ashtaroth

Daberath

En-dor

Yarmuk

Helkath

Jermuth

Helam

David pursues Hadadezer a second time and inflicts serious defeat at Helam

Dor

Megiddo

Lo-debar (?)

**LAND
OF
TOB**

Mt. Carmel

Harod

Beth-shean

Ibleam

Mt. Gilboa

Rehob

Ramoth-gilead

Dothan

Bezek

Socoh

▲ *Jebel Um ed Daraj*

Tirzah

Jordan

Zapaon

Elmattan
Pirathon

Shechem

Succoth

AMMON

Aphek

Lebonah

Mahanaim

Zarqa

Joppa

Jehud

Adam

Ramath-mizpeh

Gedor

David defeats the Ammonites

Lod

Beth-haran

Bethel

Tyre of Toblah

Rabbath-ammon

Ekron

Gezer

Gibeon

Jericho

Hisban

Heshbon

Ashdod

Kiriath

Jerusalem

Bezer

PHILISTIA

Gath

Baal-perazini

*Salt
Sea
(Dead Sea)*

Medeba

Ashkelon

Shephelah

David defeats the Philistines, and gains control of Shepelah

Gaza

Jahaz

Hebron

Aroer

Eastern Desert

Mujib

David defeats the Moabites

Gerar

Sharuen

Arad

MOAB

Beersheba

*Mizpah of Moab
(Kir-hareseth)*

Negev

Valley of Salt

David defeats the Edomites

AMELAKITES

Arabah

Hasa

Tamar

EDOM

Bozrah

David's forces Edomite king to seek sanctuary in Egypt

DAVID'S WAR OF CONQUEST	
←	David's routes of conquest
←	Edomite threat and retreat
←	Philistine threat
←	Aramean forces
▨	Saul's kingdom
▨	Territory added under David's rule
✕	Battle

0   30 km
0   30 miles

C. 1000 BC – C. 500 BC JERUSALEM

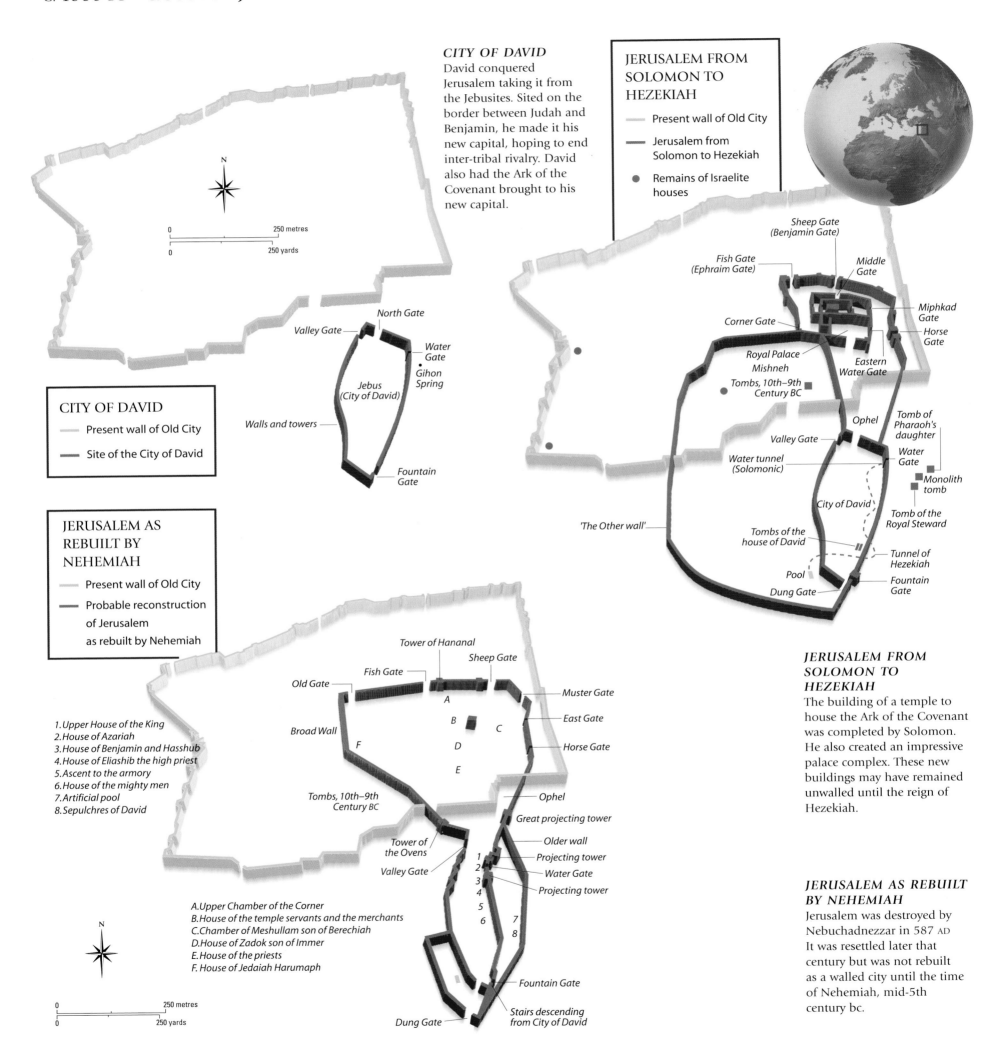

CITY OF DAVID

David conquered Jerusalem taking it from the Jebusites. Sited on the border between Judah and Benjamin, he made it his new capital, hoping to end inter-tribal rivalry. David also had the Ark of the Covenant brought to his new capital.

JERUSALEM FROM SOLOMON TO HEZEKIAH
— Present wall of Old City
— Jerusalem from Solomon to Hezekiah
● Remains of Israelite houses

N

0 ____ 250 metres
0 ____ 250 yards

CITY OF DAVID
— Present wall of Old City
— Site of the City of David

North Gate
Valley Gate
Water Gate
Jebus (City of David)
Gihon Spring
Walls and towers
Fountain Gate

Sheep Gate (Benjamin Gate)
Fish Gate (Ephraim Gate)
Middle Gate
Corner Gate
Miphkad Gate
Horse Gate
Royal Palace Mishneh
Eastern Water Gate
Tombs, 10th–9th Century BC
Ophel
Tomb of Pharaoh's daughter
Valley Gate
Water Gate
Water tunnel (Solomonic)
Monolith tomb
'The Other wall'
City of David
Tomb of the Royal Steward
Tombs of the house of David
Tunnel of Hezekiah
Pool
Dung Gate
Fountain Gate

JERUSALEM AS REBUILT BY NEHEMIAH
— Present wall of Old City
— Probable reconstruction of Jerusalem as rebuilt by Nehemiah

1. Upper House of the King
2. House of Azariah
3. House of Benjamin and Hasshub
4. House of Eliashib the high priest
5. Ascent to the armory
6. House of the mighty men
7. Artificial pool
8. Sepulchres of David

Tower of Hananal
Sheep Gate
Fish Gate
Old Gate
Muster Gate
A
East Gate
Broad Wall
B
C
F
D
Horse Gate
E
Tombs, 10th–9th Century BC
Ophel
Great projecting tower
Tower of the Ovens
Older wall
Valley Gate
Projecting tower
1
Water Gate
2
3
Projecting tower
4
5
6
7
8
Fountain Gate
Dung Gate
Stairs descending from City of David

A. Upper Chamber of the Corner
B. House of the temple servants and the merchants
C. Chamber of Meshullam son of Berechiah
D. House of Zadok son of Immer
E. House of the priests
F. House of Jedaiah Harumaph

N

0 ____ 250 metres
0 ____ 250 yards

JERUSALEM FROM SOLOMON TO HEZEKIAH

The building of a temple to house the Ark of the Covenant was completed by Solomon. He also created an impressive palace complex. These new buildings may have remained unwalled until the reign of Hezekiah.

JERUSALEM AS REBUILT BY NEHEMIAH

Jerusalem was destroyed by Nebuchadnezzar in 587 AD It was resettled later that century but was not rebuilt as a walled city until the time of Nehemiah, mid-5th century bc.

SOLOMON'S EMPIRE

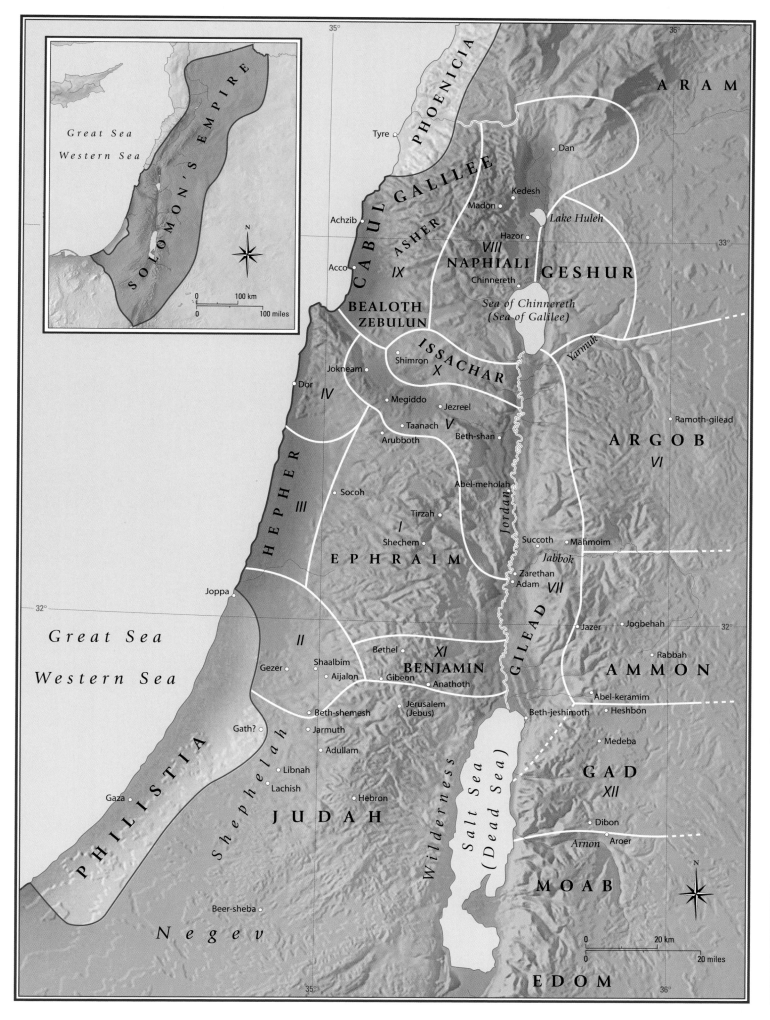

Inset map labels:
Great Sea / Western Sea
SOLOMON'S EMPIRE
0 100 km
0 100 miles

Main map labels:
35° · 36° · 33° · 32°

PHOENICIA
ARAM
Tyre
Dan
Kedesh
Madon
Lake Huleh
Hazor
Achzib
CABUL GALILEE
ASHER
NAPHTALI
VIII
GESHUR
Acco
IX
Chinnereth
BEALOTH ZEBULUN
Sea of Chinnereth (Sea of Galilee)
ISSACHAR
Shimron
X
Yarmuk
Jokneam
Dor
IV
Megiddo
Jezreel
Taanach
V
Beth-shan
Arubboth
Ramoth-gilead
ARGOB
VI
HEPHER
Socoh
Abel-meholah
III
Tirzah
I
Jordan
Shechem
Succoth
Mahmoim
Jabbok
Zarethan
Joppa
EPHRAIM
Adam
VII
GILEAD
Jazer
Jogbehah
32°
Bethel
BENJAMIN
XI
Rabbah
Shaalbim
AMMON
Gezer
Aijalon
Gibeon
Anathoth
Abel-keramim
Beth-shemesh
Jerusalem (Jebus)
Heshbon
Gath?
Jarmuth
Beth-jeshimoth
Medeba
Adullam
Great Sea / Western Sea
Shephelah
Libnah
GAD
XII
Gaza
Lachish
JUDAH
Hebron
Dibon
Wilderness
Salt Sea (Dead Sea)
Arnon
Aroer
Beer-sheba
N e g e v
MOAB
PHILISTIA
EDOM
0 20 km
0 20 miles

SOLOMON'S EMPIRE
Solomon, the second son of King David and Bathsheba, had been anointed before David's death. On his accession, Solomon ruthlessly removed any potential rivals ensuring an unthreatened transfer of power.
From the time of Solomon onwards, tension could be detected amongst the Hebrews. Some of them remained loyal to the old Hebrew religion of the nomadic shepherds, while others expressed the essentials of the covenant religion in ways that reflected the Hebrews needs in their new economic and political situation. The new stone temple built by King Solomon became a visible sign that the nomadic religion of the Hebrews was being expressed in new forms.

Legend:

SOLOMON'S EMPIRE

Maximum extent of Solomon's Kingdom (*inset map*)

Traditional tribal boundaries divided into twelve provinces with a governor for each province

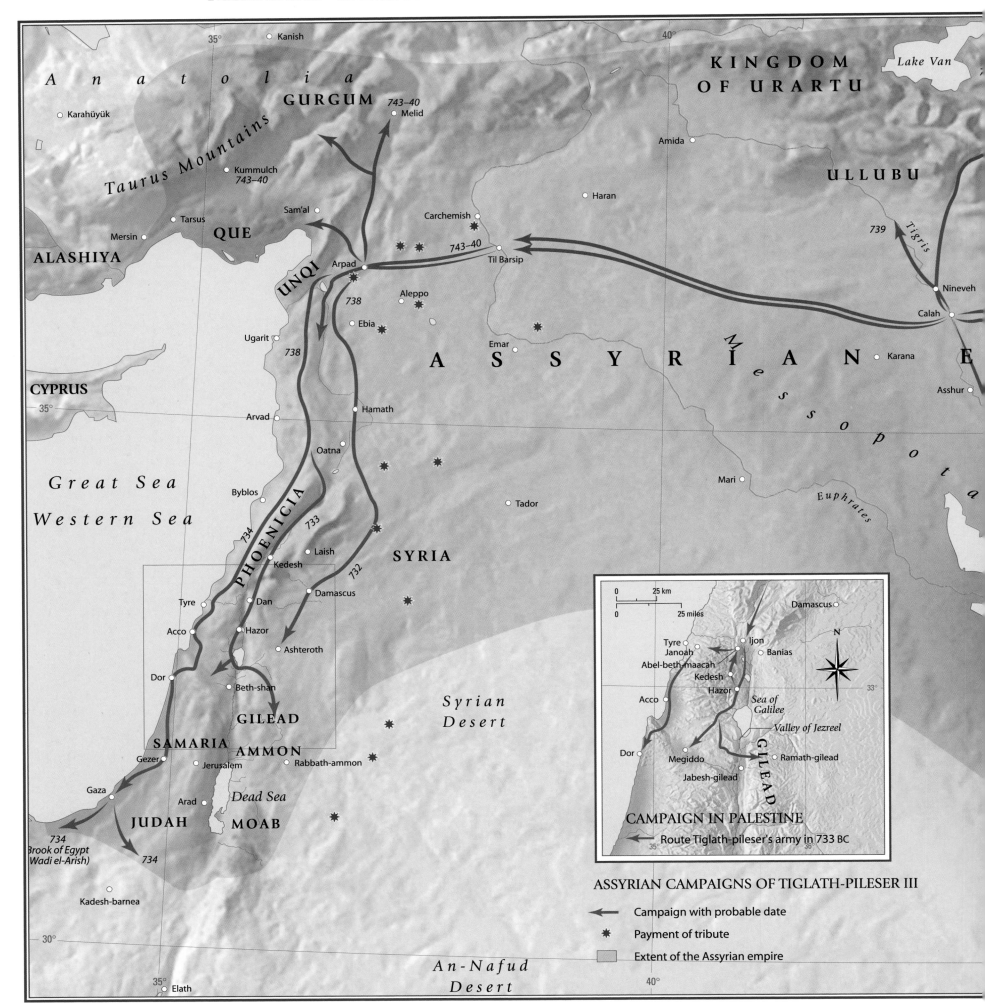

738 BC – 732 BC

ASSYRIAN CAMPAIGNS OF TIGLATH-PILESER III; MILITARY CAMPAIGN IN PALESTINE

Kanish

KINGDOM OF URARTU

Lake Van

A n a t o l i a

GURGUM 743–40

Melid

Karahüyük

Taurus Mountains

Kummulch 743–40

Amida

ULLUBU

Tarsus

Sam'al

Haran

739

Tigris

Mersin

QUE

Carchemish

ALASHIYA

UNQI

Arpad

743–40

Til Barsip

Nineveh

738

Aleppo

Calah

Ugarit

Ebia

738

Emar

A S S Y R I A N E

Karana

CYPRUS

Asshur

35°

Arvad

Hamath

Me

s

s

o

p

o

t

a

Great Sea

Byblos

Oatna

Mari

Euphrates

Western Sea

Tador

734

733

PHOENICIA

SYRIA

Laish

Kedesh

Dan

732

Tyre

Damascus

Acco

Hazor

Ashteroth

Syrian

Dor

Desert

Beth-shan

GILEAD

SAMARIA

AMMON

Gezer

Jerusalem

Rabbath-ammon

Gaza

Arad

Dead Sea

734
Brook of Egypt
(Wadi el-Arish)

734

JUDAH

MOAB

Kadesh-barnea

30°

35°

Elath

An-Nafud
Desert

40°

Inset: CAMPAIGN IN PALESTINE

0   25 km

0   25 miles

Damascus

Tyre

Ijon

Janoah

Banias

Abel-beth-maacah

Kedesh

N

Acco

Hazor

Sea of
Galilee

33°

Valley of Jezreel

Dor

GILEAD

Megiddo

Ramath-gilead

Jabesh-gilead

35°

CAMPAIGN IN PALESTINE

→ Route Tiglath-pileser's army in 733 BC

ASSYRIAN CAMPAIGNS OF TIGLATH-PILESER III

→ Campaign with probable date

✱ Payment of tribute

▬ Extent of the Assyrian empire

MILITARY ACTION AGAINST ISRAEL

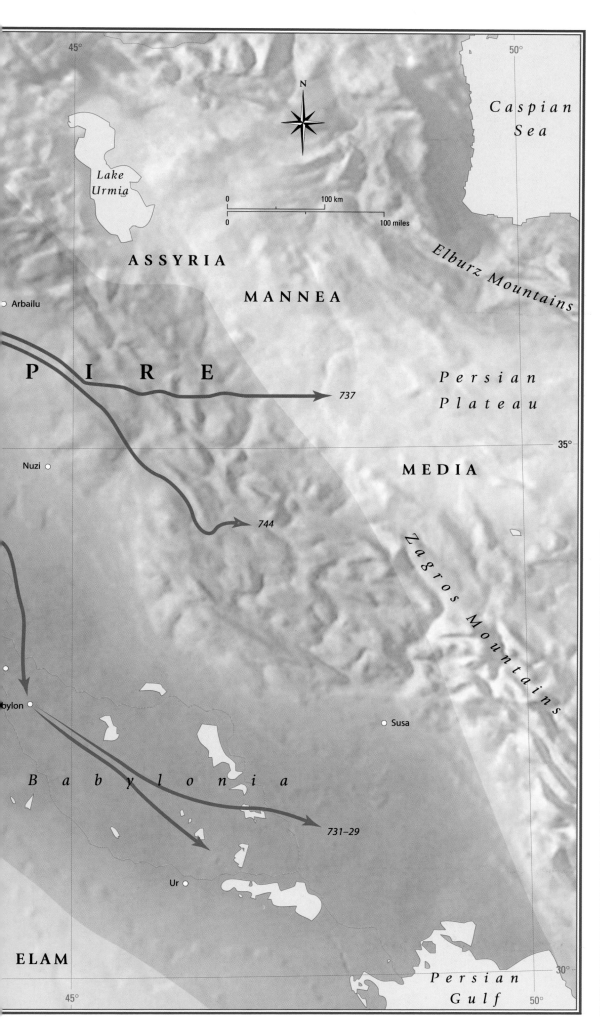

ASSYRIAN CAMPAIGNS UNDER TIGLATH-PILESER III

The Assyrians launched a series of seasonal campaigns extending their territories from the banks of the river Euphrates to the Mediterranean and the southern part of Anatolia. From 738 BC the campaigns moved southward toward Egypt and its sphere of influence. In 734 BC, Assyrian armies marched south towards Egypt, their route taking them through Israel and Judah. At this point they had no wish to occupy the area and simply brushed aside any resistance. They took up a position along the Brook of Egypt, the ancient northern border of Egypt.

MILITARY ACTION AGAINST ISRAEL

In 733 BC the Assyrians renewed their campaign. This time they focused on Israel, whose people now faced a bleak future under Assyrian control.

MILITARY ACTION AGAINST ISRAEL

← Siege by Shalmaneser V

← Hamath opposes Sargon and is defeated

← March by Sargon II

⚜ Anti-Assyrian activities

← Sennacherib's campaign of 701

← Egyptian advance

←- Egyptian retreat

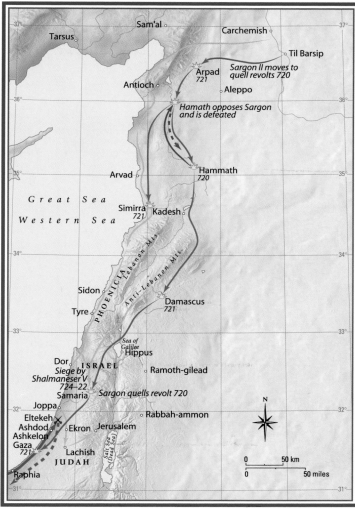

ASSYRIAN DEPORTATIONS; THE BABYLONIAN EMPIRE; THE CITY OF BABYLON

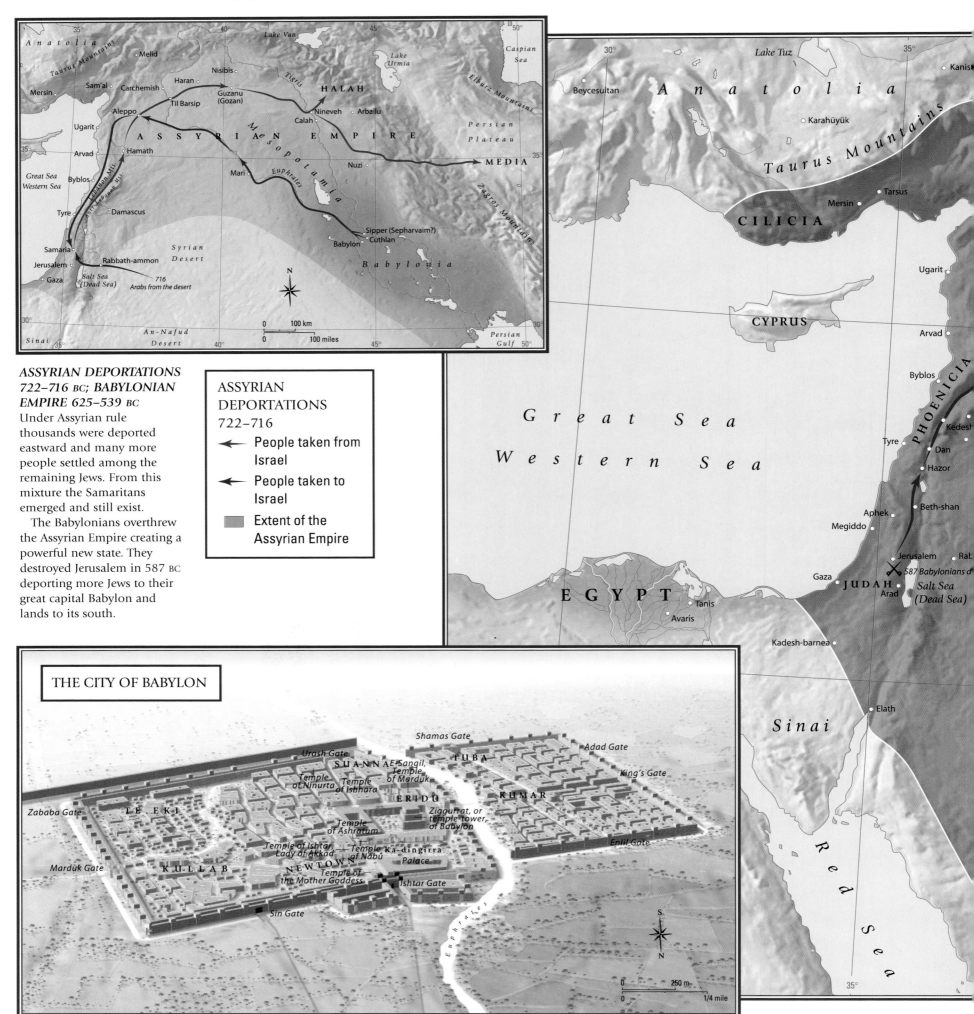

ASSYRIAN DEPORTATIONS 722–716 BC; BABYLONIAN EMPIRE 625–539 BC

Under Assyrian rule thousands were deported eastward and many more people settled among the remaining Jews. From this mixture the Samaritans emerged and still exist.

The Babylonians overthrew the Assyrian Empire creating a powerful new state. They destroyed Jerusalem in 587 BC deporting more Jews to their great capital Babylon and lands to its south.

ASSYRIAN DEPORTATIONS 722–716

⬅ People taken from Israel

⬅ People taken to Israel

▤ Extent of the Assyrian Empire

THE CITY OF BABYLON

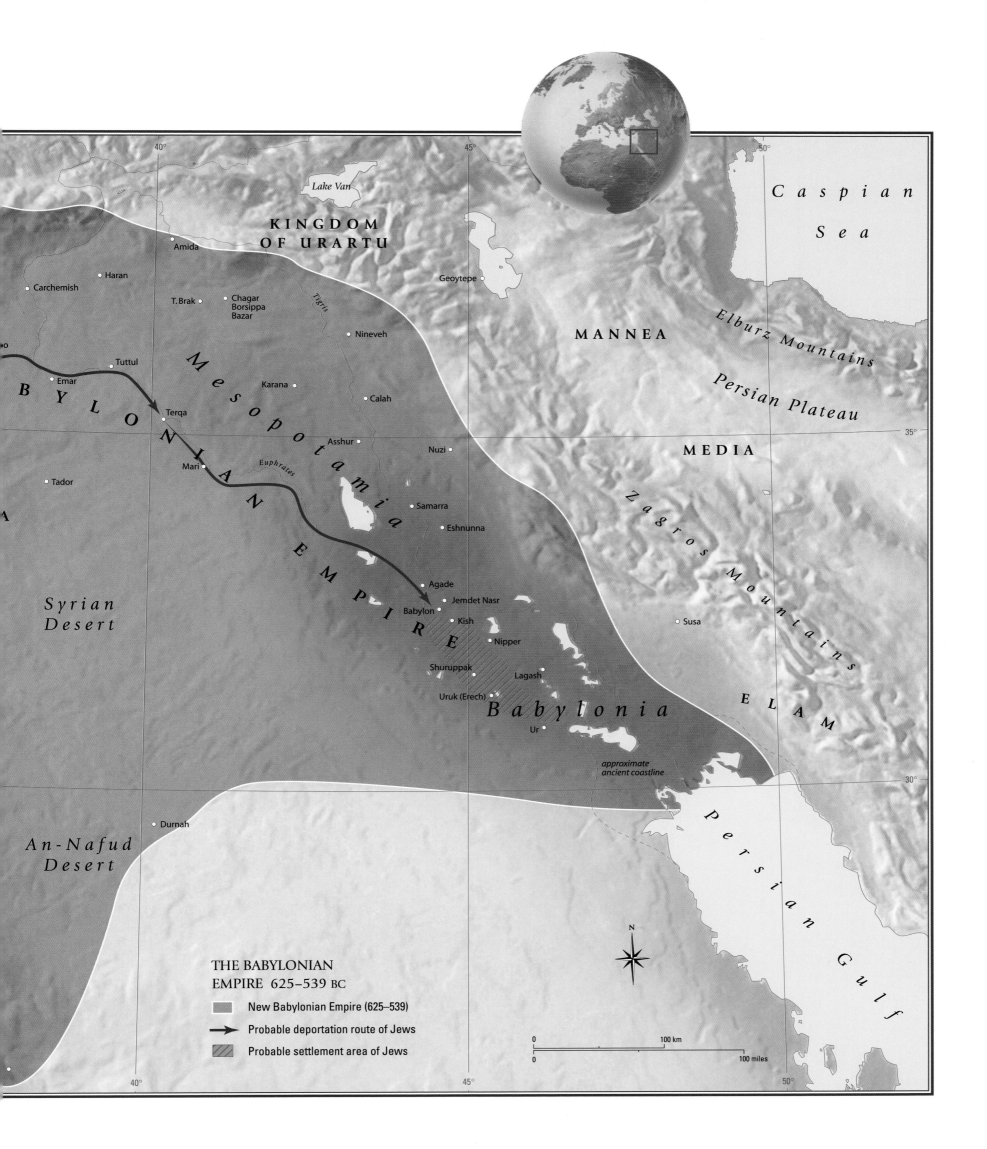

Lake Van

KINGDOM OF URARTU

Amida

Carchemish

Haran

T. Brak

Chagar
Borsippa
Bazar

Tigris

Nineveh

Geoytepe

*Caspian
Sea*

MANNEA

Elburz Mountains

Persian Plateau

o

Tuttul

Emar

M e s o p o t a m i a

Karana

Terqa

Calah

MEDIA

Zagros Mountains

Tador

Mari

Euphrates

Asshur

Nuzi

BYLONIA

B A B Y L O N I A N E M P I R E

Samarra

Eshnunna

*Syrian
Desert*

Agade

Jemdet Nasr

Babylon

Kish

Nipper

Susa

Shuruppak

Lagash

E L A M

Uruk (Erech)

B a b y l o n i a

Ur

*approximate
ancient coastline*

*An-Nafud
Desert*

Durnah

Persian Gulf

N

**THE BABYLONIAN
EMPIRE 625–539 BC**

New Babylonian Empire (625–539)

Probable deportation route of Jews

Probable settlement area of Jews

| 0 | | 100 km |
| 0 | | 100 miles |

C. 190 BC – 63 BC

JERUSALEM; SELEUCID PALESTINE; MACCABEAN REVOLT; JEWISH EXPANSION UNDER THE HASMONEAN DYNASTY

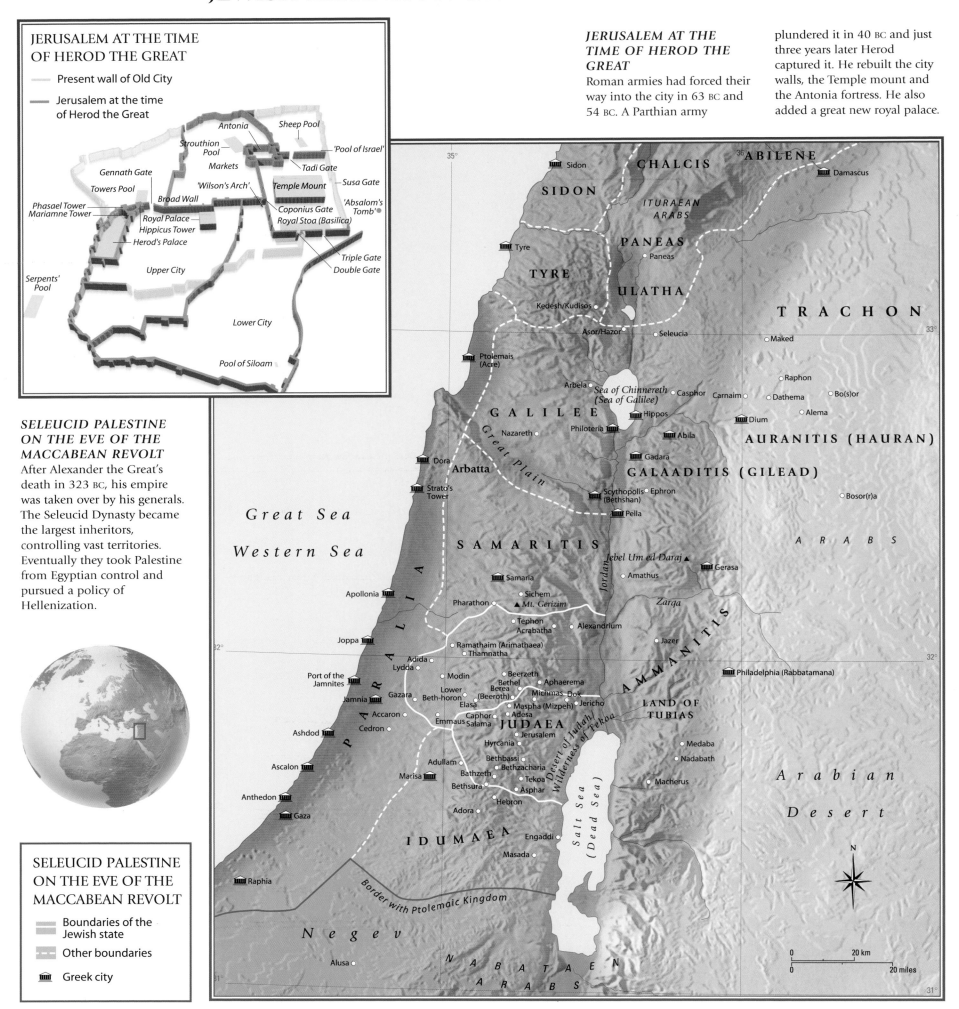

JERUSALEM AT THE TIME OF HEROD THE GREAT

— Present wall of Old City

— Jerusalem at the time of Herod the Great

Labels on Jerusalem inset map:
Antonia
Strouthion Pool
Sheep Pool
Gennath Gate
Markets
'Pool of Israel'
Tadi Gate
Towers Pool
'Wilson's Arch'
Susa Gate
Phasael Tower
Broad Wall
Temple Mount
Mariamne Tower
Royal Palace
Coponius Gate
'Absalom's Tomb'
Hippicus Tower
Royal Stoa (Basilica)
Herod's Palace
Upper City
Triple Gate
Double Gate
Serpents' Pool
Lower City
Pool of Siloam

JERUSALEM AT THE TIME OF HEROD THE GREAT

Roman armies had forced their way into the city in 63 BC and 54 BC. A Parthian army plundered it in 40 BC and just three years later Herod captured it. He rebuilt the city walls, the Temple mount and the Antonia fortress. He also added a great new royal palace.

SELEUCID PALESTINE ON THE EVE OF THE MACCABEAN REVOLT

After Alexander the Great's death in 323 BC, his empire was taken over by his generals. The Seleucid Dynasty became the largest inheritors, controlling vast territories. Eventually they took Palestine from Egyptian control and pursued a policy of Hellenization.

SELEUCID PALESTINE ON THE EVE OF THE MACCABEAN REVOLT

	Boundaries of the Jewish state
	Other boundaries
🏛	Greek city

Map labels:
Sidon
CHALCIS
ABILENE
Damascus
SIDON
ITURAEAN ARABS
PANEAS
Tyre
Paneas
TYRE
ULATHA
TRACHON
Kedesh/Kudisos
Asor/Hazor
Seleucia
Maked
Ptolemais (Acre)
Raphon
Arbela
Sea of Chinnereth (Sea of Galilee)
Casphor
Carnaim
Dathema
Bo(s)or
GALILEE
Hippos
Dium
Alema
Nazareth
Philoteria
Abila
AURANITIS (HAURAN)
Dora
Gadara
Arbatta
GALAADITIS (GILEAD)
Strato's Tower
Scythopolis (Bethshan)
Ephron
Bosor(r)a
Pella
Great Sea
Western Sea
SAMARITIS
Jebel Um ed Daraj
ARABS
Samaria
Amathus
Gerasa
Apollonia
Sichem
Pharathon
Mt. Gerizim
Zarqa
Joppa
Tephon
Alexandrium
Acrabatha
Jazer
Ramathaim (Arimathaea)
Thamnatha
AMMANITIS
Philadelphia (Rabbatamana)
Adida
Lydda
Port of the Jamnites
Modin
Bethel
Beerzeth
Aphaerema
Berea
Michmas
Dok
Gazara
Lower Beth-horon
(Beeroth)
Jamnia
Elasa
Maspha (Mizpeh)
Jericho
LAND OF TUBIAS
Accaron
Caphor
Adesa
Salama
Cedron
Emmaus
JUDAEA
Ashdod
Hyrcania
Jerusalem
Medaba
Nadabath
Bethbassi
Adullam
Bethzacharia
Ascalon
Bathzeth
Macherus
Marisa
Asphar
Arabian Desert
Bethsura
Tekoa
Anthedon
Adora
Hebron
Salt Sea (Dead Sea)
Gaza
PARALIA
Jordan
Desert of Judah/ Wilderness of Tekoa
IDUMAEA
Engaddi
Masada
Raphia
Border with Ptolemaic Kingdom
Negev
NABATAEAN ARABS
Alusa
N

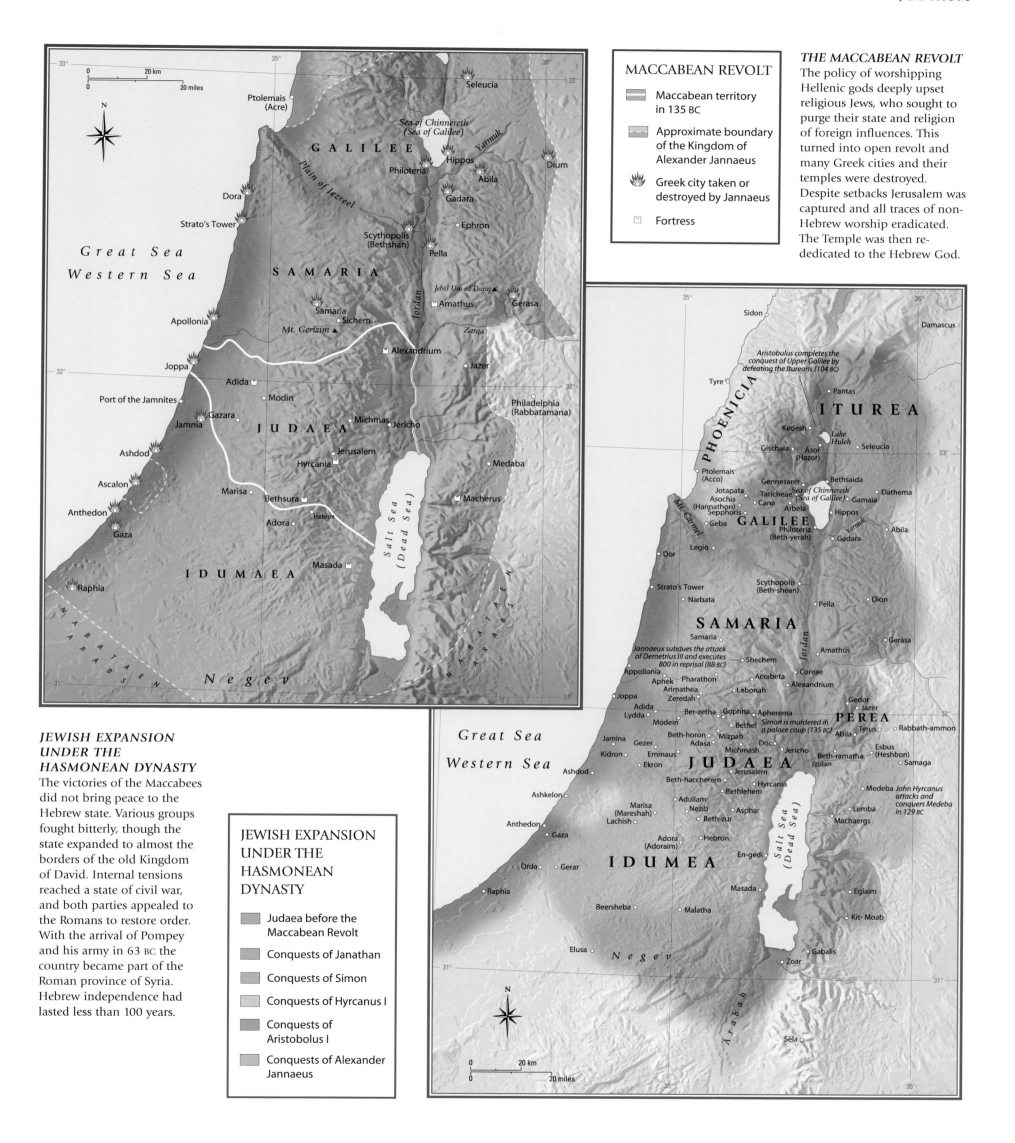

MACCABEAN REVOLT

- Maccabean territory in 135 BC
- Approximate boundary of the Kingdom of Alexander Jannaeus
- Greek city taken or destroyed by Jannaeus
- Fortress

THE MACCABEAN REVOLT

The policy of worshipping Hellenic gods deeply upset religious Jews, who sought to purge their state and religion of foreign influences. This turned into open revolt and many Greek cities and their temples were destroyed. Despite setbacks Jerusalem was captured and all traces of non-Hebrew worship eradicated. The Temple was then re-dedicated to the Hebrew God.

JEWISH EXPANSION UNDER THE HASMONEAN DYNASTY

The victories of the Maccabees did not bring peace to the Hebrew state. Various groups fought bitterly, though the state expanded to almost the borders of the old Kingdom of David. Internal tensions reached a state of civil war, and both parties appealed to the Romans to restore order. With the arrival of Pompey and his army in 63 BC the country became part of the Roman province of Syria. Hebrew independence had lasted less than 100 years.

JEWISH EXPANSION UNDER THE HASMONEAN DYNASTY

- Judaea before the Maccabean Revolt
- Conquests of Janathan
- Conquests of Simon
- Conquests of Hyrcanus I
- Conquests of Aristobulus I
- Conquests of Alexander Jannaeus

THE FIRST JEWISH REVOLT

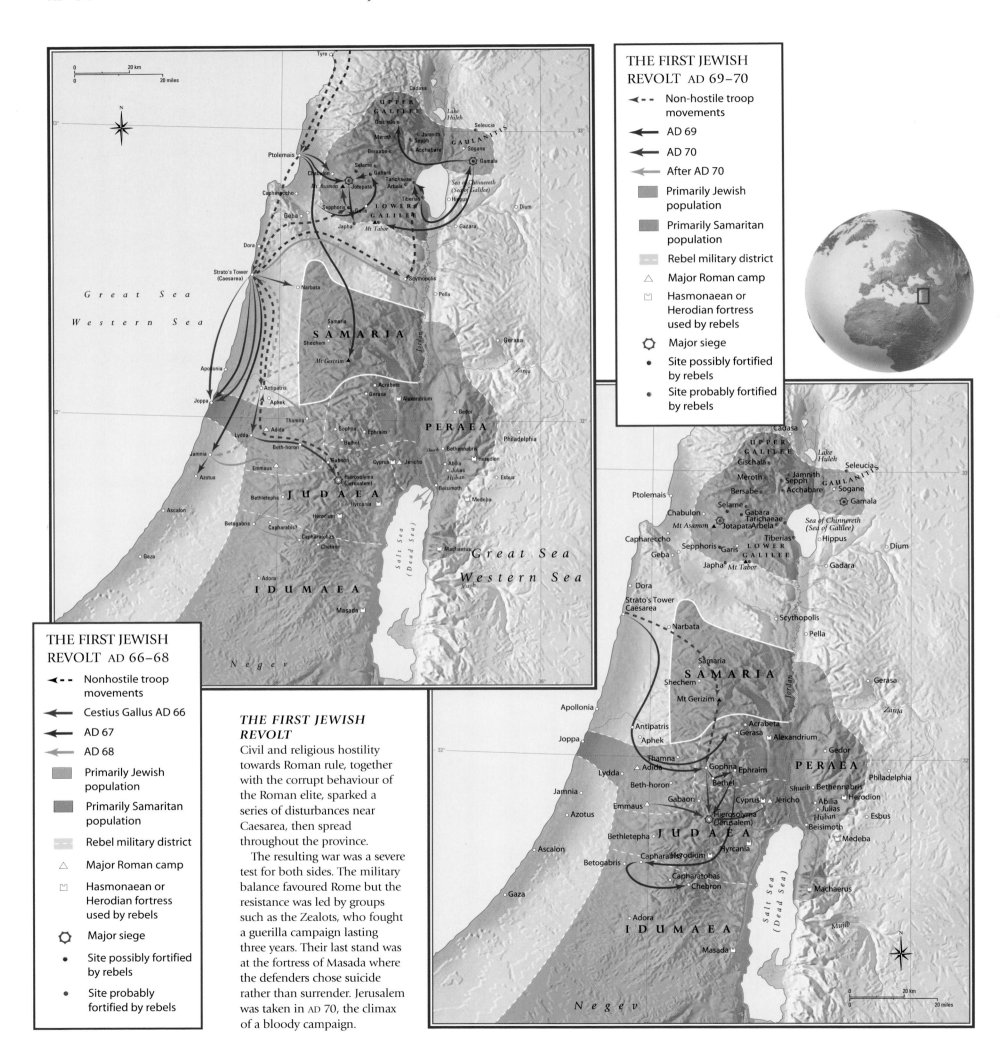

**THE FIRST JEWISH
REVOLT AD 69–70**

⊷ ‑ ‑ Non-hostile troop
movements

← AD 69

← AD 70

← After AD 70

◼ Primarily Jewish
population

◼ Primarily Samaritan
population

▦ Rebel military district

△ Major Roman camp

⌂ Hasmonaean or
Herodian fortress
used by rebels

⬡ Major siege

• Site possibly fortified
by rebels

• Site probably fortified
by rebels

**THE FIRST JEWISH
REVOLT AD 66–68**

⊷ ‑ ‑ Nonhostile troop
movements

← Cestius Gallus AD 66

← AD 67

← AD 68

◼ Primarily Jewish
population

◼ Primarily Samaritan
population

▦ Rebel military district

△ Major Roman camp

⌂ Hasmonaean or
Herodian fortress
used by rebels

⬡ Major siege

• Site possibly fortified
by rebels

• Site probably
fortified by rebels

THE FIRST JEWISH REVOLT

Civil and religious hostility towards Roman rule, together with the corrupt behaviour of the Roman elite, sparked a series of disturbances near Caesarea, then spread throughout the province.

The resulting war was a severe test for both sides. The military balance favoured Rome but the resistance was led by groups such as the Zealots, who fought a guerilla campaign lasting three years. Their last stand was at the fortress of Masada where the defenders chose suicide rather than surrender. Jerusalem was taken in AD 70, the climax of a bloody campaign.

THE SIEGE OF JERUSALEM

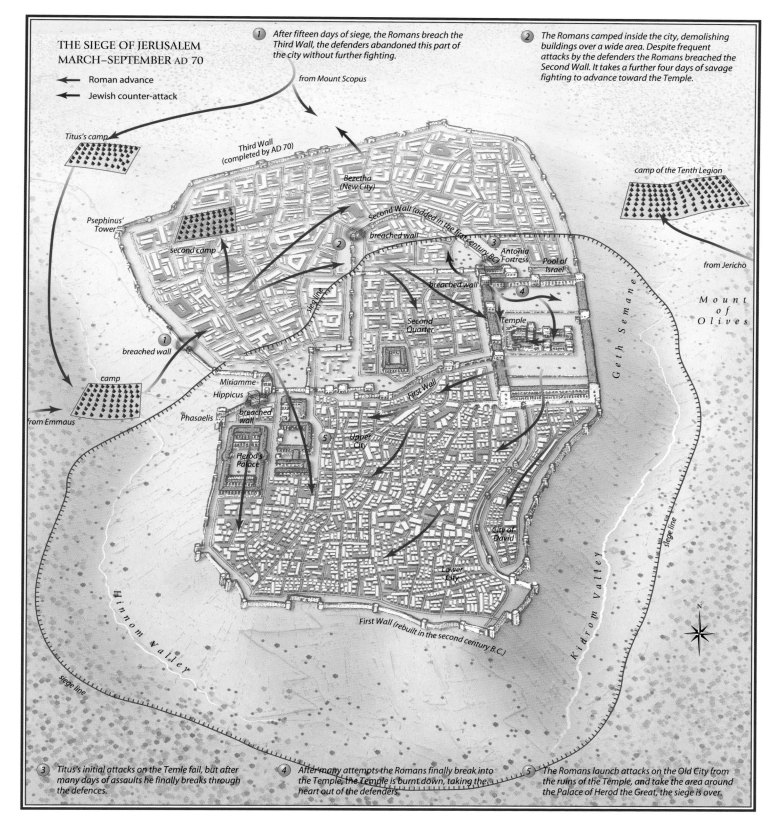

THE SIEGE OF JERUSALEM
MARCH–SEPTEMBER AD 70

→ Roman advance
→ Jewish counter-attack

from Mount Scopus

1 After fifteen days of siege, the Romans breach the Third Wall, the defenders abandoned this part of the city without further fighting.

2 The Romans camped inside the city, demolishing buildings over a wide area. Despite frequent attacks by the defenders the Romans breached the Second Wall. It takes a further four days of savage fighting to advance toward the Temple.

Titus's camp

Third Wall
(completed by AD 70)

Bezetha
(New City)

camp of the Tenth Legion

Psephinus'
Tower

Second Wall (added in the first century BC)

breached wall

from Jericho

second camp

breached wall

2

Antonia
Fortress

Pool of
Israel

*Mount
of
Olives*

Geth Semane

breached wall

3

siege line

Second
Quarter

Temple

4

1

breached wall

camp

from Emmaus

Miriamme
Hippicus

First Wall

Phasaelis

breached
wall

Herod's
Palace

5

Upper
City

Kidron Valley

Hinnom Valley

City of
David

siege line

Lower
City

siege line

First Wall (rebuilt in the second century B.C.)

N

3 Titus's initial attacks on the Temle fail, but after many days of assaults he finally breaks through the defences.

4 After many attempts the Romans finally break into the Temple, the Temple is burnt down, taking the heart out of the defenders.

5 The Romans launch attacks on the Old City from the ruins of the Temple, and take the area around the Palace of Herod the Great, the siege is over.

**THE SIEGE OF
JERUSALEM AD 70**
The First Jewish-Roman War
lasted from AD 66 to AD 73. It
started as a Jewish rebellion,
but soon became a full-scale
war. Nero appointed Vespasian
to crush it, but when Nero
died in 69, Vespasian was
proclaimed emperor. The siege
of Jerusalem had begun fairly
early in the war and the
Romans crucified anyone
trying to escape. By the end of
the siege tens of thousands of
crucified bodies encircled the
city. Vespasian's son Titus led
the final assault and the city
fell in AD 70. Most of the city
was ransacked and burnt and
the Temple was destroyed.

THE JEWISH DIASPORA

THE JEWISH DIASPORA

The Jews had suffered deportations under the Assyrians and the Babylonians, though they were allowed to return to their homeland under the Persians. Thus began the Jewish Diaspora. Trade links had also extended the number of Jewish communities around the Mediterranean. The city of Alexandria, on the Nile delta of Egypt, contained a large and thriving Jewish community. The two Jewish Revolts against Roman rule in AD 66–70 and AD 135 vastly added to the diaspora as victorious Rome sought to destroy this rebellious nation once and for all. A terrible price was paid; those who did not or could not flee the land were killed or enslaved. The Jewish religion was proscribed and Jerusalem was Romanised, resettled by non-Jews and a temple to the god Jupiter was built on the site of the Holy of Holies. The surviving Jews joined the Jewish communities abroad and became a people without a homeland.

CITY OF JERUSALEM
(INSET RIGHT)
Jerusalem as it may have looked around AD 10, after the Jewish Revolt of 135, the city was Romanised, Jews forbidden to live there and the great temple was rebuilt and dedicated to the Roman god Jupiter. Jerusalem would not be in Jewish hands again until the foundation of the modern state of Israel in 1948, and the site of the temple, by now an Islamic mosque, would not be retaken until 1967.

Following the Roman defeat of Jerusalem, the Jewish people spread throughout Babylonia and the Roman Empire

THE JEWISH DIAPSORA,
C. 1300 BC – C. AD 300

- Extent of the Roman Empire, c. AD 300
- Kingdom of David, 10th century BC
- Kingdom of Israel, 931 – 722 BC
- Kingdom of Judah, 931 – 587 BC
- Probable route of the Exodus, 13th century BC
- Route of Babylonian exile, 587 BC
- Jewish dispersion routes, c. 70 BC – c. AD 300

CITY OF JERUSALEM

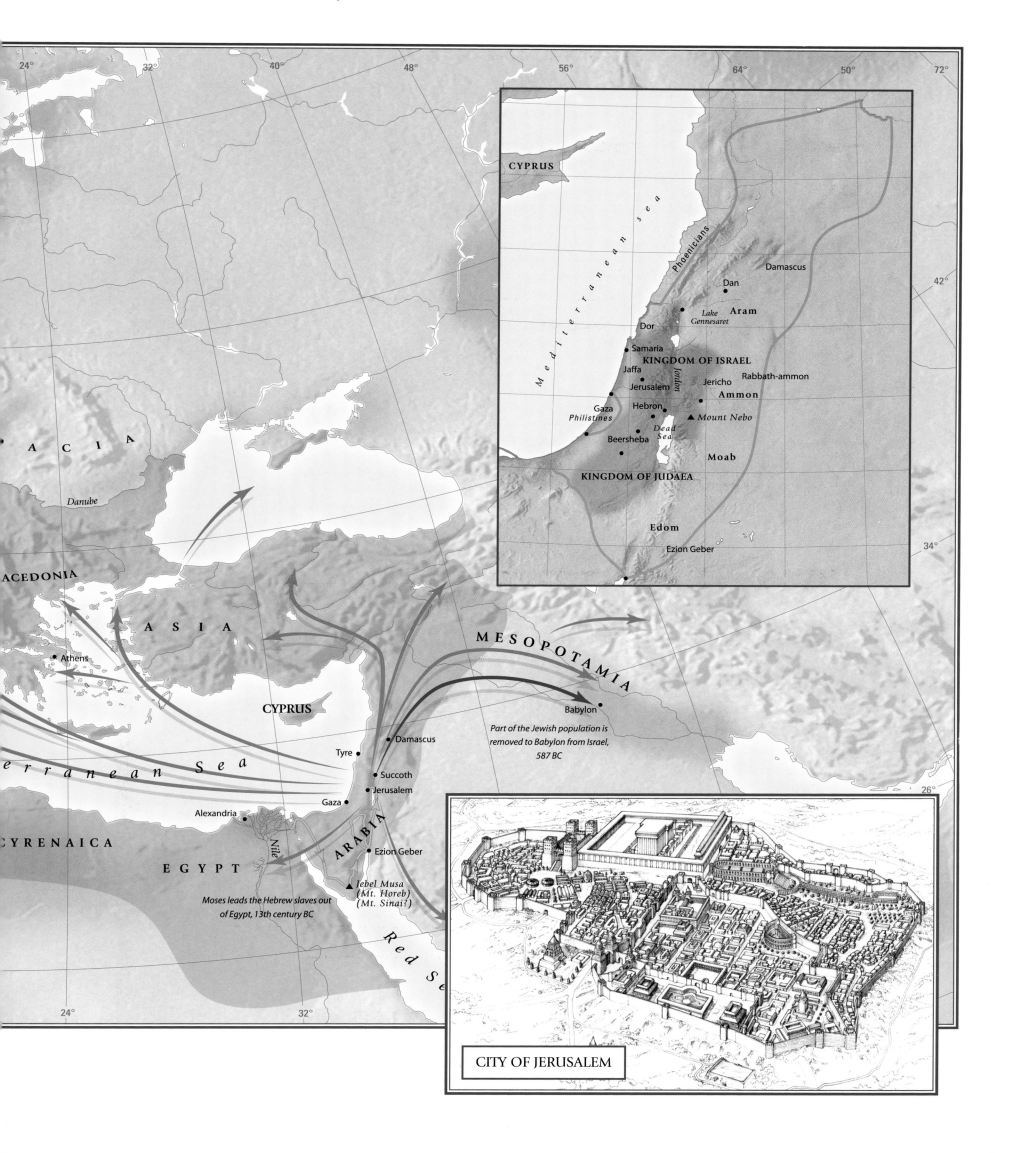

CYPRUS

Damascus

Dan

Lake Gennesaret **Aram**

Dor

Samaria

KINGDOM OF ISRAEL

Jaffa

Jerusalem *Jordan*

Jericho Rabbath-ammon

Gaza **Ammon**

Hebron

Philistines

Mount Nebo

Dead Sea

Beersheba

Moab

KINGDOM OF JUDAEA

Edom

Ezion Geber

Danube

D A C I A

MACEDONIA

A S I A

• Athens

CYPRUS

M E S O P O T A M I A

Babylon •

Part of the Jewish population is removed to Babylon from Israel, 587 BC

Mediterranean Sea

Tyre •

• Damascus

• Succoth

Gaza • • Jerusalem

Alexandria •

C Y R E N A I C A

Nile

E G Y P T

A R A B I A

• Ezion Geber

Jebel Musa (Mt. Horeb) (Mt. Sinai?)

Moses leads the Hebrew slaves out of Egypt, 13th century BC

Red Sea

CITY OF JERUSALEM

AD 1012 – 1975   # JEWS IN CHRISTIAN EUROPE

THE JEWS IN CHRISTIAN EUROPE

There were many Jewish communities around the coast of the Mediterranean, the Black Sea and the Near East. In Islamic lands the Jews were seen as 'People of the Book' who did not worship idols. However, Jewish citizens faced certain restrictions, such as as additional levels of taxation. In Europe the Jewish citizen was not looked on in such a positive light. Although Jesus was a Jew, the Gospels were critical of the Jewish leaders of his day and, of course, the Jews were blamed for the crucifixion of Jesus.

In 1144 Jews were accused of murdering Christian children, using their blood in the manufacture of unleavened bread to celebrate the Passover. In many places Jews were forbidden to own land or to practice many craft trades. In order to survive, many Jews turned to money lending, a trade forbidden to many Christians. The Jews would now be seen not only as Christ-killers but as usurers, and were thus subject to periodic persecution.

In 1290, the entire Jewish community in England was deported. In 1492, after the conquest of Islamic Granada, the Spanish Jews were expelled from the Iberian Peninsula. The exception was Poland where a large and thriving Jewish community established itself.

JEWS IN CHRISTIAN EUROPE
- ▨ Areas of Jewish communities
- → Expulsions, with date
- ○ Major centres of resettlement
- ● Main ghettoes, with date established
- ● Centres of disputations between Jews and Christians

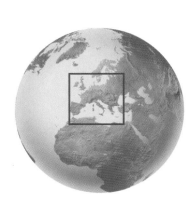

JEWISH MIGRATION; JEWS IN EUROPE AND PALESTINE

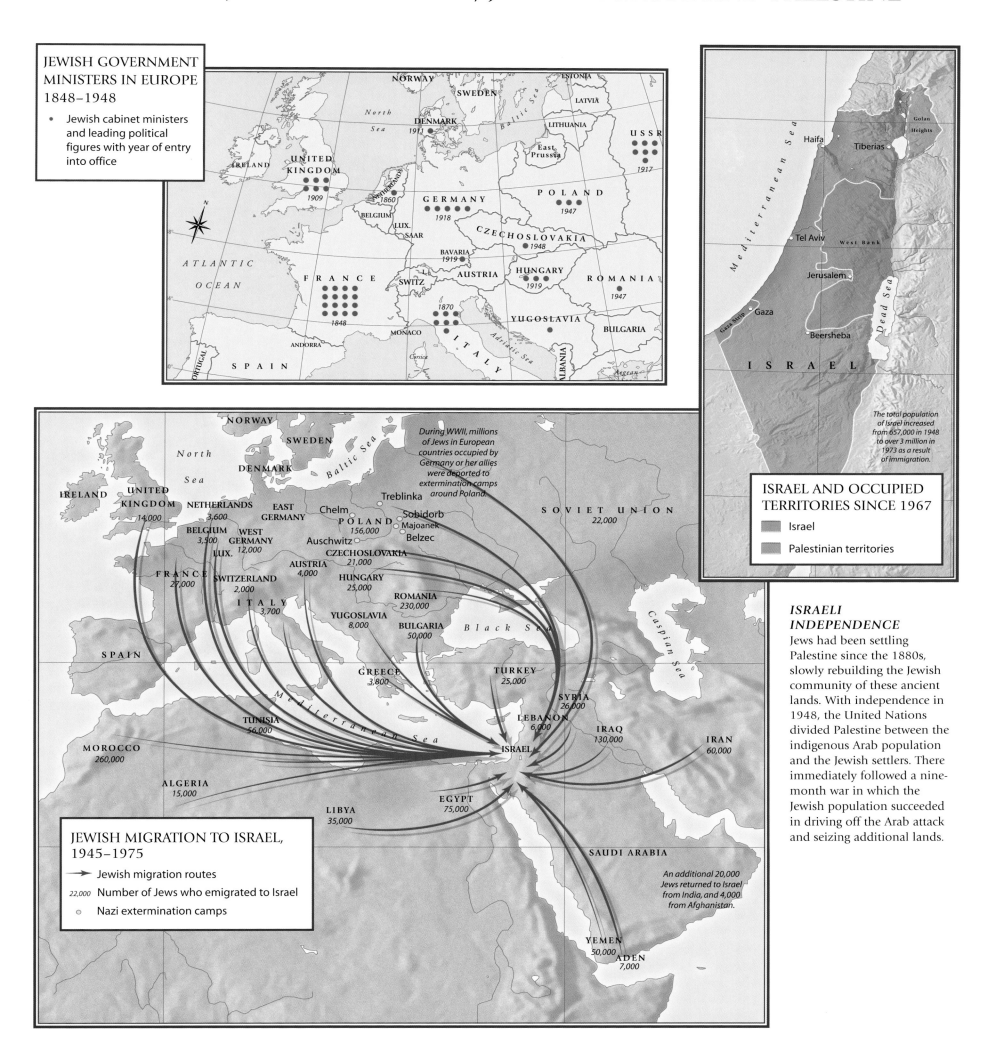

JEWISH GOVERNMENT MINISTERS IN EUROPE 1848–1948

- Jewish cabinet ministers and leading political figures with year of entry into office

The total population of Israel increased from 657,000 in 1948 to over 3 million in 1973 as a result of immigration.

ISRAEL AND OCCUPIED TERRITORIES SINCE 1967

- Israel
- Palestinian territories

During WWII, millions of Jews in European countries occupied by Germany or her allies were deported to extermination camps around Poland.

JEWISH MIGRATION TO ISRAEL, 1945–1975

→ Jewish migration routes

22,000 Number of Jews who emigrated to Israel

○ Nazi extermination camps

ISRAELI INDEPENDENCE

Jews had been settling Palestine since the 1880s, slowly rebuilding the Jewish community of these ancient lands. With independence in 1948, the United Nations divided Palestine between the indigenous Arab population and the Jewish settlers. There immediately followed a nine-month war in which the Jewish population succeeded in driving off the Arab attack and seizing additional lands.

An additional 20,000 Jews returned to Israel from India, and 4,000 from Afghanistan.

GLOBAL MIGRATION

GLOBAL MIGRATION
In the time of Catherine the Great industrial progress had led to an emergent middle class in Russia, many of whom were Jews. The Russian Imperial powers decided to limit this emergence by creating the Jewish Pale of Settlement in 1791 and so restrict Jewish areas of residence. The Pale comprised about 20 per cent of European Russia and in its heyday had a Jewish population of over 5 million, which was the largest concentration of Jewry in the world. Life in the Pale was hard and stricken by poverty. The aim of many was to get away and thousands sought a new life elsewhere.

In the early days of settlement in North America, the Jews of Spain made their home in the New World. They would later be joined by Jews from Germany and, after 1880, by a massive wave of Jews escaping persecution in eastern Europe. They also migrated in large numbers to South America and southern Africa as well as Palestine.

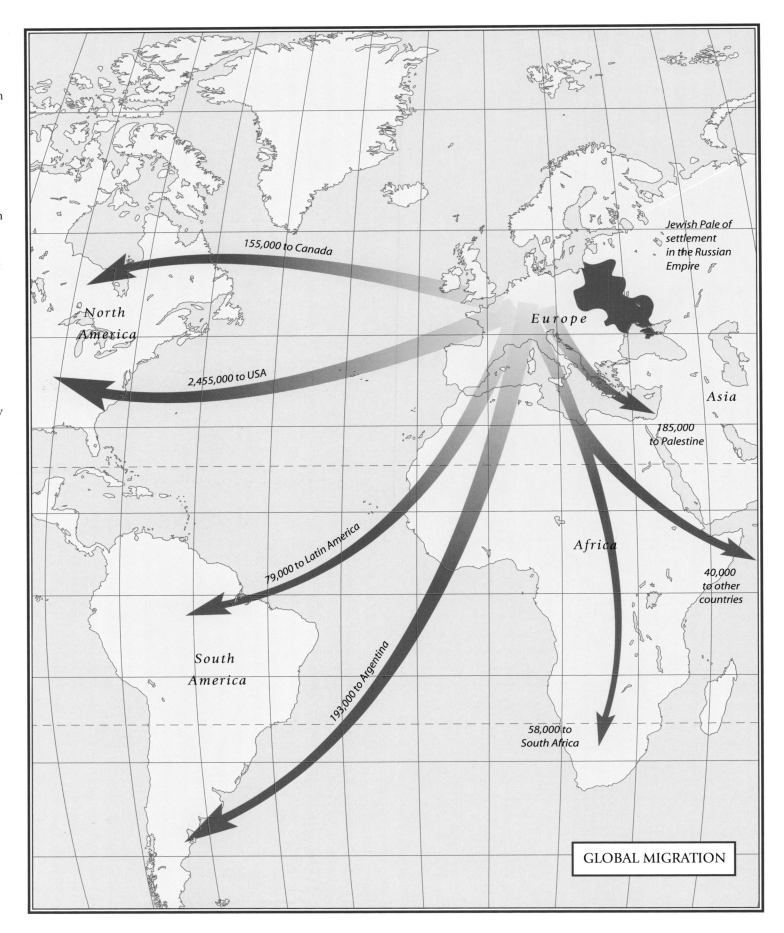

Jewish Pale of settlement in the Russian Empire

Europe

Asia

155,000 to Canada

North America

2,455,000 to USA

185,000 to Palestine

Africa

40,000 to other countries

79,000 to Latin America

South America

193,000 to Argentina

58,000 to South Africa

GLOBAL MIGRATION

JEWS IN THE USA

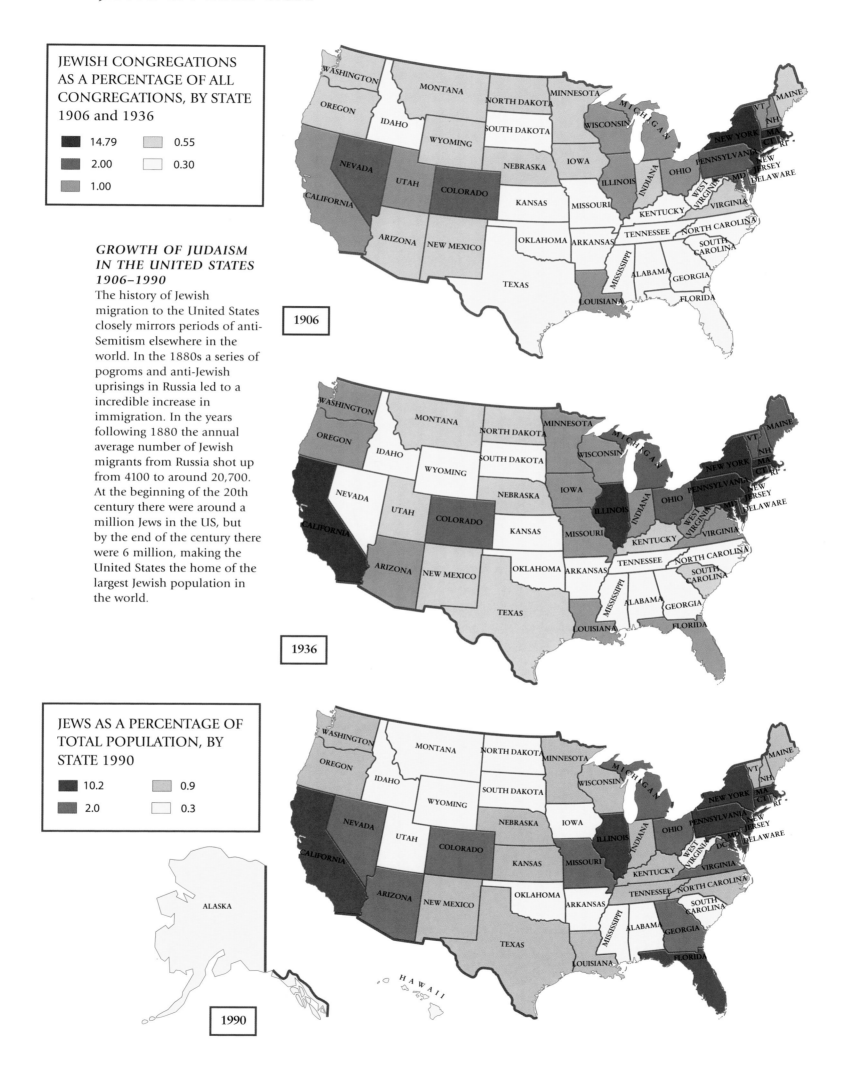

JEWISH CONGREGATIONS AS A PERCENTAGE OF ALL CONGREGATIONS, BY STATE 1906 and 1936

- 14.79
- 2.00
- 1.00
- 0.55
- 0.30

GROWTH OF JUDAISM IN THE UNITED STATES 1906–1990

The history of Jewish migration to the United States closely mirrors periods of anti-Semitism elsewhere in the world. In the 1880s a series of pogroms and anti-Jewish uprisings in Russia led to a incredible increase in immigration. In the years following 1880 the annual average number of Jewish migrants from Russia shot up from 4100 to around 20,700. At the beginning of the 20th century there were around a million Jews in the US, but by the end of the century there were 6 million, making the United States the home of the largest Jewish population in the world.

1906

1936

JEWS AS A PERCENTAGE OF TOTAL POPULATION, BY STATE 1990

- 10.2
- 2.0
- 0.9
- 0.3

1990

COUNTRIES BY JEWISH POPULATION

COUNTRIES BY JEWISH POPULATION

The worldwide Jewish population is 13.3 million, with around 4.95 million Jews based in Israel and 8.35 million scattered around the world. The country with the the largest Jewish population is the United States, with 6.5 million, or around 46 per cent of the world's total, residing there. Tel Aviv, the capital of Israel, is the world's largest Jewish City, with a population of 2.5 million Jews. The country with the highest number of Jews per 1000 population, outside of the United States and Israel, is Canada, with a ratio of 11.8. The overall Jewish population is lower than it was in the early part of the 20th century. Before 1939 there were 17 million Jews, but the Holocaust reduced the total to 11 million, which has recovered to just 13 million over the last 60 years.

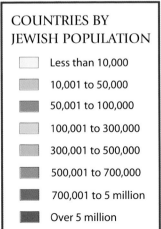

COUNTRIES BY JEWISH POPULATION

	Less than 10,000
	10,001 to 50,000
	50,001 to 100,000
	100,001 to 300,000
	300,001 to 500,000
	500,001 to 700,000
	700,001 to 5 million
	Over 5 million

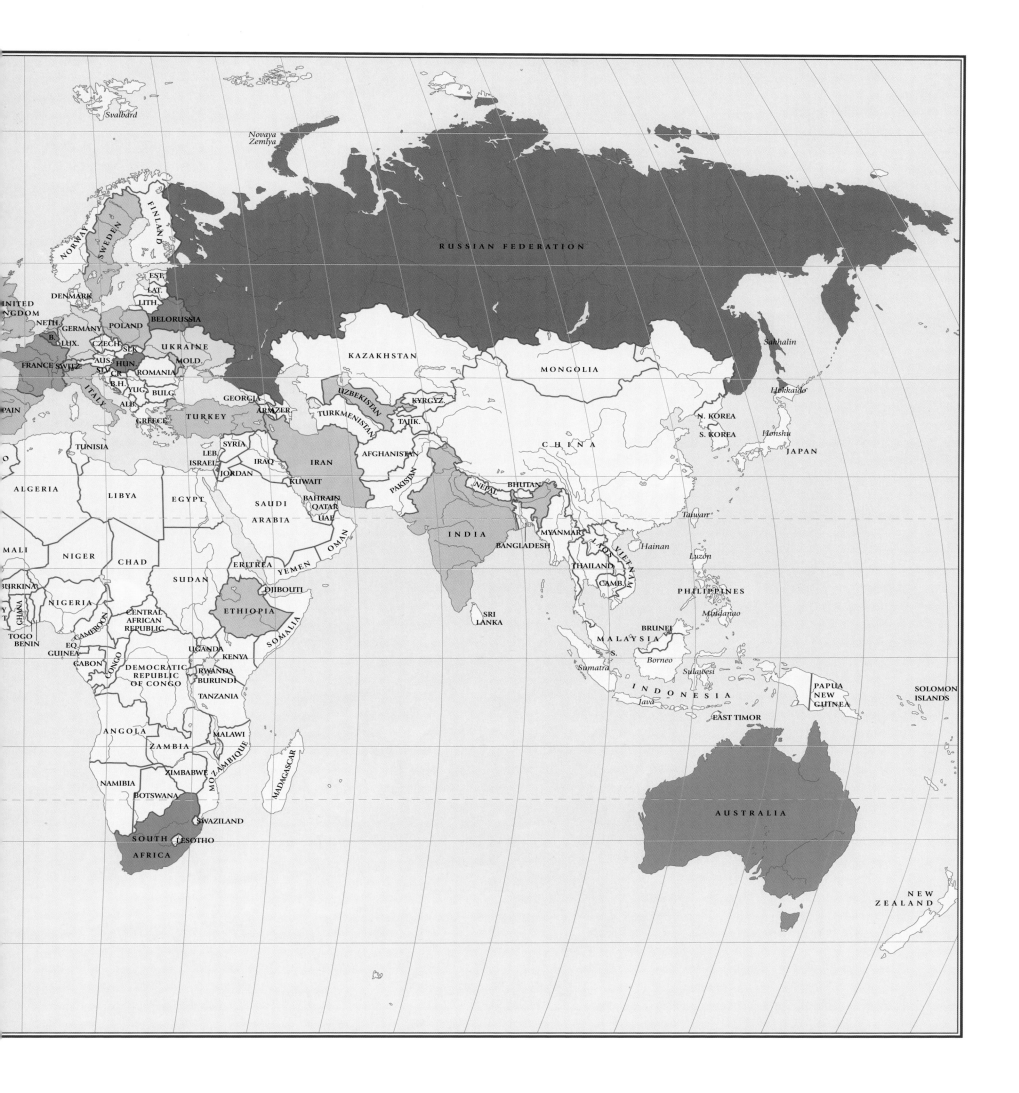

ARAB COUNTRIES INVADE; ISRAELI COUNTER-ATTACK

1948 – 1949

ARAB COUNTRIES INVADE
15 MAY–1 JUNE 1948

— Territory allocated to the State of Israel by the UN

☐ Territory overrun by the Arabs

→ Principal Arab attacks

● Jewish settlements overun by the Arabs

● Settlements remaining under Jewish control after repeated Arab attacks

ARAB COUNTRIES INVADE ISRAEL 15 MAY 1948

Palestine was under British control until 15th May 1948. The United Nations had recommended partitioning the territory into Jewish and Arab states. The Arab leaders all rejected this plan. On 14th May the State of Israel declared itself an independent nation and the surrounding Arab states mounted a concerted invasion. Over the next few days some 20,000 Arab troops from various nations invaded, although

many countries called this invasion an illegal aggression. In spite of large parts of the new state of Israel being occupied, the progressive mobilisation of Israeli society managed to prevent the country from being completely overrun.

ISRAELI COUNTER-ATTACK MAY 1948–JANUARY 1949

On 26th May the Israeli Defence Force was formally established. By July 1948 it was fielding 63,000 troops and by the following year, 115,000. The Arabs, on the other hand, had an estimated 40,000 troops in July 1948 and 55,000 in October. An Israeli Air Force had been formed and had managed to purchase 25 Czech-built versions of the Messerschmitt 109, which were soon in combat against

Egyptian Spitfires. Israel rapidly recovered from its earlier setback and tenaciously fought back. The Arabs were gradually expelled and Israel managed to secure and extend its original borders. 1n 1949 Israel signed a series of armistices with its Arab neighbours.

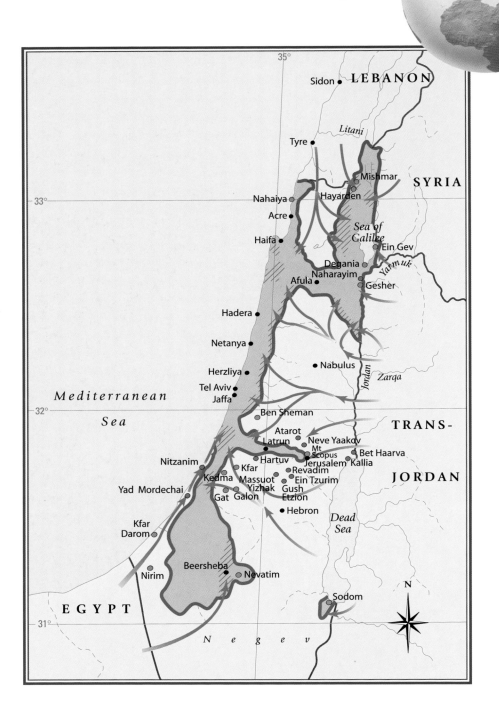

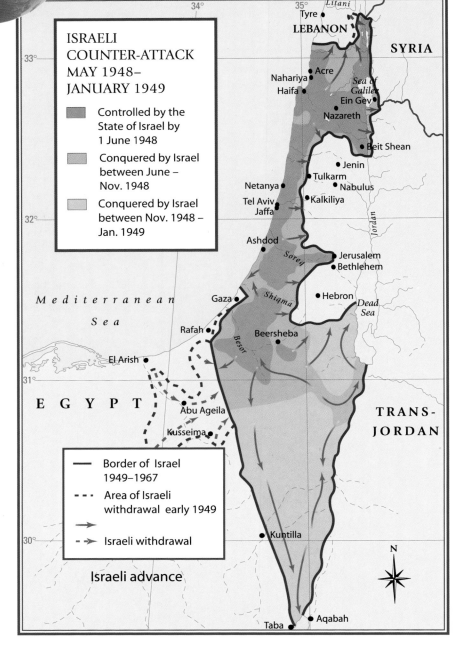

ISRAELI COUNTER-ATTACK MAY 1948– JANUARY 1949

■ Controlled by the State of Israel by 1 June 1948

■ Conquered by Israel between June – Nov. 1948

■ Conquered by Israel between Nov. 1948 – Jan. 1949

— Border of Israel 1949–1967

-- Area of Israeli withdrawal early 1949

→ Israeli withdrawal

Israeli advance

PART 4

BUDDHISM

*I*N THE 6TH CENTURY BC, in the Indian kingdom of Magadha, Gautama, the Buddha, also known as Shakyamuni or Prince Siddhartha, was born into a royal family. Feeling unhappy with his existence he left his family, setting out to search for the meaning of life. Eventually, he decided that life entails suffering and that this pain is generated by lusting after material possessions. If cravings were ended and attachments shaken off, then suffering would end and the calm and peace of nirvana could be attained.

Being thus enlightened, Gautama created a vision of the world based on Indian cosmology with its concepts of karma and reincarnation. According to Buddha, all life forms – humans, animals, gods and devils – have an infinite number of lives, and, like climbing ladder, a being can move up or down, to and from nirvana. The point achieved on this journey depended upon karma, good or bad deeds. Gautama taught that human beings can follow this route by themselves, without the help of gods or buddhas, the enlightened ones. People could end their suffering by detaching themselves from earthly possessions. Ethical living, compassion for all life, meditation, and prayer over several lifetimes might free one from suffering and allow entry into a state of calm and peace. These teachings were passed on by the Buddhist disciples and were written down as sutras.

THE BUDDHIST HEARTLAND; BUDDHISM IN INDIA

THE BUDDHIST HEARTLAND

The Buddha, originally known as Gautama, was born in c. 563 BC in the small settlement of Lumbini in the principality of Sakyan. In his early years he was discouraged from taking up a religious life. Later, however, after a series of chance encounters, he left home, becoming a mendicant. After several years of searching and religious thought, he achieved enlightenment on the banks of the River Nairanjana at a place now called Buddh Gaya. He then travelled to Sarnath, giving sermons and steadily gaining followers. He went on to found the first Buddhist religious settlement at Sangha. Missionary activities began almost immediately 60 of his disciples were sent across India to spread his word.

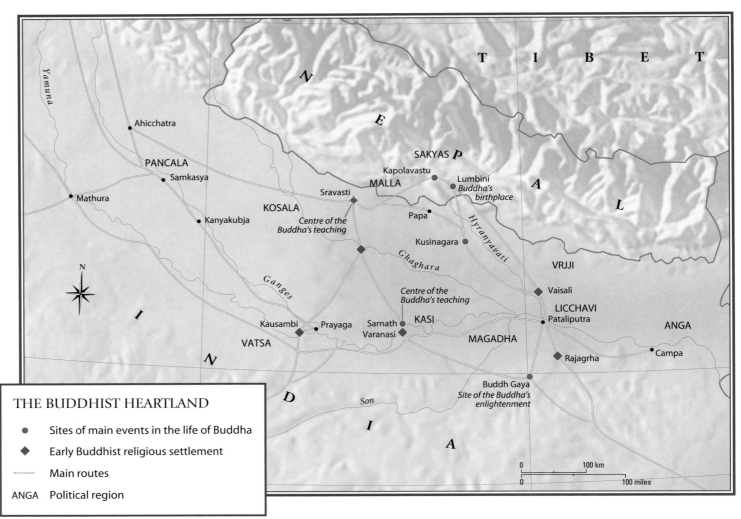

THE BUDDHIST HEARTLAND

● Sites of main events in the life of Buddha

◆ Early Buddhist religious settlement

— Main routes

ANGA Political region

BUDDHISM IN INDIA
300 BC–AD 100

▢ Mauryan Empire under Asoka

● Main Buddhist sub-schools

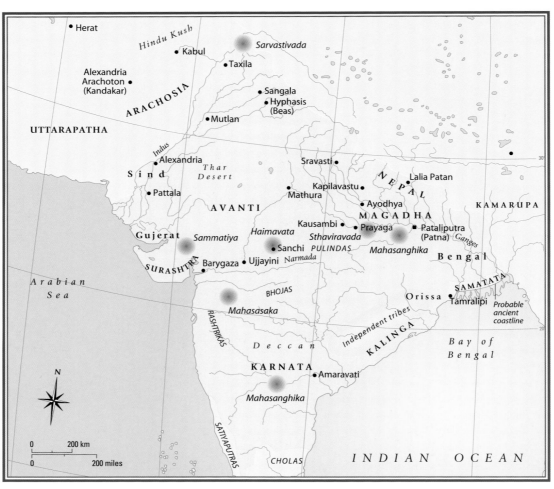

BUDDHISM IN INDIA 300 BC–AD 100

The Mauryan Empire reached its greatest extent under Asoka, 268–232 bc. The King, realising the human cost of building this Empire, converted to Buddhism becoming one of its greatest benefactors. During his rule Buddhist centres expanded and new monasteries were built, together with stupas, to house holy relics. Asoka also undertook to follow Buddhist concepts of social care throughout his domains. He also sent missionaries as far westward as Alexandria, in Egypt; Bactria, in central Asia; and to the island of Sri Lanka.

THE MAURYAN EMPIRE

THE MAURYAN EMPIRE UNDER ASOKA

Asoka, or Ashoka, was an Indian emperor of the Maurya Dynasty who ruled from 273 to 232 BC. His empire covered most of present-day India and Pakistan along with much of Afghanistan and parts of Persia. His early life was spent constantly at war, but a turning point came after the Kalinga War in 265 when his armies killed 100,000 and deported thousands more. Asoka was so appalled that he gave up war and violence and became a Buddhist. The remaining years of his reign were peaceful and prosperous, but after his death the mighty empire lasted for just 50 more years before breaking up.

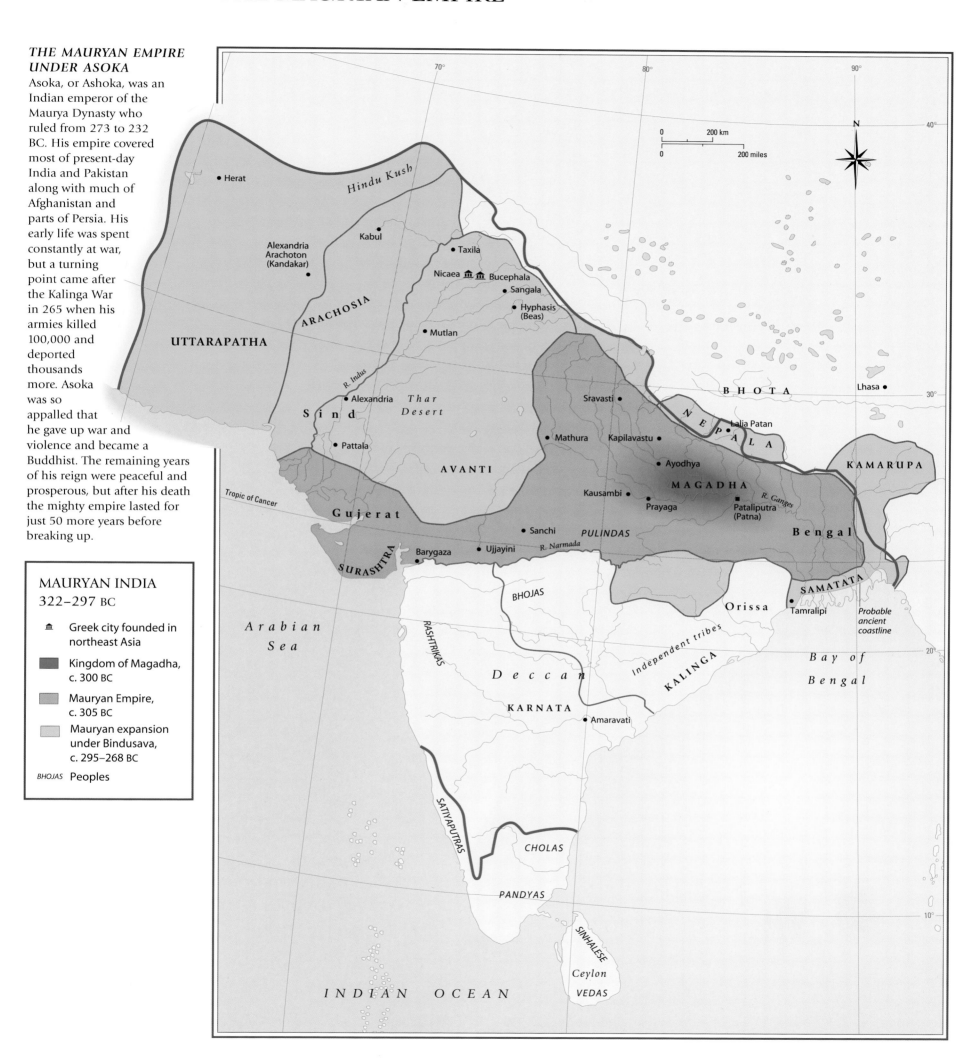

MAURYAN INDIA
322–297 BC

- 🏛 Greek city founded in northeast Asia
- ▬ Kingdom of Magadha, c. 300 BC
- ▬ Mauryan Empire, c. 305 BC
- ▬ Mauryan expansion under Bindusava, c. 295–268 BC
- *BHOJAS* Peoples

BUDDHISM IN INDIA

BUDDHISM IN INDIA 4TH TO 8TH CENTURIES
The Gupta Empire in India is regarded as a golden age that crystallised Hindu culture. While the Guptas were predominately Hindu, they were happy to embrace elements of the Buddhist religion and Buddhism quietly flourished during this time. Buddhism had already spread along the Silk Road to China, where there was great interest in the religion. A number of Chinese missionaries journeyed to India to seek further information. One of the most notable was Xuan-Zing who spent many years journeying throughout India and translated Indian Buddhist texts into Chinese.

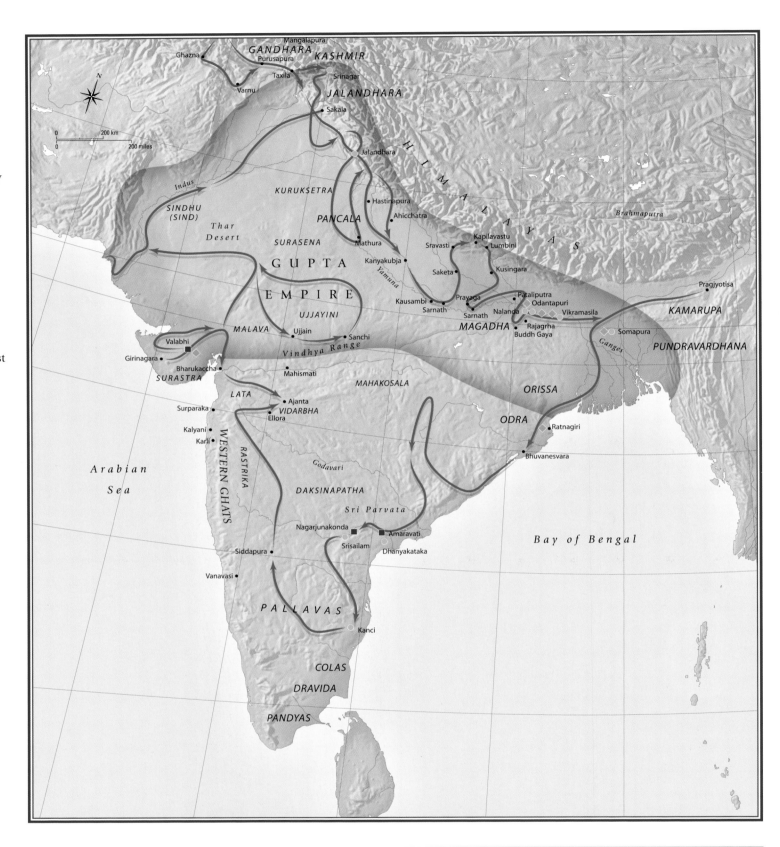

BUDDHISM IN INDIA, 4TH–8TH CENTURIES AD

- Gupta Empire at its height, 5th–6th centuries AD
- → Approximate route of Xuan-Zang, AD 629–645
- ■ Place connected with development of Mahayana Buddhism
- ● Place connected with development of Tantric Buddhism
- ◆ Buddhist university monastery

THE MUGHAL EMPIRE

**THE MUGHAL EMPIRE
1526–1707**

The Mughal Empire was an
important imperial power in
the Indian subcontinent from
the early 16th to the mid-19th
centuries. At the height of its
power, around 1700, it
controlled over 3 million
square km; most of the
subcontinent including part of
what is now Afghanistan. Its
population at that time has
been estimated as between
100 and 150 million. Babur,
the founder of the Mhugal
Dynasty, took control of Kabul
in 1504 and through conquest
he gradually acquired more
territory. He defeated the last
of the Delhi sultans in 1526
and was proclaimed the first
emperor. The empire came
to an end in 1707.

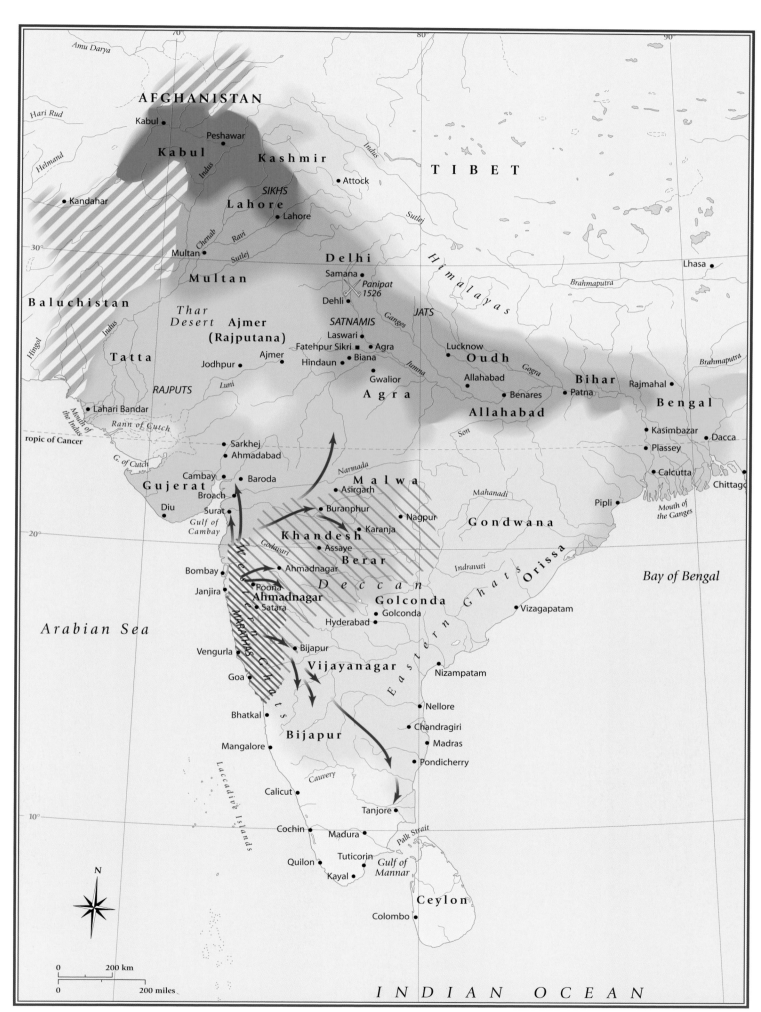

THE MUGHAL EMPIRE
1526–1707

- Mughal conquest by 1525
- Mughal conquest by 1539
- Empire at Akbar's death, 1605
- *Agra* Mughal subab (province)
- Empire at the death of Shah Jahau (Auranzeb), 1707
- → Maratha raids, 1664–1700
- Maratha territory, c.1700
- Under Maratha influence, c.1700
- *JATS* People in rebellion against the Empire, c.1700
- ✕ Battle

THE KHMER EMPIRE; THE SRIVIJAYA KINGDOM

THE KHMER EMPIRE
c. 1200

SOUTH-EAST ASIA & THE SRIVIJAYA KINGDOM

This was an ancient Malay kingdom on the island of Sumatra that lasted from the 3rd to the 14th century. It came to influence much of the Malay Archipelago. It was a stronghold of Vajrayana Buddhism and attracted pilgrims and scholars from other parts of Asia. These included the Chinese monk Yijing, who made several lengthy visits to Sumatra on his way to study at the Nalanda University in India. Another visitor was the Bengali Buddist scholar Atisha, who had a major role in the development of Vajrayana Buddhism in Tibet.

BUDDHISM: THE KHMER EMPIRE c. 1200

The Khmer Empire was the largest continuous empire of South-east Asia. King Jayavarman VII set up his capital in Angkor, which at the height of the Empire was the largest pre-industrial urban centre in the world and was larger than present-day New York. More than a thousand temples are crammed into the 310 square kilometres of the city. Jayavarman was a fervent Buddhist of the Mahayana school and there are a number of larger than life statues of him in meditation. He constructed a state temple, the Bayon, with multiple towers, each bearing faces turned in the cardinal directions.

SOUTH-EAST ASIA
AND THE SRIVIJAYA
KINGDOM, c. 1200

—— furthest extent of T'ang China

⟶ Thai peoples moving south

▲ Hindu/Buddhist temple, 600–1300

BUDDHISM IN ASIA

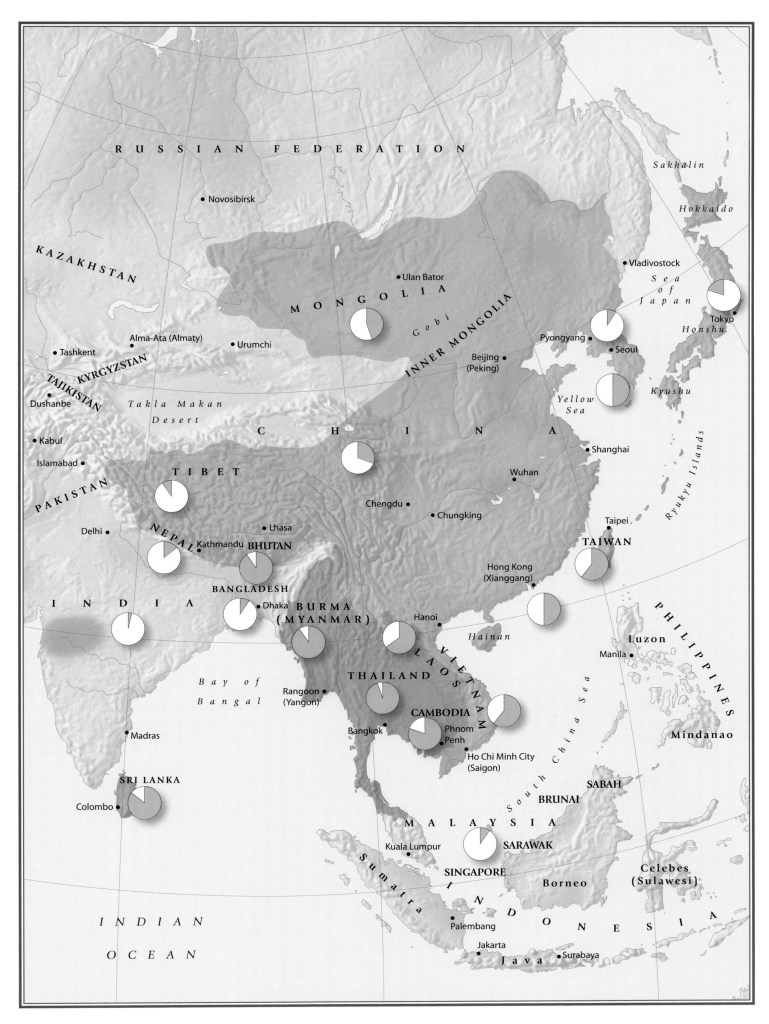

BUDDHISM IN ASIA
The two major branches of Buddhism are Theravada and Mahayana Buddhism. Theravada Buddhism is found in Burma, Thailand, Laos and Cambodia. Main centres of Mahayana Buddhism are in China Vietnam and Japan. A version of Mahayana Buddhism is the Tibetan Buddhism. Another version of Mahayana Buddhism is Zen Buddhism, which is very popular in Europe and North America.

THE SPREAD OF BUDDHISM, HINDUISM AND CHRISTIANITY

THE SPREAD OF BUDDHISM, HINDUISM AND CHRISTIANITY
Buddhism started to become established after the death of Buddha in around 483 BC. A Buddhist university was established at Taxilia and this became a jumping-off point for missionaries penetrating Central Asia. Later missionaries used the Silk Road, converting the Central Asian oasis towns and exporting Buddhism into China. Buddhism, like the older religion of Hinduism, is very much an Eastern faith, spreading no further than the western fringes of India. The spread of Christianity, on the other hand, was predominately to the west.

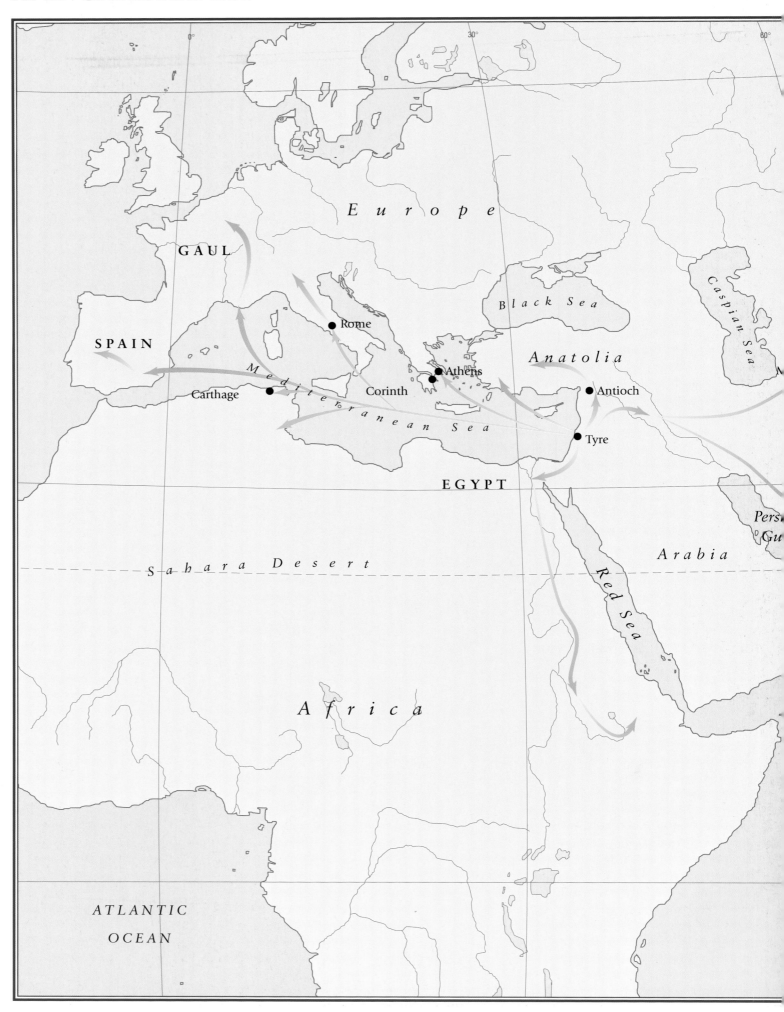

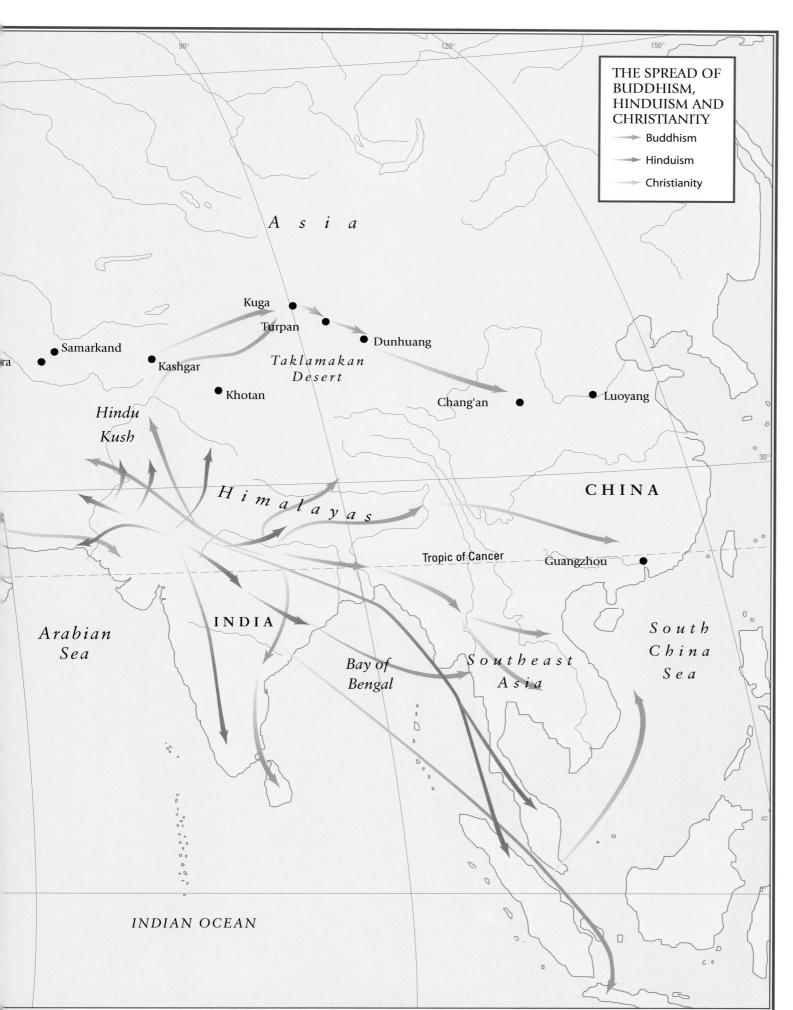

THE SPREAD OF
BUDDHISM,
HINDUISM AND
CHRISTIANITY

→ Buddhism
→ Hinduism
→ Christianity

A s i a

Kuga

Turpan

Samarkand

Kashgar

*Taklamakan
Desert*

Dunhuang

Khotan

Chang'an

Luoyang

*Hindu
Kush*

30°

H i m a l a y a s

CHINA

Tropic of Cancer

Guangzhou

*Arabian
Sea*

INDIA

*Bay of
Bengal*

*Southeast
Asia*

*South
China
Sea*

INDIAN OCEAN

BUDDHISM IN JAPAN
(OVERLEAF)
There is a long history of
Buddhism in Japan. It was
brought to China by the Silk
Road in around the 1st century
AD and it reached Japan in
around the 5th century. In
modern times there are three
main paths of Buddhism to
which all Japanese schools of
Buddhism belong; the Amidst
(Pure Land) schools, Nichiren
Buddhism and Zen Buddhism.
The Todaiji Temple in Nara
is one of the major historical
temples of Japan and dates
from the year 743. Among
its many treasures is the
world's largest gilded bronze
Buddha, that stands 15 metres
(49 feet) tall.

BUDDHISM IN JAPAN

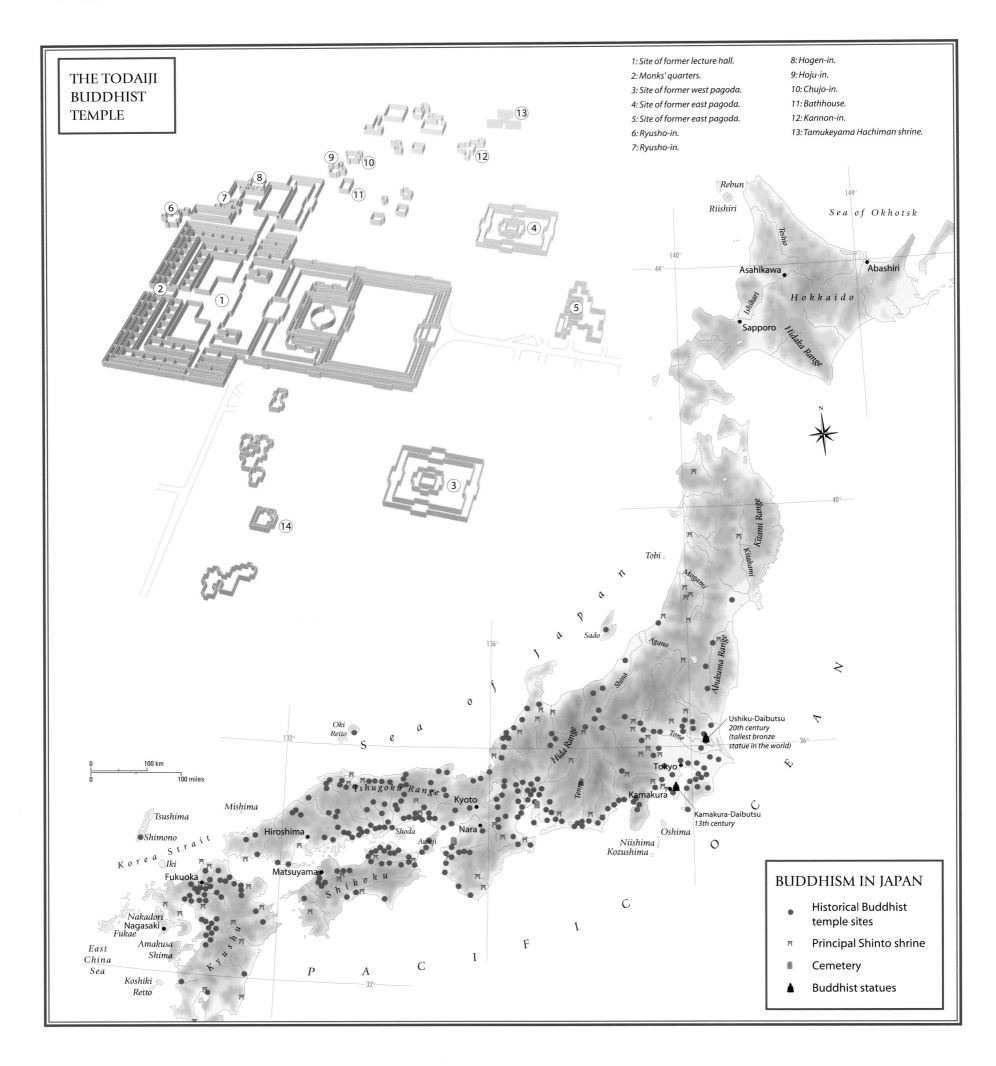

THE TODAIJI
BUDDHIST
TEMPLE

1: Site of former lecture hall.
2: Monks' quarters.
3: Site of former west pagoda.
4: Site of former east pagoda.
5: Site of former east pagoda.
6: Ryusho-in.
7: Ryusho-in.
8: Hogen-in.
9: Hoju-in.
10: Chujo-in.
11: Bathhouse.
12: Kannon-in.
13: Tamukeyama Hachiman shrine.

Ushiku-Daibutsu
20th century
(tallest bronze
statue in the world)

Kamakura-Daibutsu
13th century

BUDDHISM IN JAPAN

- Historical Buddhist temple sites
- Principal Shinto shrine
- Cemetery
- ▲ Buddhist statues

PART 5

CHRISTIANITY

CHRISTIANITY IS THE FAITH based upon the teachings off Jesus of Nazareth as expounded in his three-year ministry of preaching, parables, and miracles before his crucifixion. Jesus' mission on earth was not to restore the old kingdom of David by military force but to work in the spiritual realm. He personified the promises recorded in ancient Jewish holy books and, morere importantly, he was to bring about God's universal kingdom of love and peace. His crucifixion was an act of redemption decreed by God to free the world from sin. Because Jesus accepted theis death from God's hand he was invested with God's power to make the kingdom of God a reality on earth. Jesus Christ's teachings took place amongst his disciples, in synagogues or in mass open-air meetings. His preaching proclaimed the fatherhood and authority of God and the need for righteousness and selfless love. His famous Sermon on the Mount stated that happiness could be found by eschewing wealth and success and accepting instead mercy, humility, peace-making and spiritual hunger. He condemned anger and lust, equating them with murder and adultery. The Sermon's beatitudes are coreements of Christianity as is the legacy expressed in The Lord's Prayer.

AREA AROUND JERUSALEM

AREA AROUND JERUSALEM 1ST CENTURY AD

The 1st century AD is a period of great significance for both Christians and Jews. For Christians it includes the period of Jesus' life, death and resurrection. By the end of the century Christian influence extended throughout the Eastern Mediterranean. For the Jews it was the time of the First Roman War. Jerusalem was besieged and anyone caught trying to escape was crucified. By the end of the siege in AD 70, there were tens of thousands of crucified bodies surrounding the city. Jerusalem was looted and burned and apart from one wall, Solomon's temple was flattened.

JESUS' BIRTH AND EARLY CHILDHOOD

Mary and Joseph lived in Nazareth but had to travel to Bethlehem to be registered for tax purposes. Here Jesus was born in around 7–6 BC. After his birth he was taken to Jerusalem for the ritual sacrificial ceremony, before being taken by his parents to Egypt after Joseph had been warned in a dream about King Herod's impending slaughter of male babies. A further dream told him when it was safe to return. When Jesus was 12 he went to Jerusalem with his parents. He was so engrossed with the elders at the Temple that his parents nearly went home without him.

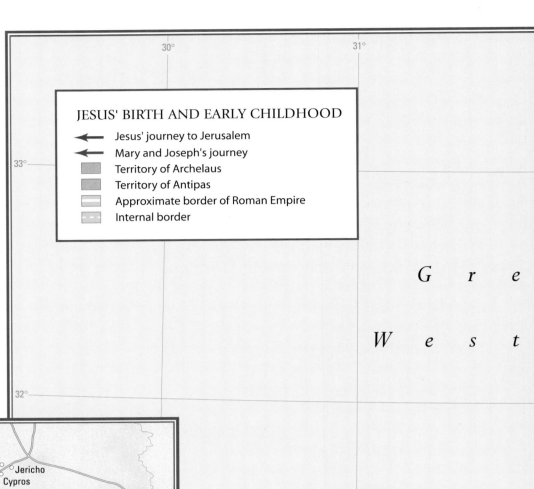

JESUS' BIRTH AND EARLY CHILDHOOD
← Jesus' journey to Jerusalem
← Mary and Joseph's journey
▢ Territory of Archelaus
▢ Territory of Antipas
▭ Approximate border of Roman Empire
▭ Internal border

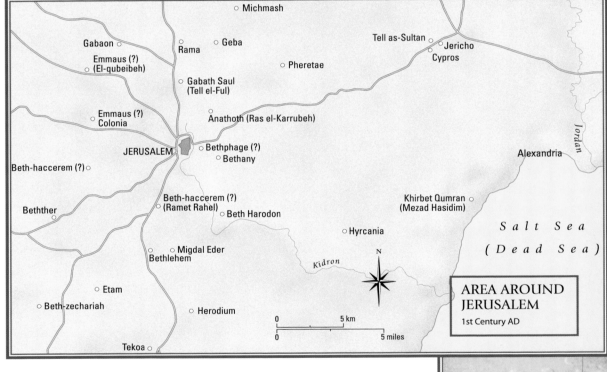

Michmash
Gabaon
Rama · Geba
Emmaus (?) (El-qubeibeh)
Pheretae
Tell as-Sultan
Jericho
Cypros
Gabath Saul (Tell el-Ful)
Emmaus (?) Colonia
Anathoth (Ras el-Karrubeh)
JERUSALEM
Bethphage (?)
Bethany
Beth-haccerem (?)
Alexandria
Jordan
Beth-haccerem (?) (Ramet Rahel)
Beth Harodon
Khirbet Qumran (Mezad Hasidim)
Beththter
Migdal Eder
Bethlehem
Hyrcania
Kidron
N
Salt Sea (Dead Sea)
Etam
Beth-zechariah
Herodium
Tekoa

AREA AROUND JERUSALEM
1st Century AD

0   5 km
0   5 miles

G r e
W e s t

A E G Y P T U S
(E G Y P T)

On (Hellopolis)

Noph (Memphis)

Nile

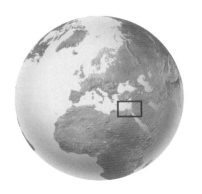

JESUS' BIRTH AND EARLY CHILDHOOD

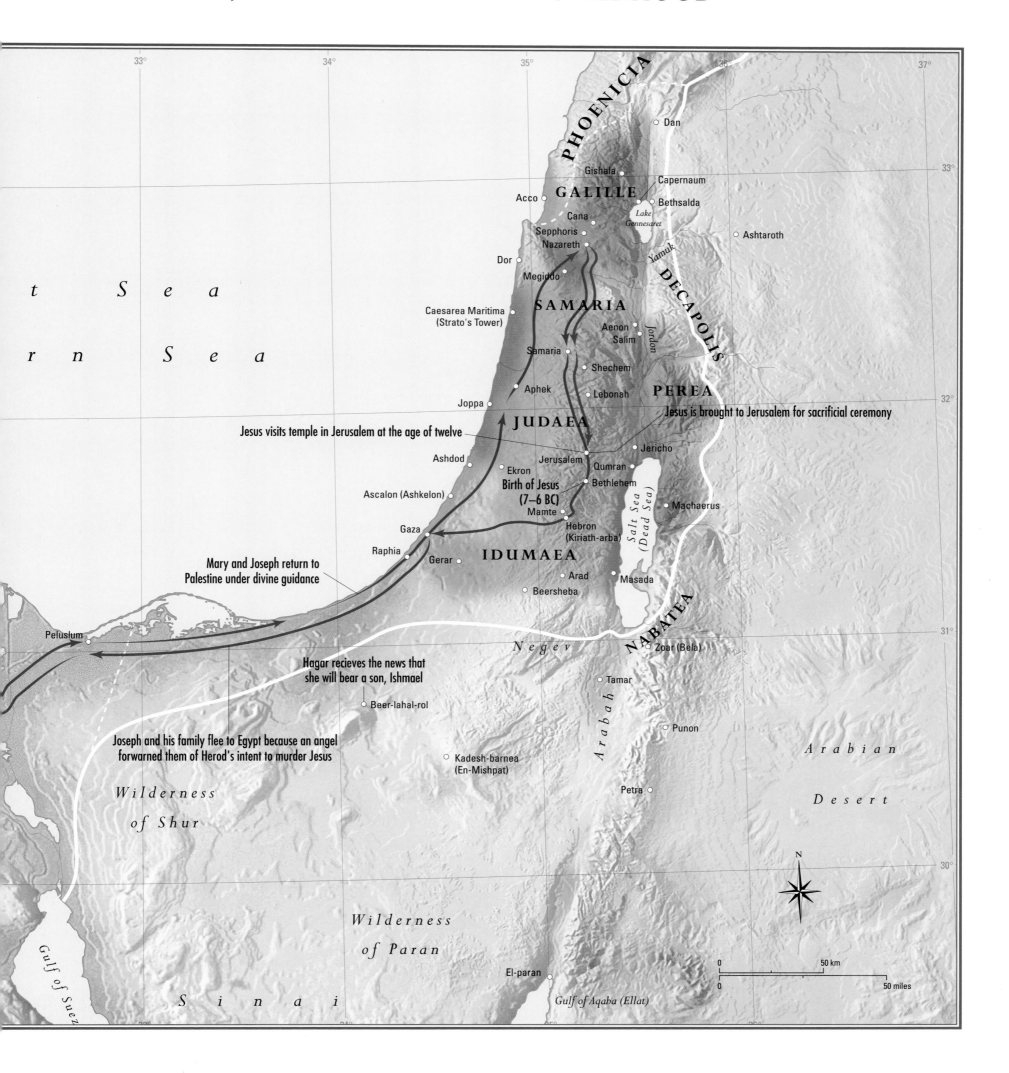

PHOENICIA

Dan

Gishala

GALILLE

Capernaum

Acco

Bethsalda

Cana

Lake
Gennesaret

Sepphoris

Ashtaroth

Nazareth

Dor

DECAPOLIS

Megiddo

Yamuk

Caesarea Maritima
(Strato's Tower)

SAMARIA

Aenon
Salim

Jordan

Samaria

Shechem

Aphek

Lebonah

PEREA

Joppa

Jesus is brought to Jerusalem for sacrificial ceremony

JUDAEA

Jesus visits temple in Jerusalem at the age of twelve

Jericho

Ashdod

Jerusalem

Qumran

Ekron

Bethlehem

Birth of Jesus
(7–6 BC)

Ascalon (Ashkelon)

Machaerus

Mamte

Gaza

Hebron
(Kiriath-arba)

Salt Sea
(Dead Sea)

Raphia

Gerar

IDUMAEA

Mary and Joseph return to
Palestine under divine guidance

Arad

Masada

Beersheba

NABATEA

Pelusium

Negev

Zoar (Bela)

Hagar recieves the news that
she will bear a son, Ishmael

Tamar

Beer-lahal-rol

Arabah

Punon

Joseph and his family flee to Egypt because an angel
forwarned them of Herod's intent to murder Jesus

Arabian

Wilderness

Desert

of Shur

Kadesh-barnea
(En-Mishpat)

Petra

N

Wilderness

of Paran

0   50 km

El-paran

0   50 miles

Gulf of Suez

Sinai

Gulf of Aqaba (Ellat)

t   S e a

r n   S e a

THE HOLY LAND AFTER HEROD AND THE RULE OF THE TETRARCHS

THE HOLY LAND AFTER HEROD AND THE RULE OF THE TETRARCHS
When Herod the Great died in 4 BC, his kingdom was divided between his sons who ruled as Tetrarchs. Archelaus, Herod's son by his fourth wife, received the largest area, Idumaea, Judaea and Samaria. Archelaus's brother Antipas became Tetrarch of Galilee and Perea, while Philip, who was Herod's son by his fifth wife, became Tetrarch of the northern part of Herod's kingdom. Herod Archelaus was removed by Emperor Augustus in AD 6 following complaints about his cruelty and his territory was reorganised as a Roman province with a Roman governor.

THE HOLY LAND AFTER HEROD, THE RULE OF THE TETRARCHS
- Tetrarchy of Achelaus
- Tetrarchy of Antipas
- Tetrarchy of Philip
- Salome's inheritance
- Major roads
- minor roads

PHOENICIA

GAULANITES

GALILEE

BATANAEA

Tyre

Caesarea

Lake Huleh

Ptolemais

Sea of Chinnereth (Sea of Galilee)

Hippus

Gadara

Dora

Caesarea

Great Sea

Western Sea

SAMARIA

Jordan

Samaria

Amathus

Mt Gerizim ▲

Shechem

Zarqa

Joppa

Phasaelis

Gedor

JUDAEA

PERAEA

Shueib

Jamnia

Jericho

Hisban

Esbus

Azotus

Hierosolyma (Jerusalem)

Ascalon

Betogabris

Salt Sea (Dead Sea)

Gaza

Mujib

the King's Highway

IDUMAEA

NABATAEA

0   20 km
0   20 miles

Negev

THE MINISTRY OF JESUS

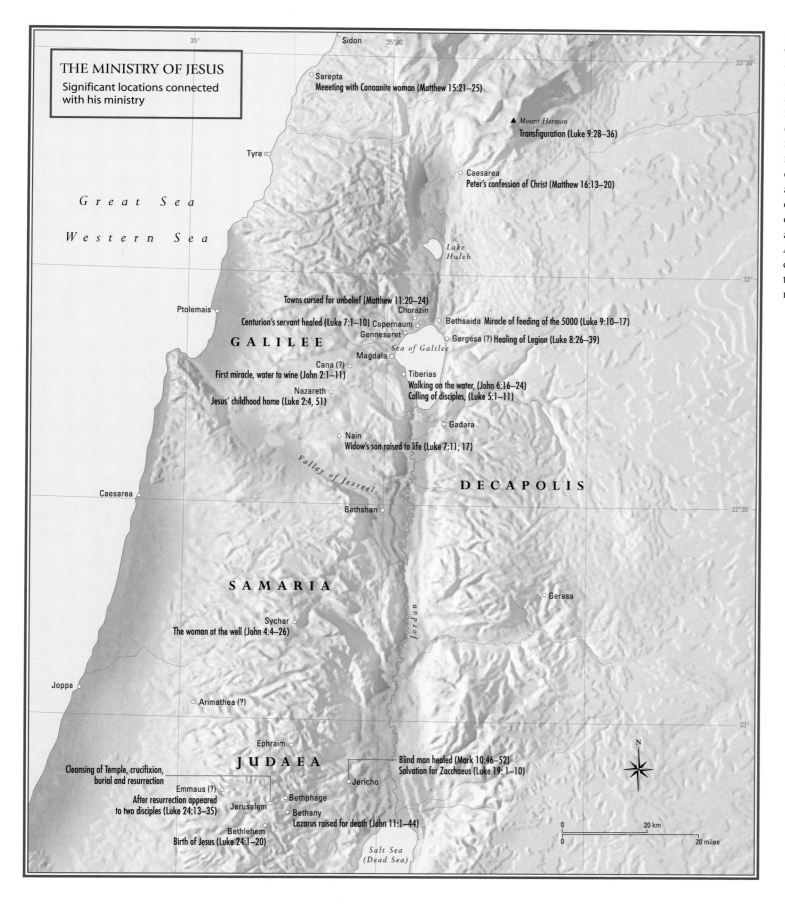

THE MINISTRY OF JESUS
Significant locations connected
with his ministry

Sidon

Sarepta
Meeeting with Canaanite woman (Matthew 15:21–25)

▲ Mount Hermon
Transfiguration (Luke 9:28–36)

Tyre

Caesarea
Peter's confession of Christ (Matthew 16:13–20)

Great Sea

Western Sea

Lake Huleh

Towns cursed for unbelief (Matthew 11:20–24)
Chorazin
Ptolemais
Centurion's servant healed (Luke 7:1–10) Capernaum Bethsaida Miracle of feeding of the 5000 (Luke 9:10–17)
Gennesaret Gergesa (?) Healing of Legion (Luke 8:26–39)
GALILEE Magdala *Sea of Galilee*
Cana (?)
First miracle, water to wine (John 2:1–11) Tiberias
Nazareth Walking on the water, (John 6:16–24)
Jesus' childhood home (Luke 2:4, 51) Calling of disciples, (Luke 5:1–11)

Nain Gadara
Widow's son raised to life (Luke 7:11; 17)

Valley of Jezreel **DECAPOLIS**

Caesarea

Bethshan

SAMARIA Gerasa

Sychar *Jordan*
The woman at the well (John 4:4–26)

Joppa

Arimathea (?)

Ephraim Blind man healed (Mark 10:46–52)
JUDAEA Salvation for Zacchaeus (Luke 19: 1–10)
Cleansing of Temple, crucifixion,
burial and resurrection Jericho
Emmaus (?) Bethphage
After resurrection appeared
to two disciples (Luke 24:13–35) Jerusalem Bethany
Bethlehem Lazarus raised for death (John 11:1–44)
Birth of Jesus (Luke 24:1–20)

*Salt Sea
(Dead Sea)*

N

0   20 km
0   20 miles

THE MINISTRY OF JESUS
The four Gospels were all
written by different people at
different times, for different
audiences, but all describe
important happenings before,
during and after Jesus'
ministry. The length of his
ministry is unclear, but it was
certainly more than one year
and less than three. Various
events in Jesus' life appear in
each of the Gospels and some
appear in more than one.
Although there is no
chronology, it is possible
to plot the locations of
many of these events.

THE EARLY SPREAD OF THE GOSPEL

THE EARLY SPREAD OF THE GOSPEL

St Peter was very successful in taking the Christian message to Jewish people. Initially many Jews regarded Christianity as something of a 'bolt-on' religion and they still regarded it as very important to maintain their Jewish traditions. Meanwhile evangelists such as St Paul and St Philip were particularly active in taking the Christian message to non-Jewish people, where it became very popular. St Philip is especially remembered for preaching the Gospel outside Judaea and spending some time preaching to the Samaritans. Conflict arose when Jewish converts insisted that Gentile converts could only be admitted if they abided by Jewish law.

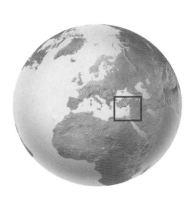

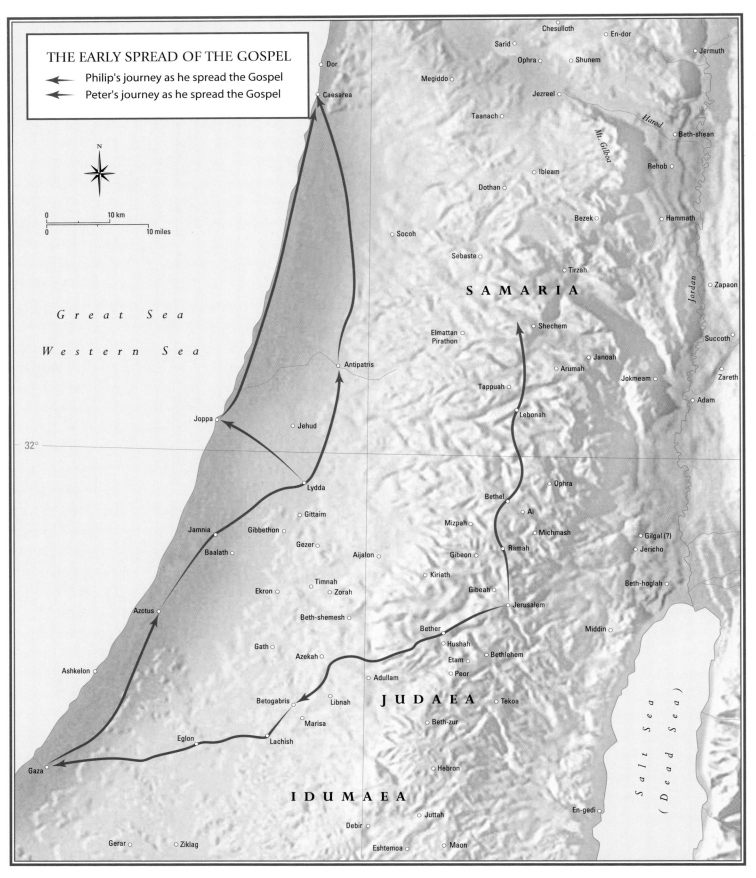

THE EARLY SPREAD OF THE GOSPEL

⬅ Philip's journey as he spread the Gospel

⬅ Peter's journey as he spread the Gospel

PAUL'S JOURNEYS (RIGHT)

St Paul made three major missionary journeys. There is some speculation about the precise timings of these and, particularly with the Third Journey, the precise route that Paul took. Much has to be gleaned from references he made in various letters and there is even some speculation that not all of the letters attributed to Paul were actually written by him. The three journeys took place during a period of 10 to 14 years between AD 44 and 58. In AD 60 Paul was taken to Rome as a prisoner. He was finally released in AD 63, but was probably martyred in AD 67.

THE JOURNEYS OF ST PAUL; EARLY ROMAN CHRISTIAN CHURCH

EARLY ROMAN CHRISTIAN CHURCH

The first Christian Emperor of Rome was Constantine the Great (285–337). He was originally a pagan who worshipped the sun but when he was going into battle in 312 he started to pray to the 'Supreme God' for help. Jesus came to him in a dream and he was converted to Christianity, although he was not baptised until his old age. Christianity became the favoured religion of the Empire and many churches were built. Initially many existing buildings were adapted and in some cases had a dual use. New buildings followed very much the same design as Roman secular buildings.

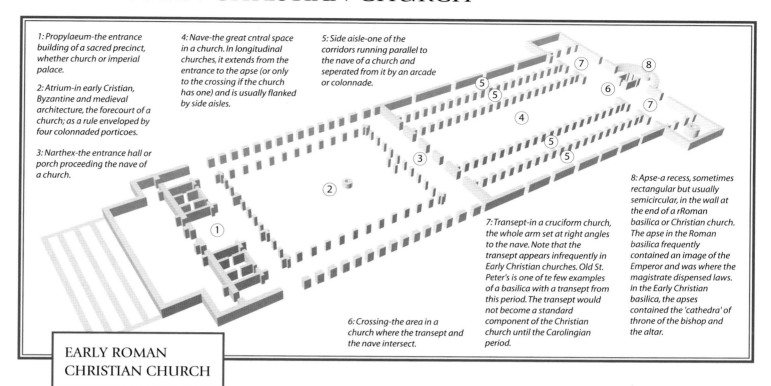

1: Propylaeum-the entrance building of a sacred precinct, whether church or imperial palace.

2: Atrium-in early Cristian, Byzantine and medieval architecture, the forecourt of a church; as a rule enveloped by four colonnaded porticoes.

3: Narthex-the entrance hall or porch proceeding the nave of a church.

4: Nave-the great cntral space in a church. In longitudinal churches, it extends from the entrance to the apse (or only to the crossing if the church has one) and is usually flanked by side aisles.

5: Side aisle-one of the corridors running parallel to the nave of a church and seperated from it by an arcade or colonnade.

6: Crossing-the area in a church where the transept and the nave intersect.

7: Transept-in a cruciform church, the whole arm set at right angles to the nave. Note that the transept appears infrequently in Early Christian churches. Old St. Peter's is one of te few examples of a basilica with a transept from this period. The transept would not become a standard component of the Christian church until the Carolingian period.

8: Apse-a recess, sometimes rectangular but usually semicircular, in the wall at the end of a rRoman basilica or Christian church. The apse in the Roman basilica frequently contained an image of the Emperor and was where the magistrate dispensed laws. In the Early Christian basilica, the apses contained the 'cathedra' of throne of the bishop and the altar.

EARLY ROMAN CHRISTIAN CHURCH

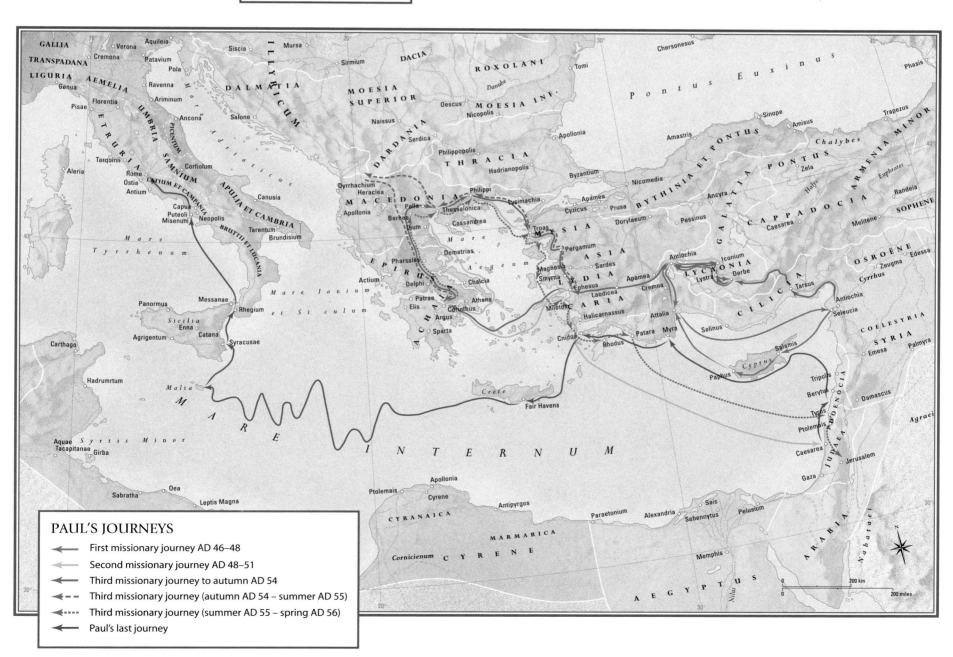

PAUL'S JOURNEYS

- First missionary journey AD 46–48
- Second missionary journey AD 48–51
- Third missionary journey to autumn AD 54
- Third missionary journey (autumn AD 54 – summer AD 55)
- Third missionary journey (summer AD 55 – spring AD 56)
- Paul's last journey

THE CITY OF ROME C. AD 500

THE CITY OF ROME
C. AD 500

By AD 100 Rome had one and a half million citizens and Christianity was beginning to gain ground, even though Christians usually met in secret. Meanwhile the Roman military was losing ground and in AD 476 the last Roman emperor, Romulus Augustulus was defeated. By AD 500 the Lombards had invaded the city. Pope Gregory I negotiated a peace with the Lombards and this led eventually to the emergence of the Papal States. During Gregory's reign four of Rome's great basilicas were built and he sent missionaries to what is now the United Kingdom.

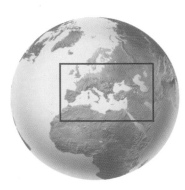

THE CITY OF ROME
c. AD 500

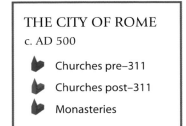

- Churches pre–311
- Churches post–311
- Monasteries

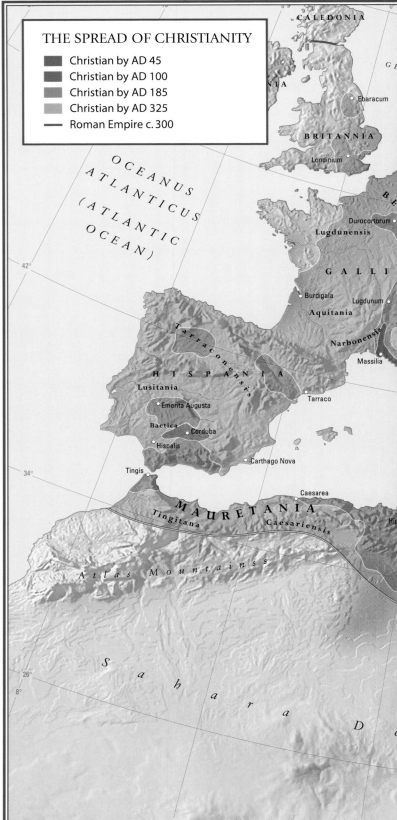

THE SPREAD OF CHRISTIANITY
- Christian by AD 45
- Christian by AD 100
- Christian by AD 185
- Christian by AD 325
- — Roman Empire c. 300

CALEDONIA

OCEANUS ATLANTICUS (ATLANTIC OCEAN)

Ebaracum

BRITANNIA

Londinium

GALLI

Durocortorum

Lugdunensis

Burdigala

Lugdunum

Aquitania

Narbonensis

Massilia

HISPANIA

Lusitania

Tarraco

Emerita Augusta

Baetica

Corduba

Hispalis

Carthago Nova

Tingis

Caesarea

MAURETANIA

Tingitana

Caesariensis

Atlas Mountains

Sahara

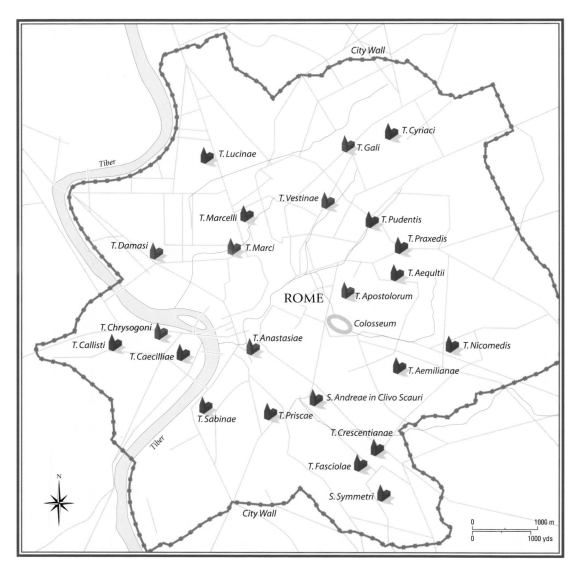

City Wall

Tiber

T. Lucinae

T. Gali

T. Cyriaci

T. Vestinae

T. Marcelli

T. Pudentis

T. Damasi

T. Marci

T. Praxedis

T. Aequltii

T. Apostolorum

ROME

Colosseum

T. Chrysogoni

T. Anastasiae

T. Nicomedis

T. Callisti

T. Caecilliae

T. Aemilianae

S. Andreae in Clivo Scauri

T. Sabinae

T. Priscae

T. Crescentianae

T. Fasciolae

Tiber

S. Symmetri

City Wall

N

0   1000 m
0   1000 yds

THE SPREAD OF CHRISTIANITY

THE SPREAD OF CHRISTIANITY

Within 20 years of the death of Jesus Christ, Christianity spread throughout the Middle East as far as Rome, where a Christian community became well established. Within the next 300 years it spread throughout most of the Roman world. During that time it was subjected to a pattern of alternate persecution and toleration, depending largely on the whim of the particular Emperor who happened to be ruling at the time. This situation lasted until Emperor Constantine made Christianity the state religion in AD 312.

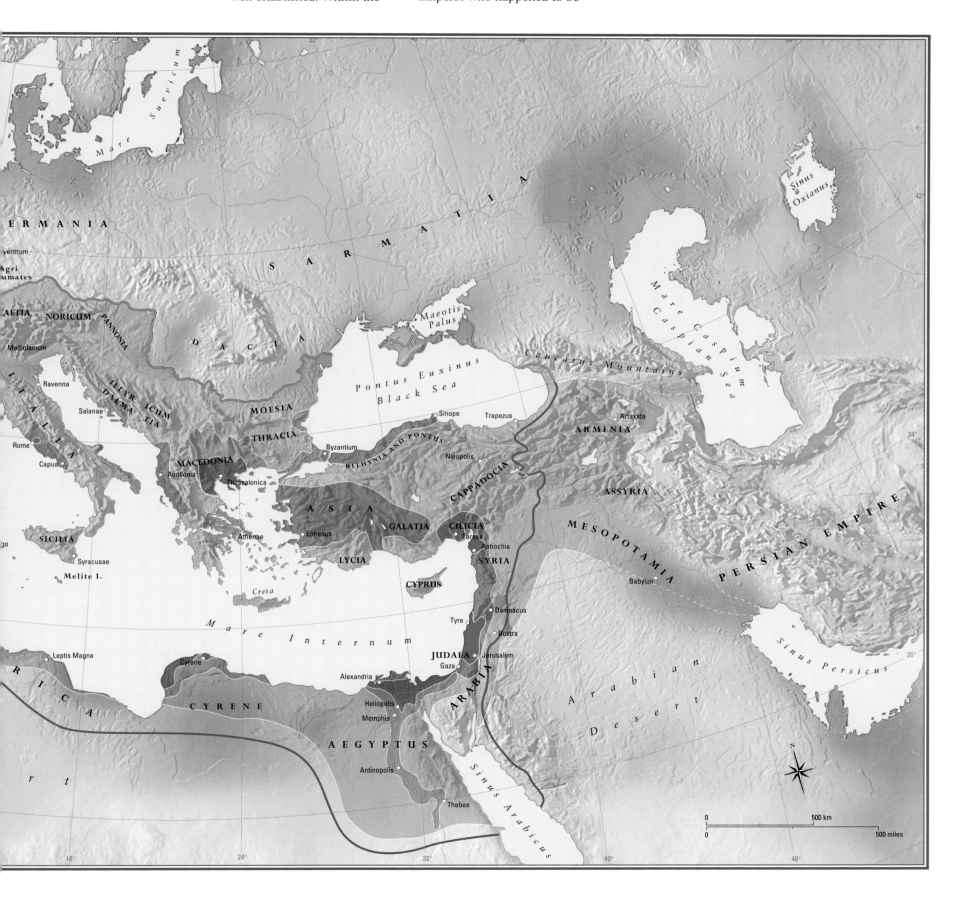

THE REACH OF ROME

THE REACH OF ROME
Within a few hundred years the
Roman Church had reached
out to embrace most of Europe
from Northern Spain in the
west to Poland and Hungary in
the east, and as far north as the
British Isles and a large part of
Scandinavia. A pattern of
bishops had been established,
that remains very much as it
was to this day. Southern Spain

at this time was still Muslim
and the Balkan states belonged
to the Byzantine Orthodox
Christian Communion. The
Baltic states remained pagan.

THE REACH
OF ROME

 extent of Catholicism

✝ archbishoprics

KINGDOM OF
ORKNEY

*North
Sea*

Kaupang •   • Birka

SCOTLAND

IRISH
KINGDOMS
Armagh ✝
Tuam ✝
✝ Dublin
Cashel ✝

• Lindisfarne

ENGLAND

✝ York

*Baltic
Sea*

DENMARK

Ripen •
✝ Hamburg
Bremen ✝

✝ Gniezo   *Vistula*

WELSH
STATES

London •✝
Canterbury ✝

Saxony
Magdeburg ✝

POLAND

✝ Rouen

Britanny

Paris • • Reims

Aachen ✝ ✝ Cologne

Trier ✝
✝ Mainz

EAST
FRANKISH
KINGDOM
(GERMANY)

✝ Gran

HUNGARY

*ATLANTIC
OCEAN*

Tours ✝
✝ Bourges

WEST
FRANKISH
KINGDOM
(FRANCE)

✝ Salzburg

Danube

Bordeaux ✝

✝ Lyon
Vienne ✝
BURGUNDY
Embrun ✝
✝ Avignon

✝ Tarantaise

Milan ✝
Turin •

Aquilea ✝ ✝ Grado
Venice ✝

CROATIA

• Nish

NAVARRE

Auch ✝ • Toulouse
✝ Aix

Santiago ✝
LEÓN
Oporto • ✝ Braga

Burgos ✝
CASTILE

Narbonne

Gerona ✝

SMALL
COUNTIES

Barcelona •

✝ Genoa
Pisa ✝ ✝ Florence
✝ Sienna

Ravenna ✝

Corsica

Rome ✝

*Adriatic
Sea*

✝ Ragusa

BULGARIA

Trivento ✝
Sant' Angelo
✝ Trani
✝ Bari

EMIRATE OF CORDOVA

Balearic Is.

Mediterranean Sea

Sardinia

Naples ✝✝
Sorento ✝
Amalfi
Salerno

✝ Conza
✝
Brindisi
Taranto ✝
Otranto ✝

Cordova •   Cartagena •

0   200 km

0   200 miles

Palermo •

Monreale ✝ ✝

✝✝ Reggio
Messina

Sicily   • Catania

CATHOLICISM AND ORTHODOXY

CATHOLICISM AND ORTHODOXY c. *1100*
In 1054 Christianity experienced the trauma of the Great Schism. This was when the Eastern and Western churches split from each other. The result was Western Catholicism and Eastern Orthodoxy. The primary cause of the Schism was a dispute over papal authority.

The church split along doctrinal, theological, linguistic, political and geographic lines and the fundamental breach has never been healed. The Western Catholic churches included most of Europe, while the Eastern Orthodox churches included Greece, Russia, Armenia, the Balkans, parts of Eastern Europe and Asia Minor.

THE HOLY ROMAN EMPIRE AND THE PAPACY

***THE HOLY ROMAN
EMPIRE AND THE PAPACY***

The Holy Roman Empire was
a monarchy in Central Europe
during the Middle Ages. It was
based on the Kingdom of
Germany and was a
conglomeration of states of
various sizes. There were
kingdoms, principalities,
duchies, counties and free
cities, some of which were not
much bigger than large
villages. At its peak it consisted
of Germany, Austria,
Switzerland, Liechtenstein,
Luxembourg, the Czech
Republic, Slovenia, Belgium,
the Netherlands and large
parts of modern Poland,
France and Italy. The first
emperor was Charlemagne the
Great, but the continuous line
of emperors from the
Kingdom of Germany did not
begin until Otto the Great.

THE PROTESTANT REFORMATION

THE PROTESTANT REFORMATION 1560–1572

The Protestant Reformation was the movement in Europe that began with Martin Luther's activities in 1517. It began as an attempt to reform the Catholic Church, but it eventually led to the fracturing of Christendom. By the 16th century many Christians had become disenchanted with what they saw as false doctrines and malpractices within the Church. Corruption was rife and it was quite normal for the buying and selling of church positions to take place. Although some countries remained true to the Pope, many, especially those in Northern Europe, rapidly welcomed the new reforming movement.

THE PROTESTANT REFORMATION, c. 1560–72

- Reformed faith dominant, c. 1560–72
- Reformed faith growing, c. 1560–72
- Considerable local reformed faith, c. 1560–72
- Catholic area
- Seigneurial lands of the King of Navarre in France
- ■ Catholic mission and reform endeavours
- ■ Reformed community discovered by the inquisition in Italy
- ⚲ Papal nunciature, with date
- ⑥ Number of legates sent to the last session of the Council of Trent
- ✳ Iconoclastic riots in Netherlands, 1566
- ✳ Sectarian riots following the Saint Bartholomew massacre in Paris, 1572

THE BEGINNING OF THE PAPAL STATES

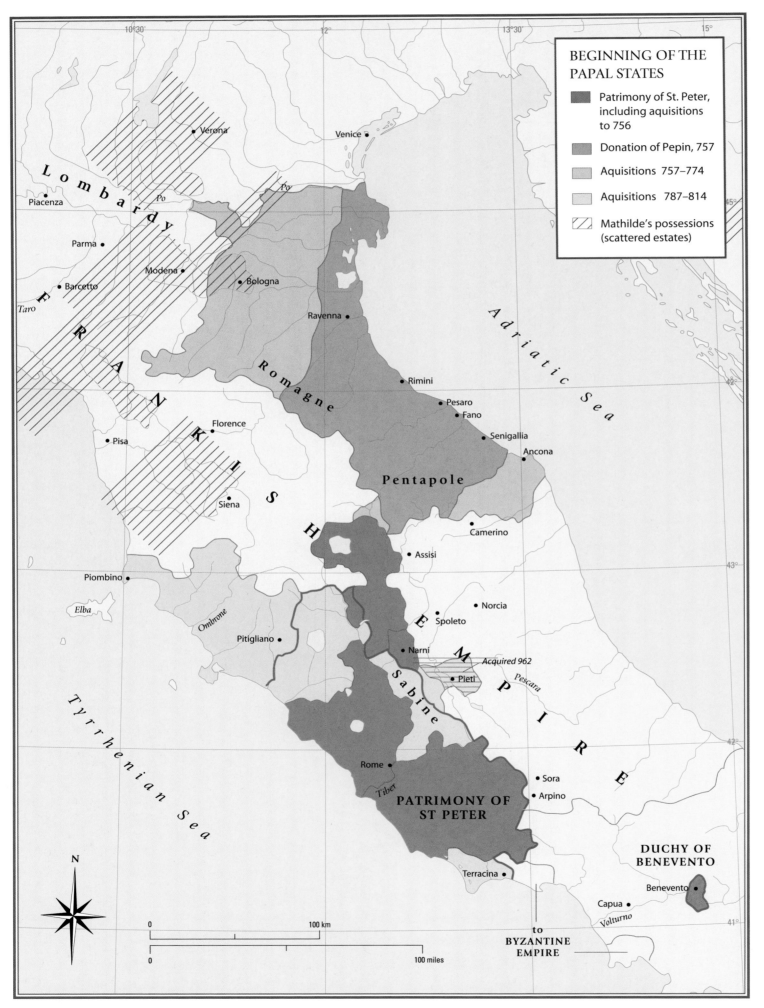

BEGINNING OF THE PAPAL STATES

- Patrimony of St. Peter, including aquisitions to 756
- Donation of Pepin, 757
- Aquisitions 757–774
- Aquisitions 787–814
- Mathilde's possessions (scattered estates)

Lombardy

Verona

Venice

Po

Piacenza

Parma

Modena

Barcetto

Bologna

Taro

Ravenna

Romagne

Adriatic Sea

Rimini

Pesaro
Fano

Florence

Senigallia

Pisa

Ancona

Pentapole

Siena

Camerino

Assisi

Piombino

Norcia

Elba

Spoleto

Ombrone

Pitigliano

Narni

Acquired 962

Sabine

Pieti

Pescara

Tyrrhenian Sea

Rome

Sora

Tiber

Arpino

PATRIMONY OF ST PETER

DUCHY OF BENEVENTO

Terracina

Benevento

N

Capua

Volturno

BYZANTINE EMPIRE

0   100 km

0   100 miles

to
BYZANTINE
EMPIRE

THE BEGINNING OF THE PAPAL STATES

The Papal States were a group of territories that were ruled by the papacy from 759 to 1870. As early as the 4th century the papacy had acquired a considerable amount of property around Rome. This was known as the Patrimony of St Peter. From the 5th century as the imperial authority of Rome gradually began to fall apart, people increasingly relied on papal influence to protect them from barbarian invasion. When the Lombards threatened to take over the whole of the Italian peninsula, Pope Stephen appealed to the Frankish King Pippin who restored central Italy to the Holy See. This became known as the Donation of Pippin.

PAPAL STATES IN THE 16TH CENTURY

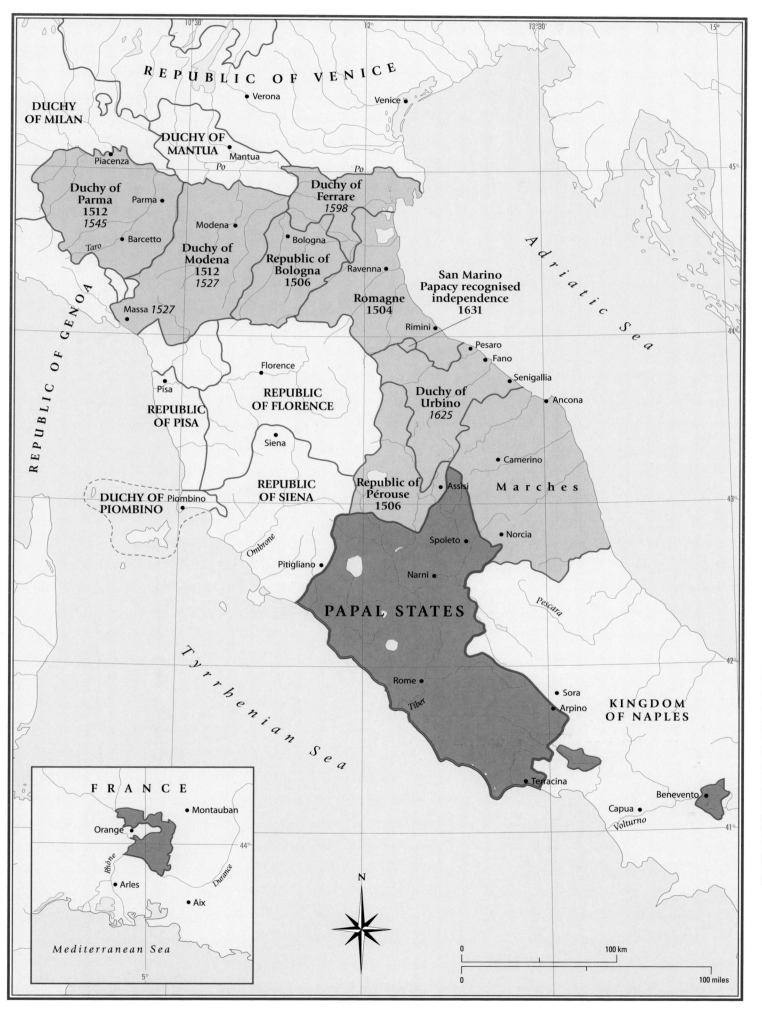

PAPAL STATES IN
THE 16th CENTURY

Papal territory c. 1500

Claimed or controlled
by the Papal States
by 1512

1506 Date of acquisition by
Rome, where known

1506 Date of autonomy or
independence from
Rome

CHRISTIANITY IN THE WORLD BY 1600

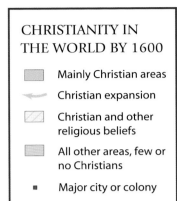

CHRISTIANITY IN
THE WORLD BY 1600

▨ Mainly Christian areas

↢ Christian expansion

▨ Christian and other
religious beliefs

▨ All other areas, few or
no Christians

■ Major city or colony

***CHRISTIANITY IN THE
WORLD BY 1600***
Its adoption as the official
religion of the Roman Empire
firmly established Christianity
in Europe and by 1600 it had
spread throughout the
continent and far into the
Russian Empire. Here it was
effectively the only religion.
This was the period of great
maritime exploration and in
Central and South America in
particular, missionaries had
followed the Spanish and
Portuguese explorers and there
was now a significant Christian
presence, at least along the
coastal areas. Explorers and
merchants had taken
Christianity to other areas in
the world. Here it existed
alongside other religions in
varying degrees of harmony.

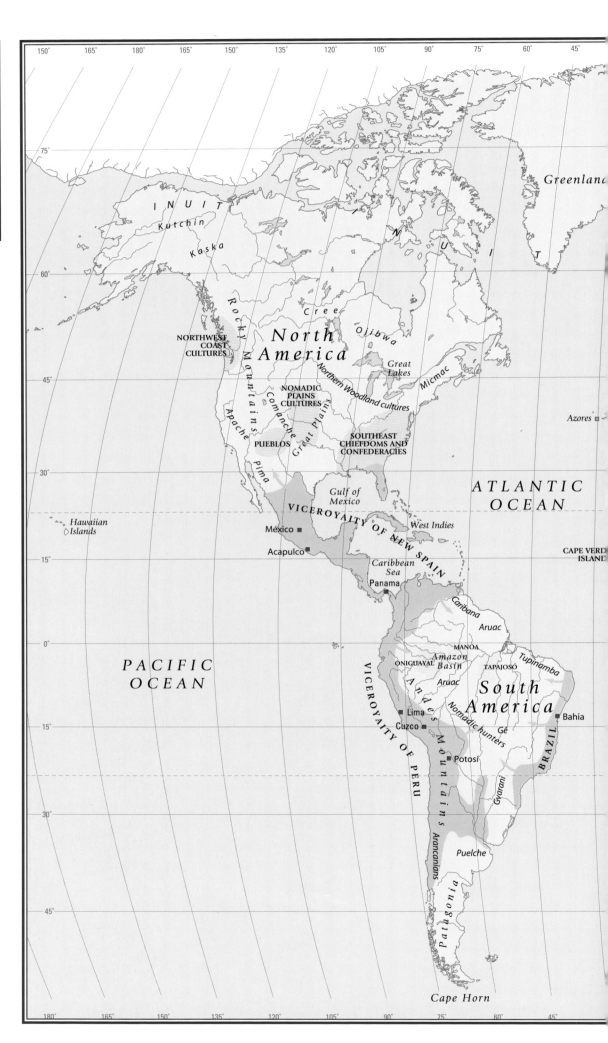

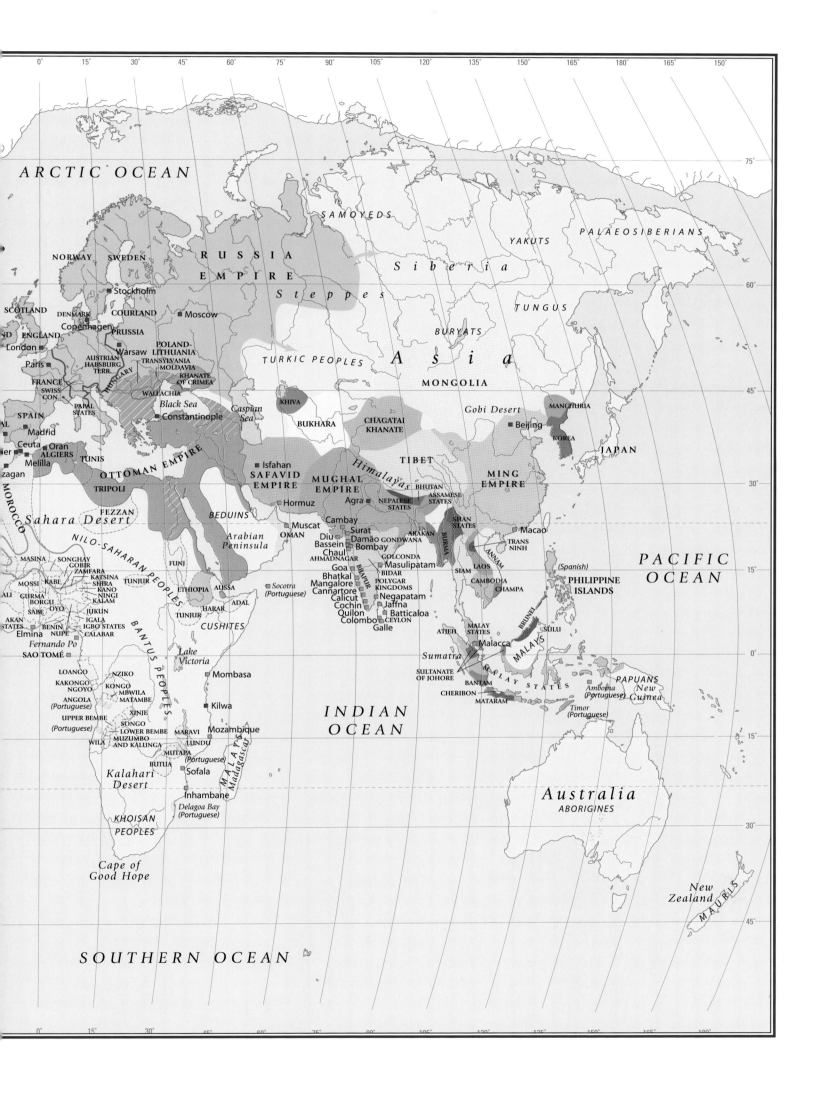

ARCTIC OCEAN

SAMOYEDS

YAKUTS

PALAEOSIBERIANS

NORWAY SWEDEN

RUSSIA

EMPIRE

Siberia

Steppes

Stockholm

SCOTLAND

DENMARK COURLAND

Copenhagen

Moscow

TUNGUS

BURYATS

ND ENGLAND

London

PRUSSIA

Paris

FRANCE
SWISS
CON.

POLAND-
LITHUANIA

Warsaw

AUSTRIAN
HABSBURG
TERR.

TRANSYLVANIA
MOLDAVIA

KHANATE
OF CRIMEA

TURKIC PEOPLES

Asia

MONGOLIA

SPAIN

PAPAL
STATES

WALLACHIA

Black Sea

Caspian
Sea

KHIVA

Gobi Desert

MANCHURIA

Madrid

Constantinople

BUKHARA

CHAGATAI
KHANATE

Beijing

Ceuta Oran
ALGIERS TUNIS
Melilla

OTTOMAN EMPIRE

Isfahan

SAFAVID
EMPIRE

TIBET

MING
EMPIRE

KOREA

JAPAN

zagan

TRIPOLI

FEZZAN

Hormuz

MUGHAL
EMPIRE

Himalayas

BHUTAN

Agra

NEPALESE
STATES

ASSAMESE
STATES

Macao

MOROCCO

Sahara Desert

BEDUINS

SHAN
STATES

TRANS
NINH

PACIFIC
OCEAN

NILO-SAHARAN PEOPLES

Muscat
OMAN

Cambay

Surat
Diu
Bassein
Damão
Bombay

GONDWANA

ARAKAN

BURMA

ANNAM

Arabian
Peninsula

MASINA

SONGHAY
GOBIR
ZAMFARA

FUNJ

Chaul
AHMADNAGAR

GOLCONDA

Masulipatam

SIAM

LAOS

CAMBODIA

(Spanish)

PHILIPPINE
ISLANDS

MOSSI
BORGU

KATSINA
SHIRA
KANO
NINGI
KALAM

TUNJUR

Ethiopia

AUSSA

Socotra
(Portuguese)

Bhatkal
Mangalore
Cannartore
Calicut
Cochin
Quilon
Colombo

BIDAR

POLYGAR
KINGDOMS

BIJAPUR

Negapatam
Jaffna
Batticaloa
CEYLON

CHAMPA

ALI

GURMA

OYO

SABE

JUKUN

IGALA

HARAR

ADAL

AKAN
STATES

BENIN
NUPE

IGBO STATES
CALABAR

TUNJUR

CUSHITES

Galle

Elmina

Fernando Po

SAO TOMÉ

Lake
Victoria

Sumatra

ATJEH

MALAY
STATES

Malacca

MALAYS

BRUNEI

SULU

LOANGO

NZIKO

Mombasa

SULTANATE
OF JOHORE

MALAY STATES

PAPUANS

KAKONGO
NGOYO

KONGO
MBWILA
MATAMBE

Kilwa

BANTAM

CHERIBON

MATARAM

Amboina
(Portuguese)

New
Guinea

ANGOLA
(Portuguese)

XINJE

INDIAN
OCEAN

Timor
(Portuguese)

UPPER BEMBE
(Portuguese)

SONGO
LOWER BEMBE

MUZUMBO
AND KALUNGA

MARAVI

Mozambique

WILA

LUNDU

BANTUS PEOPLES

MUTAPA

BUTUA

(Portuguese)

Sofala

MALAYS
Madagascar

Australia
ABORIGINES

Kalahari
Desert

Inhambane

Delagoa Bay
(Portuguese)

KHOISAN
PEOPLES

Cape of
Good Hope

New
Zealand

MAORIS

SOUTHERN OCEAN

HABSBURG EMPIRE 1618

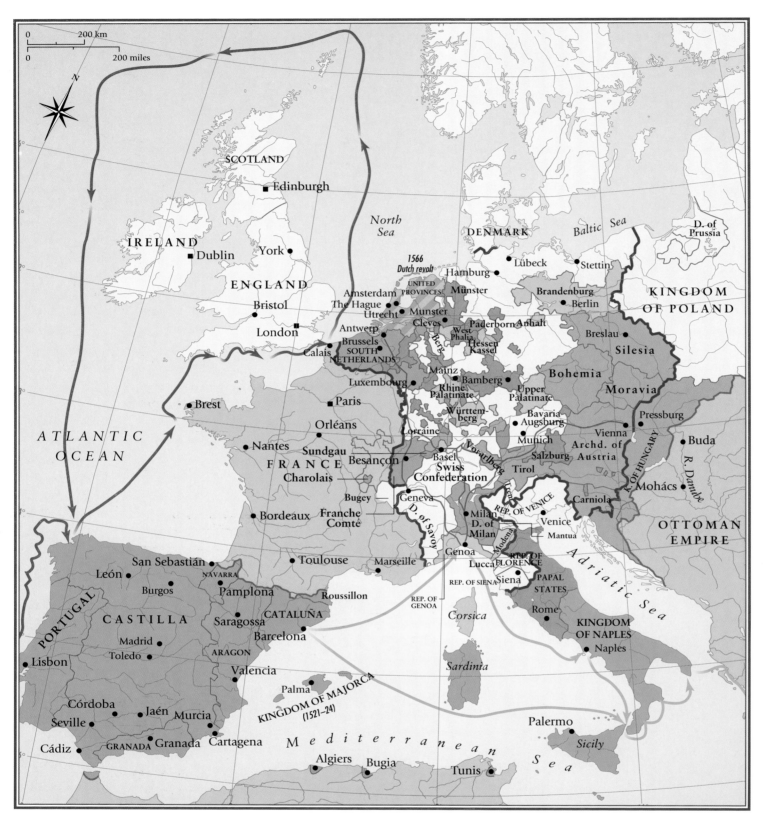

THE HABSBURG EMPIRE c. 1600

Around the turn of the 16th century the Catholic Habsburgs of Austria and Spain ruled much of Eastern Europe, the whole of Iberia and large areas elsewhere. In 1571 the Spanish had been very successful when as part of a coalition fleet they had defeated the Muslim Ottomans at the Battle of Lepanto, but they were not so successful 17 years later when in 1588 they sent a huge fleet of 130 ships to England with aim of landing the Duke of Parma and reversing the Protestant revolution. The expedition was a complete failure and only 67 ships returned to Spain.

EUROPE IN 1700

EUROPE IN 1700
By 1700 Europe had settled down into broad religious divisions. Generally speaking the north of Europe was predominately Protestant, countries to the south and east of Europe were predominately Roman Catholic, while Russia and the Baltic nations were predominately Orthodox

Christian. At that time the Balkan countries formed part of the Muslim Ottoman Empire and here Christianity was heavily oppressed and any Christian activity had to be carried out in conditions of great secrecy. In many regions there was a considerable amount of overlap. While countries such as Spain, Italy,

Portugal and France were almost entirely populated by Roman Catholics, Britain, though officially Protestant, was more heterogeneous in its religious make-up.

EUROPE IN 1700

☐ Austrian Habsburgs

☐ Spanish Habsburgs

☐ Ottoman Empire

— Holy Roman Empire

CHRISTIANITY IN THE WORLD BY 1700

CHRISTIANITY IN THE WORLD BY 1700

By 1700 missionary activity and settlement had increased, particularly in the Americas. The Spanish and the Portuguese continued to develop their territories and religious orders had moved in to bring Christianity to the indigenous population. In North America the population had been boosted by Christian settlers from Europe who were either there for speculative reasons, or because they were fleeing from religious persecution. In Russia the spread of Christianity throughout Siberia was the result of policies by the Orthodox Church and the government that alternated between forced conversion and gradual spiritual and educational enlightenment.

CHRISTIANITY IN THE WORLD BY 1700

- Mainly Christian areas
- Christian and other religious beliefs
- All other areas, few or no Christians
- ■ Major city or colony

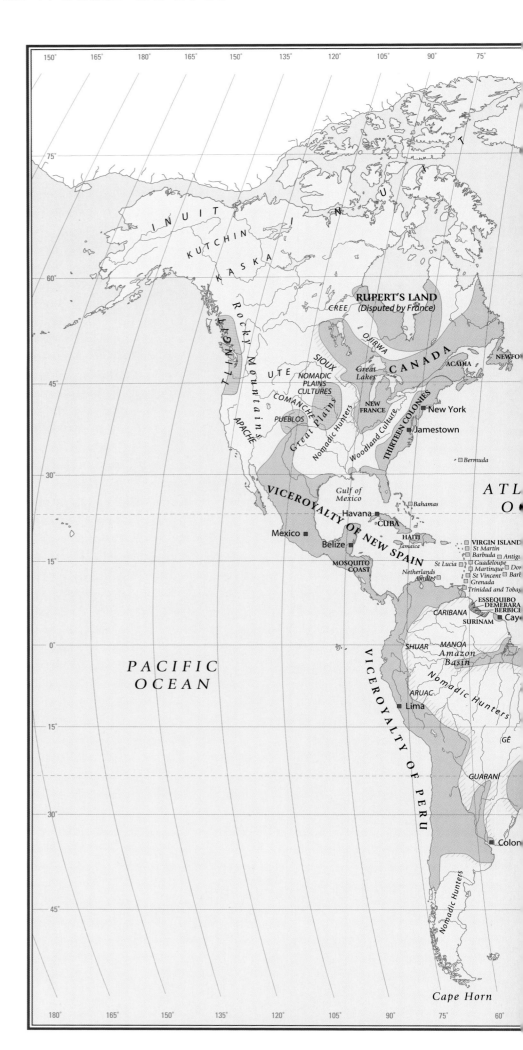

ARCTIC OCEAN

Iceland

NORWAY
SWEDEN
Stockholm

Siberia

RUSSIAN EMPIRE

CHUKCHI

SCOTLAND
DENMARK
Copenhagen
NETHER-
LAND
IRELAND ENGLAND
London
PRUSSIA
Warsaw
POLAND-
LITHUANIA
COURTLAND

Nerchinsk

KORYAKS

Paris
FRANCE
Vienna
HUNGARY
MOLDAVIA
ZAPOROGIAN
COSSACKS
KHANATE
OF CRIMEA

KZAKHS

SWISS
CONFEDERATION
PAPAL
STATES
VENETIAN REPUBLIC
WALLACIA
Black Sea
TURKMENS
KHIVA

Gobi Desert

Beijing

PORTUGAL SPAIN
Lisbon Madrid
NAPLES
SARDINIA
SICILY
Constantinople
Caspian Sea
BUKHARA
KHANATE OF
THE DZUNGARS

QING
EMPIRE

KOREA

JAPAN
Kyoto
Nagasaki

Ceuta ALGIERS
Melilla Oran TUNIS
Mediterranean Sea

OTTOMAN EMPIRE

SAFAVID
EMPIRE
Isfahan

Himalayas

TIBET

Delhi
BHUTAN ASSAM
MANIPUR

Madeira
MOROCCO
TRIPOLI

*Canary
Islands*

FEZZAN
(*Vassal of Tripoli*)

BEDUINS

NEPALESE
PRINCIPALITIES

BEDUINS

Sahara Desert
TUAREGS

*Arabian
Peninsula*
OMAN
Cambrey
MUGHAL
EMPIRE

ARAKAN BURMA
CHIENGMAI

Macao

PACIFIC
OCEAN

Africa
NILO-SAHARANS

Diu
Bassein Damão
Chaul Bombay

*Bay of
Bengal*

KAABU
WALO KAARTA
St Louis
Gorée
MOSSI
KINGDOMS
BORGU
KINGDOMS
BORNU
WADAI DARFUR
*Arabian
Sea*
YEMEN
Goa
Bhatkal
Mangalore
Cannartore
Calicut
Masulipatam
Pulicat
Madras
Pondicherry
Sadras
Tranquebar
LAOS
ANNAN
Manila
PHILIPPINE
ISLANDS

ames Island
eda Cacheu
FUTA
TORO SEGU
HAUSA
STATES
ETHIOPIA
Cochin
Quilon
Tuticorin
CEYLON
KINGDOM
OF KANDY
SIAM
CAMBODIA
(*to Annan*)

SIERRA LEONE
FUTA
JALLON
MAMPRUSI
GONJA
BANDA
BONO
KWARARAFA
*SMALL
OROMO
STATES*
HARAR
KUSHITES
TRAN NINH

DENKYERA
GOLD COAST
BENIN
OYO IGALA
ASANTE
SMALL
STATES
DAHOMEY

POLYGAR
KINGDOMS

MALAY
STATES
Malacca
BRUNEI
SULU

ALLADA
Fernando Po
SAO TOME

BANTUS

BUNYORO
TORO
ANKOLE
BUGANDA
BUSOGA
*Lake
Victoria*

ATJEH
MAMPAVA
MALAY
STATES
KUTEI
Moluccas

LOANGO
KAKONGO
NGOYO
KONGO
TEKE
RWANDA
KARAGWE
BURUNDI
KALUNDE
KUBA
KANIOK LUBA
Mombasa
(*To Oman*)

Sumatra
Benkulen
Silebar
East Indies
BANDJAR
MASIN

PAPUANS
New
Guinea

MATAMBA
ANGOLA
NDONGO
KASANJE
UPPER BEMBE
LUNDA
XINJE
SONGO
KIKONJA
Zanzibar
(*To Oman*)
Kilwa
(*To Oman*)

INDIAN
OCEAN

Batavia

MATARAM
MALAY
STATES

PORTUGUESE
TIMOR

WILA
MUZUMBO
A KALUNGA
LOWER BEMBE
LOZI
KAEONGA
LINDI
LUNDU
MERINA
KINGDOM
ROZWI

MALAYS

Madagascar

Mauritius
Réunion

Australia
ABORIGINES

*Kalahari
Desert*
Delagoa Bay

KHOISAN
PEOPLES

DUTCH
SOUTH AFRICA
*Cape of
Good Hope*

*New
Zealand*
MAURIS

SOUTHERN OCEAN

C. 1000 – 1643

EUROPEAN EXPLORATION AND COLONIZATION

EUROPEAN EXPLORATION AND COLONISATION

Once the Western European states developed ocean-going ships, they began a concentrated programme of exploration and colonisation. When an explorer discovered a new territory, one of the top priorities was to "convert the natives". The belief was that it was impossible to go to Heaven without being baptised as a Christian, so every effort was made to persuade the indigenous population to discard their pagan ways and embrace the true faith. If this was not accomplished by gentle persuasion, more violent methods would usually be employed. The result was that by the 18th century – the end of the great period of world exploration – Christianity had been exported to every continent and was the world's most practised religion

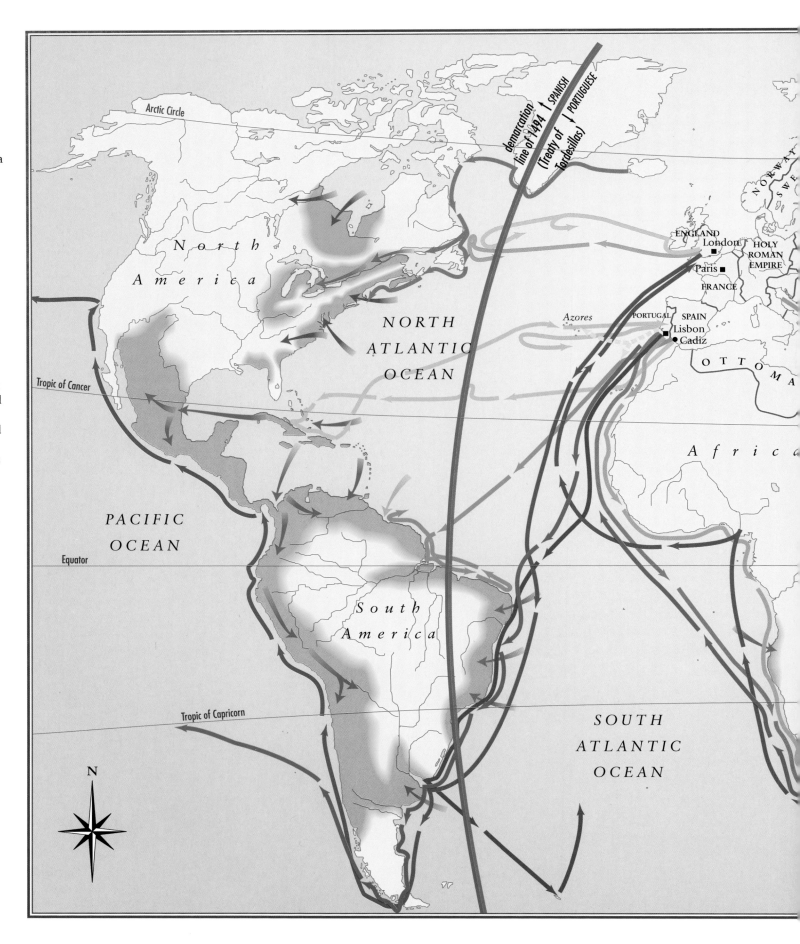

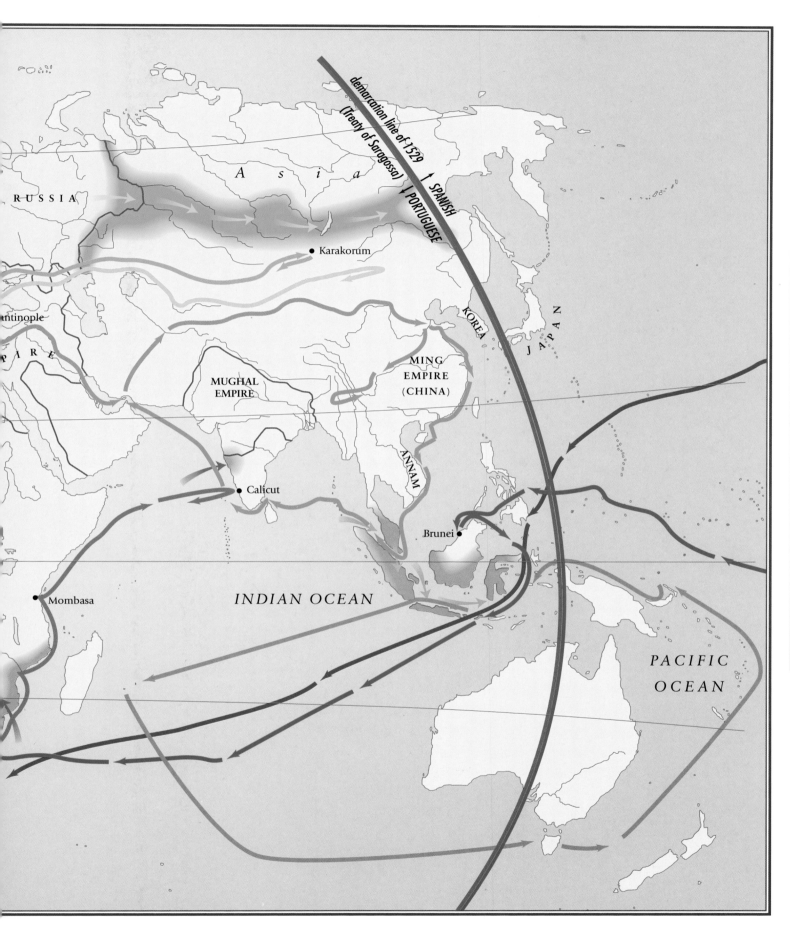

Norwegians,
Icelanders, c. 1000

Friar Rubruck, 1253–55

Nicolo and Maffeo
Polo, 1262

Marco Polo, 1272–95

Portugese discover Madeira
c. 1419, Azores c. 1427

King Manuel of Portugal
sends expedition west to
locate Antillia, unsuccessful

Bristol Merchants attempt
to find "Isles of Brazil",
1480–81

Bartholomew Diaz,
1496–88

Christopher Columbus,
1492–93 (1st voyage)

John Cabot, 1497
(1st voyage)

Amerigo Vespucci,
1499 (2nd voyage)

Vasco de Gama, 1427–98

Amerigo Vespucci,
1501

Magellan (del Cano after
Magellan's death), 1521–22

Drake, 1577–80

Abel Tasman,1642–43

**main directions of European
colonization or control,
1450–1600**

Spanish

Portuguese

English

French

Dutch

Russian

under European
colonization or
control mid. 17th C.

On the map:

RUSSIA

Asia

Karakorum

antinople

IRE

MUGHAL
EMPIRE

MING
EMPIRE
(CHINA)

KOREA

JAPAN

ANNAM

Calicut

Brunei

Mombasa

INDIAN OCEAN

demarcation line of 1529
(Treaty of Saragossa)

SPANISH | PORTUGUESE

*PACIFIC
OCEAN*

1494 – C. 1780 — HISPANIC AMERICA

HISPANIC AMERICA
c. 1780

From 1493 Spain began to maintain a number of missions throughout what became known as New Spain. These had a dual purpose; one was to spread the Catholic faith among the aboriginal people and the other was to facilitate colonisation. These religious outposts were established primarily by Franciscans and the missions introduced European livestock, fruits, vegetables and industry to the region. They also introduced European diseases. The English and the French had different priorities and were not really interested in the conversion of the native population.

HISPANIC AMERICA
c. 1780

- Spanish territory
- Portuguese territory
- British territory
- French territory
- Dutch territory

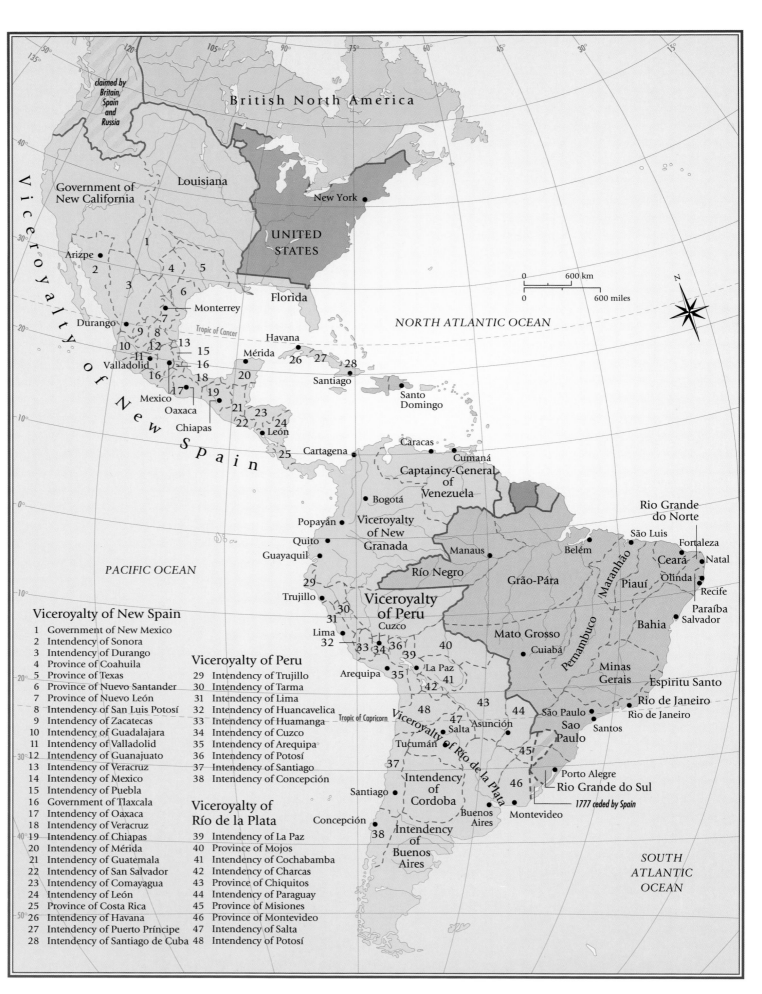

Viceroyalty of New Spain

1 Government of New Mexico
2 Intendency of Sonora
3 Intendency of Durango
4 Province of Coahuila
5 Province of Texas
6 Province of Nuevo Santander
7 Province of Nuevo León
8 Intendency of San Luis Potosí
9 Intendency of Zacatecas
10 Intendency of Guadalajara
11 Intendency of Valladolid
12 Intendency of Guanajuato
13 Intendency of Veracruz
14 Intendency of Mexico
15 Intendency of Puebla
16 Government of Tlaxcala
17 Intendency of Oaxaca
18 Intendency of Veracruz
19 Intendency of Chiapas
20 Intendency of Mérida
21 Intendency of Guatemala
22 Intendency of San Salvador
23 Intendency of Comayagua
24 Intendency of León
25 Province of Costa Rica
26 Intendency of Havana
27 Intendency of Puerto Príncipe
28 Intendency of Santiago de Cuba

Viceroyalty of Peru

29 Intendency of Trujillo
30 Intendency of Tarma
31 Intendency of Lima
32 Intendency of Huancavelica
33 Intendency of Huamanga
34 Intendency of Cuzco
35 Intendency of Arequipa
36 Intendency of Potosí
37 Intendency of Santiago
38 Intendency of Concepción

Viceroyalty of Río de la Plata

39 Intendency of La Paz
40 Province of Mojos
41 Intendency of Cochabamba
42 Intendency of Charcas
43 Province of Chiquitos
44 Province of Paraguay
45 Province of Misiones
46 Province of Montevideo
47 Intendency of Salta
48 Intendency of Potosí

HISPANIC SOUTH AMERICA

**HISPANIC SOUTH
AMERICA
c. 1780**

By the late 1700s Spain held
large areas of North America,
Central American, the
Caribbean and most of South
America. The major part of
South America that was not
Spanish was Portuguese. The
Spanish, the Portuguese and
to a lesser extent the French
colonisers were Roman
Catholics, so their influence
was considerable and remains
so to this day.

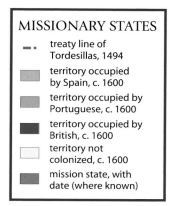

MISSIONARY STATES

- – ·· – treaty line of
  Tordesillas, 1494
- territory occupied
  by Spain, c. 1600
- territory occupied by
  Portuguese, c. 1600
- territory occupied by
  British, c. 1600
- territory not
  colonized, c. 1600
- mission state, with
  date (where known)

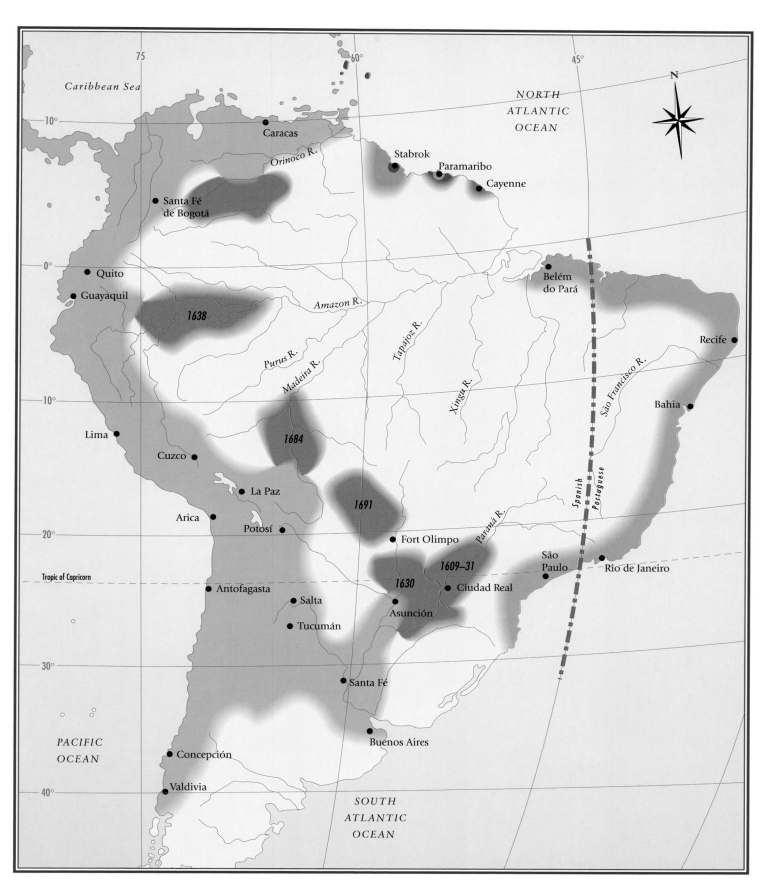

CHURCH FORMATION IN THE AMERICAN COLONIES

CHURCH FORMATION IN THE AMERICAN COLONIES 1607–1770

During this period as the population began to grow, so did the number of churches. There were few Catholics in the Middle and Southern Colonies, so the vast majority of Christians were Protestant. In the New England Colonies Congregationalists far outnumbered any other group, while in the Middle Colonies, where the ethic origin was more diverse, there were large number of groups such as German Lutherans and the Dutch Reformed Church. In the Southern Colonies, with their large plantations, the Anglicans were in the majority, with the Baptists and Presbyterians close behind.

SPANISH MISSIONS

Following the Spanish Conquistadors came another army, smaller in numbers and fired up by the zeal of their mission. They were not after gold and glory; their mission was to spread the gospel among the remote tribes in the jungles and mountains. The Jesuits developed a series of missions where, in contrast to what was happening elsewhere, education, commercial endeavours and trade were developed. These settlements were a great success and grew rapidly. The Spanish and Portuguese feared that the Jesuits were becoming too powerful and too independent. In 1756 the missions were attacked, many were killed and the Jesuits were expelled from South America.

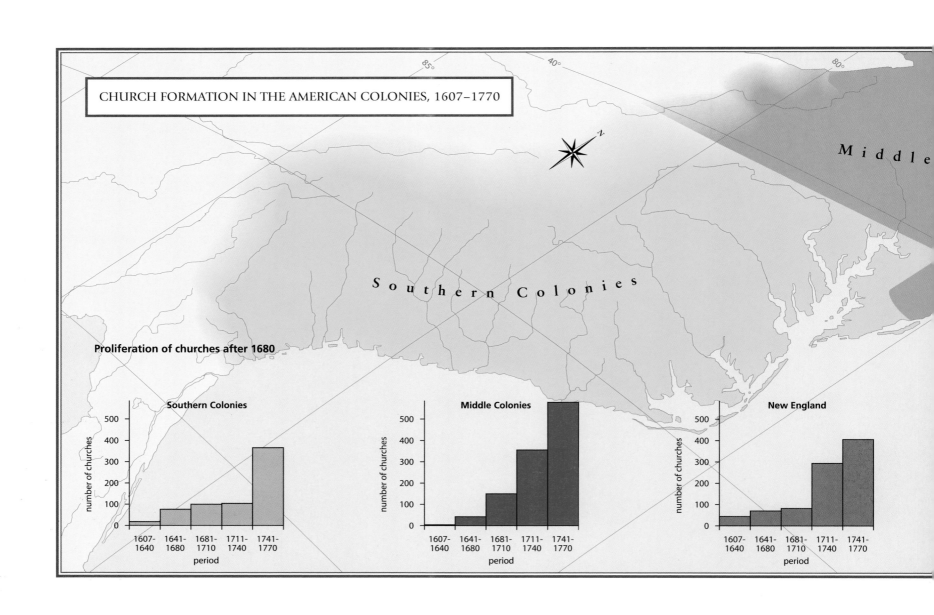

CHURCH FORMATION IN THE AMERICAN COLONIES, 1607–1770

Southern Colonies

Middle

Proliferation of churches after 1680

Southern Colonies

number of churches

500 / 400 / 300 / 200 / 100 / 0

1607-1640 / 1641-1680 / 1681-1710 / 1711-1740 / 1741-1770

period

Middle Colonies

number of churches

500 / 400 / 300 / 200 / 100 / 0

1607-1640 / 1641-1680 / 1681-1710 / 1711-1740 / 1741-1770

period

New England

number of churches

500 / 400 / 300 / 200 / 100 / 0

1607-1640 / 1641-1680 / 1681-1710 / 1711-1740 / 1741-1770

period

SPANISH MISSIONS

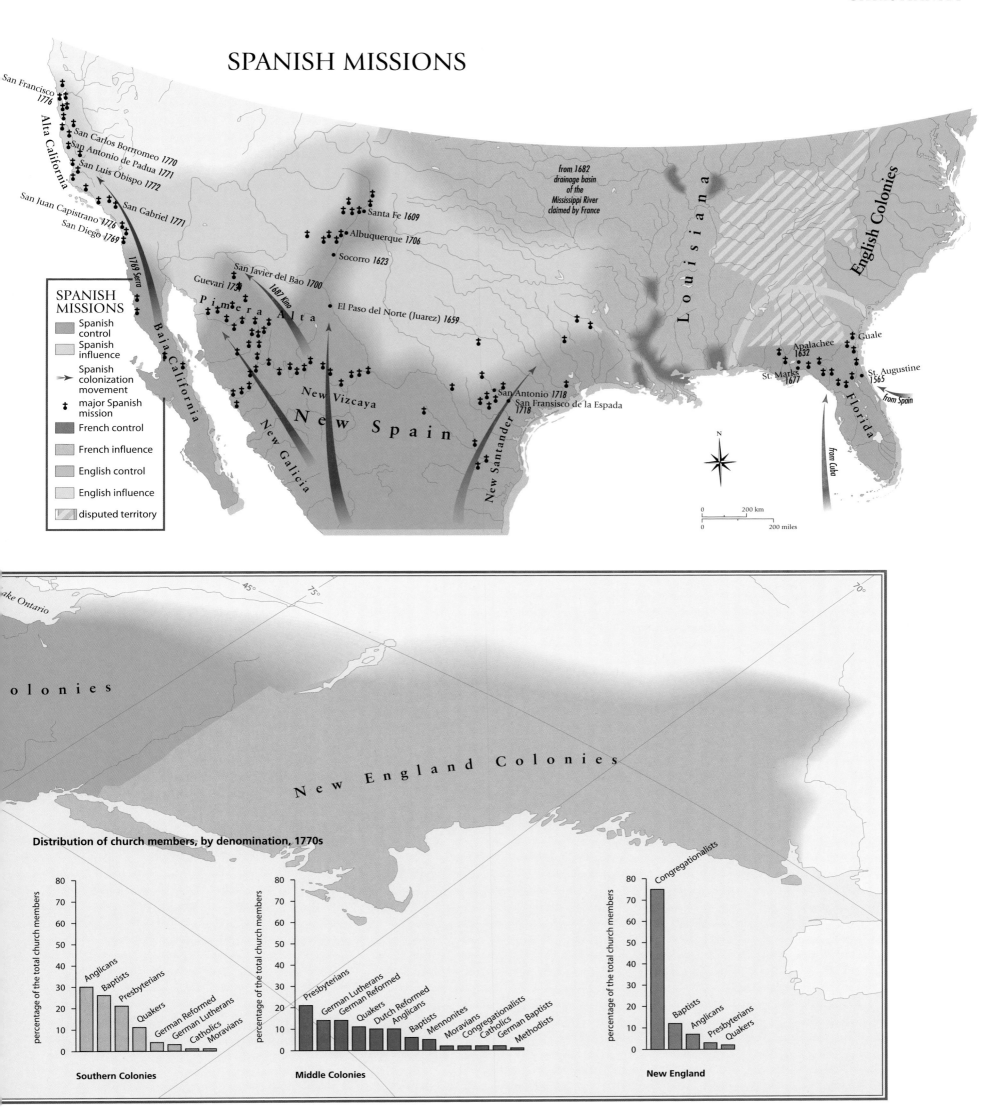

San Francisco 1776

Alta California

San Carlos Borromeo 1770
San Antonio de Padua 1771
San Luis Obispo 1772

San Gabriel 1771

San Juan Capistrano 1776
San Diego 1769

1769 Serra

Baja California

SPANISH MISSIONS
- Spanish control
- Spanish influence
- → Spanish colonization movement
- ✝ major Spanish mission
- French control
- French influence
- English control
- English influence
- ▨ disputed territory

Guevari 1751
San Javier del Bao 1700
1687 Kino
Pimería Alta
El Paso del Norte (Juarez) 1659

Socorro 1623
Albuquerque 1706
Santa Fe 1609

from 1682 drainage basin of the Mississippi River claimed by France

Louisiana

English Colonies

New Vizcaya

New Galicia

New Spain

New Santander

San Antonio 1718
San Fransisco de la Espada 1718

Apalachee 1632
Guale
St. Marks 1677
St. Augustine 1565
from Spain

Florida

from Cuba

N

0   200 km
0   200 miles

Lake Ontario

45°   75°

...olonies

New England Colonies

70°

Distribution of church members, by denomination, 1770s

Southern Colonies

percentage of the total church members

- Anglicans
- Baptists
- Presbyterians
- Quakers
- German Reformed
- German Lutherans
- Catholics
- Moravians

Middle Colonies

percentage of the total church members

- Presbyterians
- German Lutherans
- German Reformed
- Quakers
- Dutch Reformed
- Anglicans
- Baptists
- Mennonites
- Moravians
- Congregationalists
- Catholics
- German Baptists
- Methodists

New England

percentage of the total church members

- Congregationalists
- Baptists
- Anglicans
- Presbyterians
- Quakers

THE GREAT AWAKENING

THE GREAT AWAKENING

The 'Great Awakening' can best be described as a revitalisation of religious piety that swept through the American Colonies between the 1730s and 1770s. This was part of a broad movement of evangelical upsurge that was taking place, notably in England, Scotland and Germany. In America it first appeared among Presbyterians in Pennsylvania and New Jersey and was led by the Reverend William Tennent and his four sons, all clergymen. It quickly spread to the Congregationalists and Baptists of New England and emotionally charged sermons evoked vivid and terrifying images of the terrors that awaited the unrepentant.

CHURCH MEMBERSHIP DURING THE COLONIAL PERIOD

This map gives a very clear picture of the relative populations of the different colonies and the size of their church membership. As can be seen, the numbers of church members were by no means huge and were generally quite mixed, apart from those in the New England Colonies where Congregationalists made up a clear majority. Most colonies had a sprinkling of Anglicans and Presbyterians and in some, such as Pennsylvania, the influence of non-English immigrants can be seen by the number of German churches.

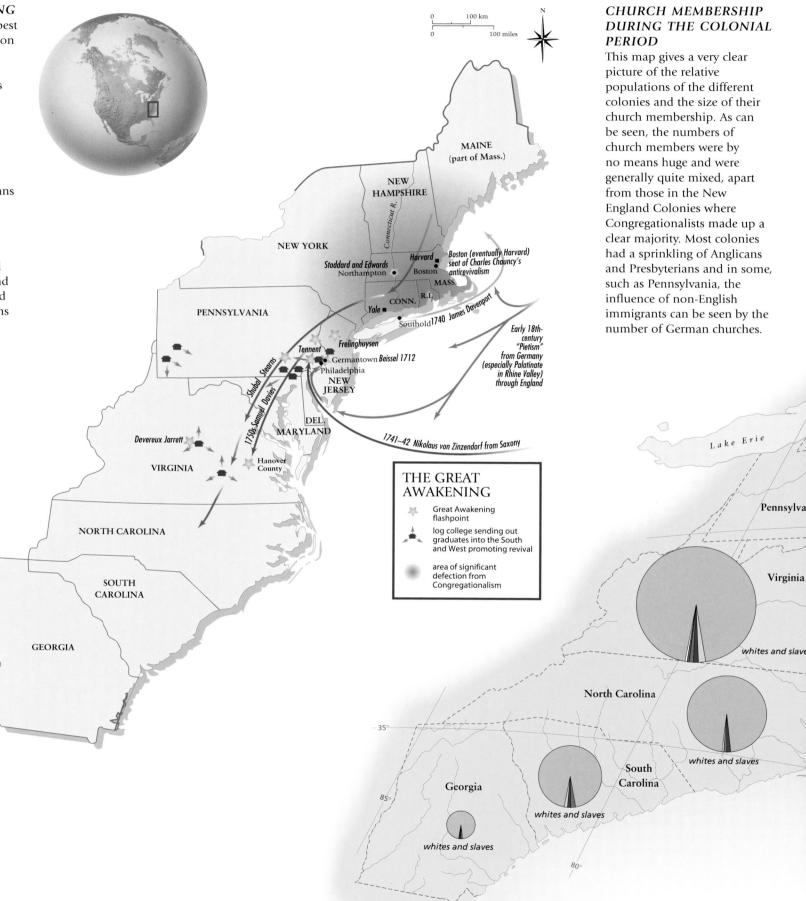

THE GREAT AWAKENING

⭐ Great Awakening flashpoint

⬥ log college sending out graduates into the South and West promoting revival

⬤ area of significant defection from Congregationalism

COLONIAL AMERICAN RELIGIOUS REGIONS; CHURCH MEMBERSHIP IN COLONIAL AMERICA

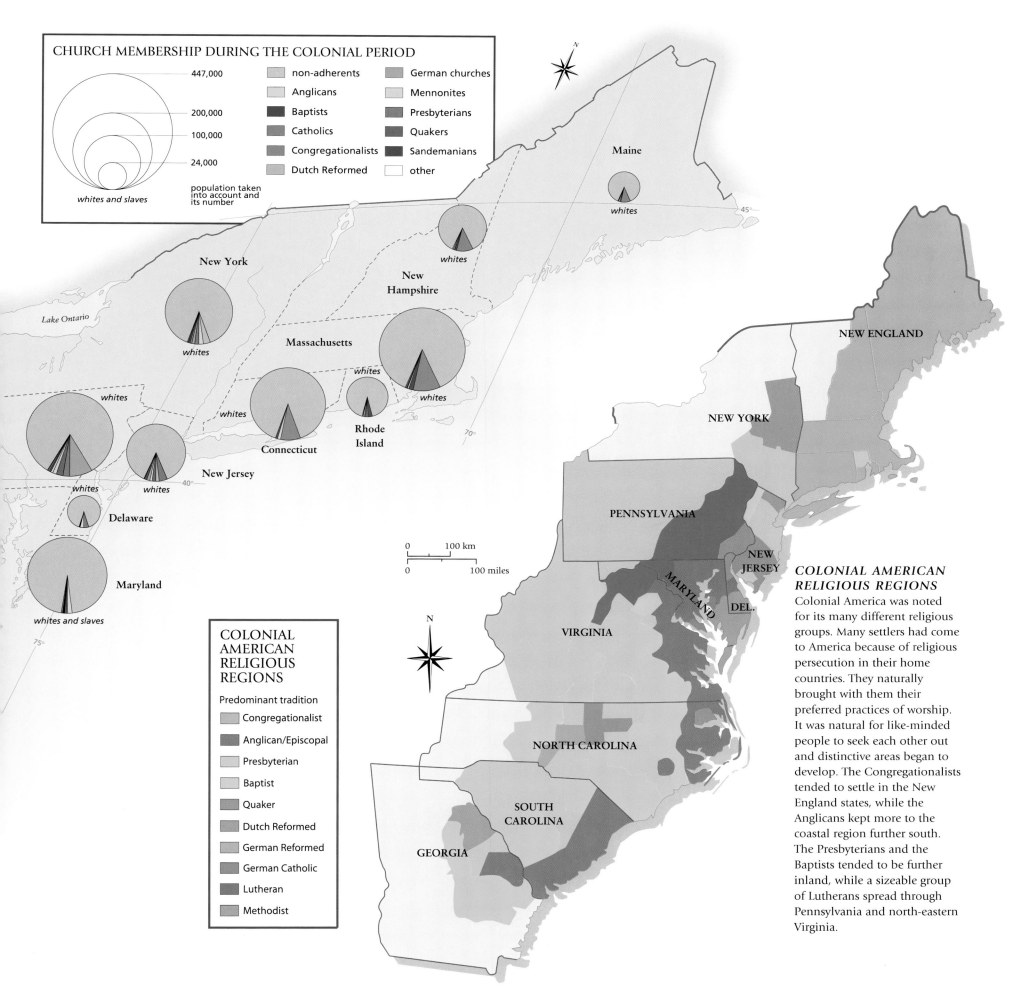

CHURCH MEMBERSHIP DURING THE COLONIAL PERIOD

447,000
200,000
100,000
24,000

whites and slaves

non-adherents	German churches
Anglicans	Mennonites
Baptists	Presbyterians
Catholics	Quakers
Congregationalists	Sandemanians
Dutch Reformed	other

population taken into account and its number

Maine
whites

New York
whites

New Hampshire
whites

Massachusetts
whites

Connecticut
whites

Rhode Island
whites

New Jersey
whites

Delaware
whites

Maryland
whites and slaves

Lake Ontario

COLONIAL AMERICAN RELIGIOUS REGIONS

Predominant tradition

- Congregationalist
- Anglican/Episcopal
- Presbyterian
- Baptist
- Quaker
- Dutch Reformed
- German Reformed
- German Catholic
- Lutheran
- Methodist

0   100 km
0   100 miles

NEW ENGLAND

NEW YORK

PENNSYLVANIA

NEW JERSEY

MARYLAND

DEL.

VIRGINIA

NORTH CAROLINA

SOUTH CAROLINA

GEORGIA

COLONIAL AMERICAN RELIGIOUS REGIONS
Colonial America was noted for its many different religious groups. Many settlers had come to America because of religious persecution in their home countries. They naturally brought with them their preferred practices of worship. It was natural for like-minded people to seek each other out and distinctive areas began to develop. The Congregationalists tended to settle in the New England states, while the Anglicans kept more to the coastal region further south. The Presbyterians and the Baptists tended to be further inland, while a sizeable group of Lutherans spread through Pennsylvania and north-eastern Virginia.

CHRISTIANITY IN THE WORLD BY 1850

CHRISTIANITY IN THE WORLD BY 1850

By the mid-19th century Christianity had swept through the world. Europe and the Russian Empire were entirely Christian and so was almost all of North and South America. In the developing British Empire the English-speaking territories such as Australia and New Zealand were Christian. European missionaries had taken Christianity to large parts of Africa where, in most cases it continued to exist alongside established local beliefs. Away from the coastal areas most of Africa was yet to be explored by Europeans and the traditional beliefs and religions continued to be uninfluenced by Christian missionaries.

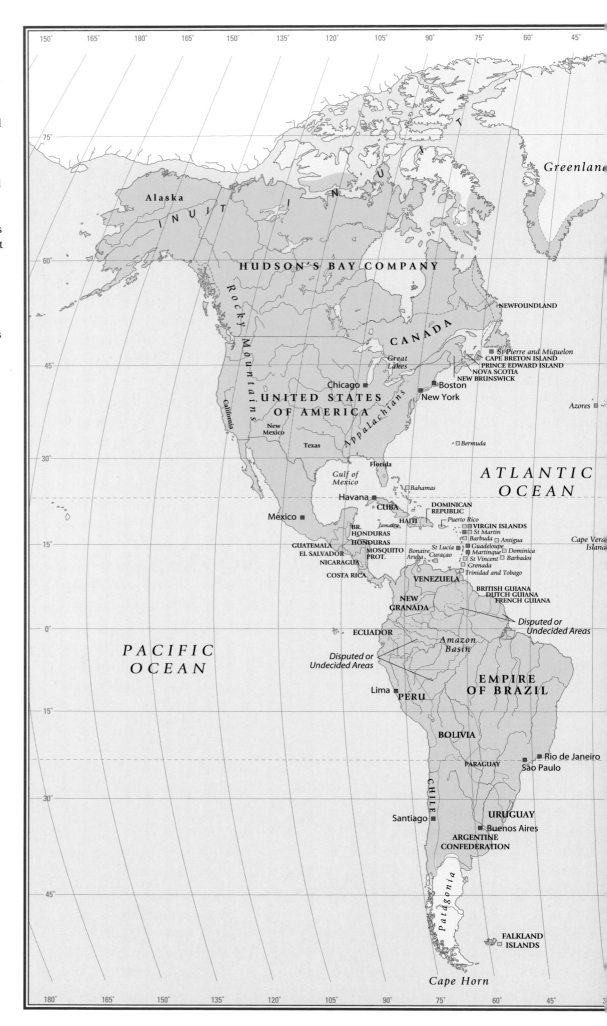

ARCTIC OCEAN

Siberia

RUSSIAN EMPIRE

NORWAY
SWEDEN
FINLAND

■ St. Petersburg

■ Moscow

DENMARK
BRITAIN
NETH.
ondon
BELGIUM
Paris
PRUSSIA
POLAND
SAXONY
BAVARIA

FRANCE
RLAND
BADEN

AUSTRIAN
EMPIRE
MOLDAVIA
TUSCANY
WALLACHIA
PAPAL
STATES
SERBIA
MONTENEGRO
Rome
Sardinia
KINGDOM
OF THE TWO
SICILIES
GREECE

KAZAKHS

Black Sea

*Caspian
Sea*
KHIVA

SMALL
TURKMEN
STATES
BUKHARA
KOKAND
KUNDUZ
BADAKHSHAN

Gobi Desert

QING
EMPIRE

■ Beijing

KOREA

JAPAN
■ Tokyo

SPAIN
■ Madrid

a
Gibraltar
ALGERIA
TUNIS
Malta
Mediterranean Sea

Constantinople

■ Tehran
BAEKH

PERSIA
AFGHANISTAN

Himalayas

■ Nanjing

OROCCO
*French conquest
in progress*
OTTOMAN EMPIRE
■ Cairo

BEDUINS

Sahara Desert

EGYPT
(Viceroyalty)

BALUCHISTAN

Delhi ■
Gwadar
(To Oman)

NEPAL
BHUTAN

INDIA

MANIPUR

■ Hong Kong
Macao

BAHRAIN

*Arabian
Peninsula*
OMAN

Diu
Damão

Chandernagore
BURMA

LUANG
PRABANG

TUAREGS
BORGU
KINGDOMS
MARADI
NILO-SAHARAN
PEOPLES
DAMARGAM
WADAI
DARFUR

YEMEN

*Arabian
Sea*

Goa ■
Yanaon

*Bay of
Bengal*

SIAM

ANNAM

PACIFIC
OCEAN

GU
MOSSI
KINGDOMS
AMPRUSI
AGOMBA
GOBIR
SOKOTO
BORNU

ETHIOPIA
■ Aden

HARAR

Mahé
Pondicherry
Karikal

TENASSERIM

■ Bangkok
CAMBODIA

■ Manila

PHILIPPINE
ISLANDS

MAGINDANAO

ASANTE
Whydah
ABUJA
IGALA
BENIN
DAHOMEY
GOLD
COAST
SAO TOME

Socotra

Ceylon

KUSHITES

NILO-SAHARAN
PEOPLES

*Nicobar
Islands*

MALAY
STATES

SULU

Fernando Po

*Maldive
Islands*

Malacca
Singapore

BRUNEI
SARAWAK

BANTUS

Sumatra

BUNYORO
BUGANDA
TORO
BUSOGA
ANKOLE
RWANDA
KARAGWE
BURUNDI

Labuan

MALAY STATES

*New
Guinea*
PAPUANS

TEKE
KUBA
KANIOK
LUBA
KIKONJA
NGONI
KASANJE

*Lake
Victoria*
■ Mombasa
(To Oman)
■ Zanzibar
(To Oman)
■ Kilwa (To Oman)

Seychelle Islands
Amirante Islands

Batavia ■
Java

DUTCH POSSESSIONS
AND DEPENDENCIES

KALUNDE

ANGOLA
LUNDA
CHOKWE
NGONI
KAZEMBE

INDIAN
OCEAN

PORTUGUESE
TIMOR

cension

MBAILUNDU
KIAKA
BIHE
LOZI
WAMBU
GALANGI
NDULU
KAKONDA
NDEBELE

PORTUGUESE EAST AFRICA

Madagascar

■ Nossi-Bé Island

MERINA
KINGDOM
Mauritius
Réunion

AUSTRALIAN
COLONIES

*Kalahari
Desert*

KHOISAN
PEOPLES
REPUBLIC OF
WINBURG-
POTCHEFSTROOM
GRIQUA
BASUTO
SWAZI
ZULU
NATAL
GAZA

a ■

CAPE
COLONY
PONDO

Cape Town ■
*Cape of
Good Hope*

■ Perth

Adelaide ■
■ Sydney

Lord Howe
Island

■ Melbourne

NEW
ZEALAND

SOUTHERN OCEAN

CHRISTIANITY IN
THE WORLD BY 1850

Mainly Christian areas

Christian and other
religious beliefs

All other areas, few or
no Christians

■ Major city or colony

CHRISTIANITY IN THE NAPOLEONIC EMPIRE

1812 – 1883

THE NAPOLEONIC EMPIRE

Napoleon had an uneasy relationship with the Vatican. In 1796 his troops had invaded Italy and defeated the papal army. The Pope sued for peace, but rioters killed the French ambassador. The French then marched on Rome and Napoleon proclaimed it a Roman republic. The Pope was captured and subsequently died in captivity in 1799. The papal regalia were melted down and the new Pope had to be crowned with a papier-mâché tiara. The French invaded the Papal states again in 1808 and the new Pope was imprisoned for six years until he was released following British victories in Europe.

THE NAPOLEONIC EMPIRE, c. 1812

- ruled directly by Napoleon
- ruled by members of Napoleon's family
- dependent state

MISSIONS IN THE UNITED STATES

MISSIONS IN THE UNITED STATES 1817–1883

During the early to mid-19th century a number of missionaries were actively working with the Native American tribes. Samuel Worcester worked with the Cherokees and established a Cherokee newspaper. Jason Lee was a Canadian Methodist who helped to establish the first permanent school in Oregon. Pierre-Jean de Smet was a Belgian Jesuit who worked with tribes in the Rocky Mountains. Marcus and Narcissa Whitman crossed the Rocky Mountains and spent six unsuccessful years at Waiilatpu trying to convert the Cayuse Indians and were eventually killed by them. Stephen Riggs worked with the Sioux in Dakota.

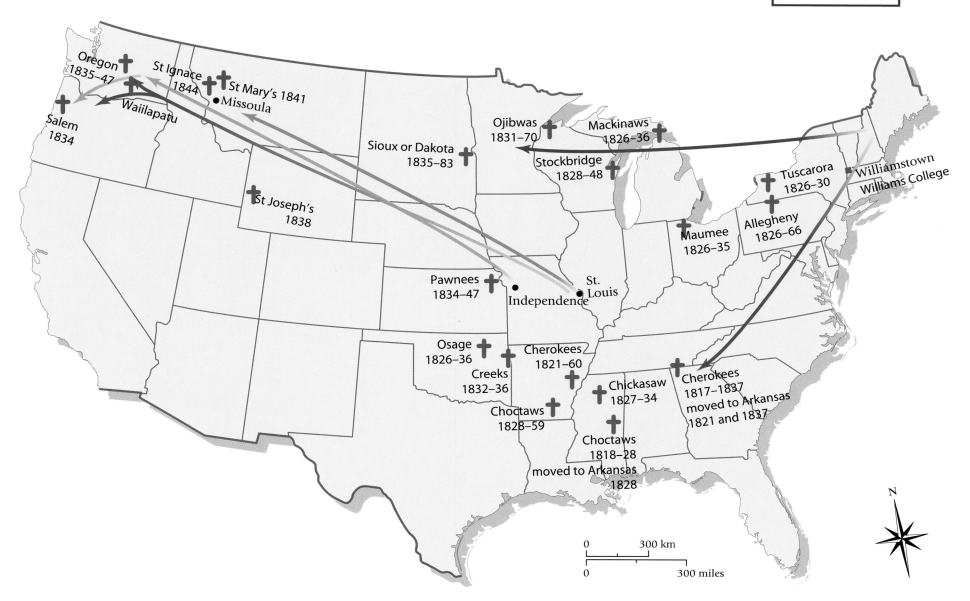

MISSIONS IN
THE UNITED
STATES, 1817–83

✝ mission

MISSIONARIES' TREKS

→ De Smet, 1840

→ Lee, 1834

→ Whitmans, 1836

→ Worcester, 1825

→ Riggs, 1837

Borders and states as of 1880

UTOPIAN COMMUNITIES IN THE USA

CHURCH FAMILY MAIN DWELLING, HANCOCK

This was a Shaker house. The Shakers originally came to London following persecution in France. They gained converts from Quakers and Methodists and eventually emigrated to New England. They lived as extended families in communal houses of about 50 people. Each family would look after its own finances and would have its own plot of land to till for vegetables and food.

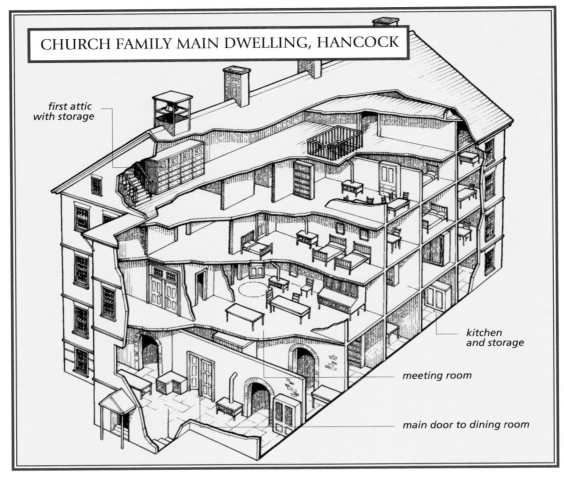

CHURCH FAMILY MAIN DWELLING, HANCOCK

first attic with storage

kitchen and storage

meeting room

main door to dining room

ONEIDAN HOUSE

The Oneida Community Mansion House was built for a community of 300 members who lived as one family. Between 1848 and 1880, under the leadership of John Humphrey Noyes, this religiously based perfectionist community challenged contemporary social views on property ownership, gender roles, child-rearing practices, monogamous marriage and work. Succumbing to pressures from within and without, the Community disbanded in 1881 and formed a joint-stock company Oneida Community Ltd. The name eventually changed to Oneida Ltd and found worldwide fame producing fine cutlery such as Community Plate.

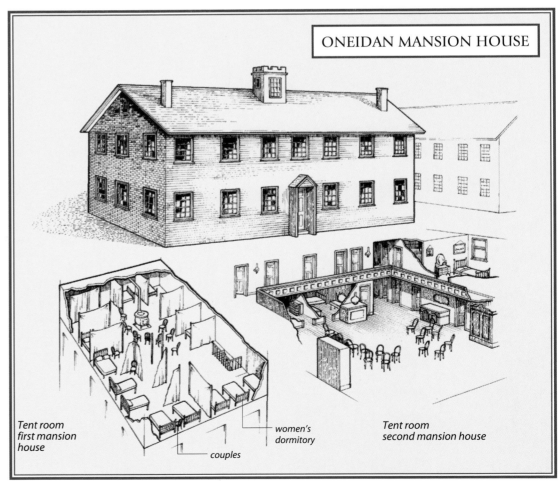

ONEIDAN MANSION HOUSE

Tent room first mansion house

couples

women's dormitory

Tent room second mansion house

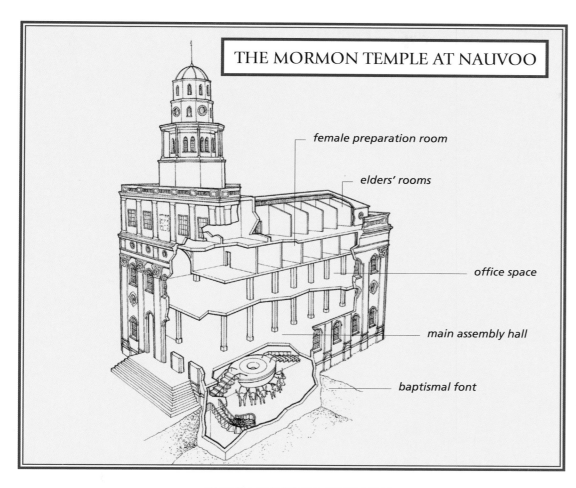

THE MORMON TEMPLE AT NAUVOO

- female preparation room
- elders' rooms
- office space
- main assembly hall
- baptismal font

THE MORMON TEMPLE AT NAUVOO

The Mormons (Church of Latter Day Saints) arrived in Illinois in 1832 after fleeing from persecution in Missouri. By 1842 Nauvoo had a population of at least 12,000 and was the largest city in Illinois. The Church built a massive temple, but attempted to gain control over all local institutions. This led to conflict with other Illinoisans and the murder of the Mormon leader, John Smith and his brother Hyrum. In 1846 the Mormons decided to leave Illinois, and under the leadership of Brigham Young made the long trek across the desert to Utah where they founded Salt Lake City.

THE SHAKER COMMUNITY, HANCOCK MASSACHUSETTS

The Shaker Community was established at Hancock in 1783. Shakers believed in pacifism, celibacy and communal living. Worship would be in the form of singing and ecstatic dancing, which was why they were called Shakers. The movement reached its peak in the 1840s, when there were 19 Shaker societies. Today there is only one. The Hancock Shaker Village was named the City of Peace and is famous for its 'Round Stone Barn' built in 1826 and its communal houses. At its peak it had 300 believers, but closed as a community in 1960 and now operates as a museum.

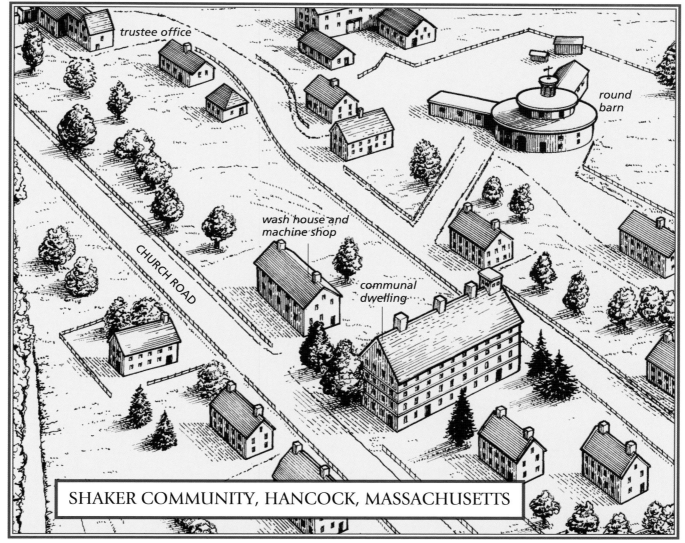

- trustee office
- round barn
- wash house and machine shop
- communal dwelling
- CHURCH ROAD

SHAKER COMMUNITY, HANCOCK, MASSACHUSETTS

MORMONISM; MORMON ADHERENTS

1800 – 1990

MORMONISM

In 1820 John Smith, the founder of Mormonism, had a vision. This vision told him where to find three gold plates containing ancient inscriptions. Smith translated these to his wife and the resulting writings were later published as the Book of Mormon in 1830. The Mormons became centred in Illinois and built a large temple at Nauvoo, but there was trouble with the local people and Smith and his brother Hyrum were both imprisoned and subsequently murdered by a rioting mob. The whole community then moved to Utah where a new headquarters was set up at Salt Lake City.

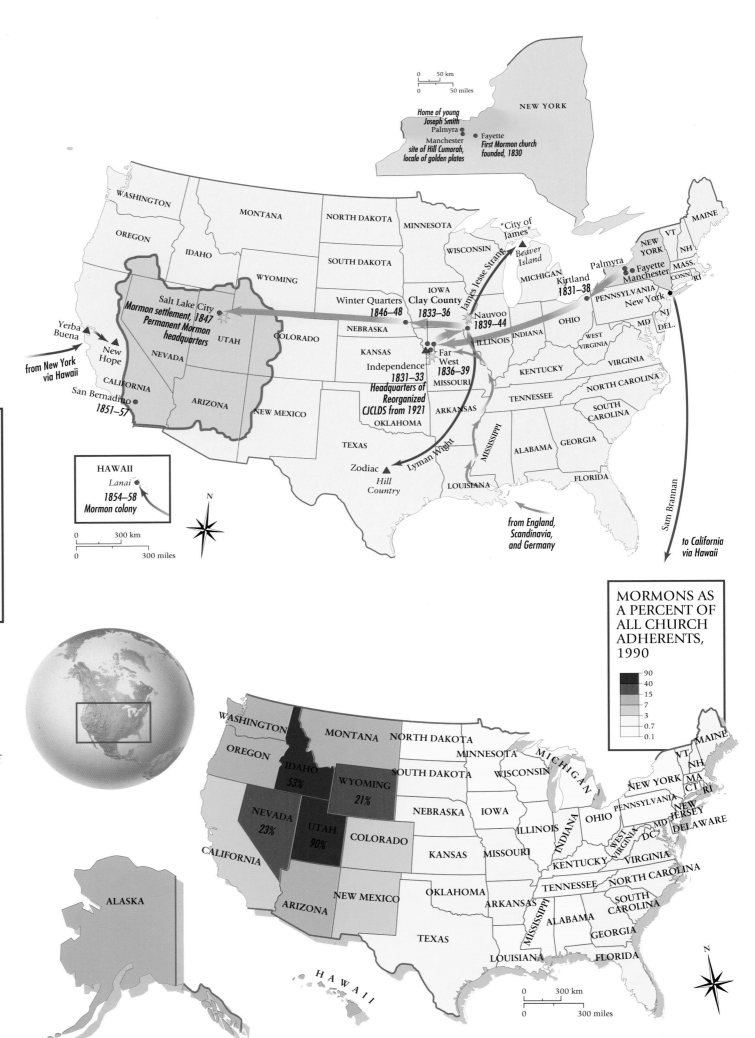

MORMONISM

- ● Important Mormon locale
- → Mormon exodus
- ▢ Proposed Mormon state of Deseret, 1849
- ✳ Violence against Mormons
- → Immigration of European converts
- ▲ Mormon splinter group
- → Mormon splinter spread
- New York's "burned-over district"

MORMONS AS A PERCENTAGE OF ALL CHURCH ADHERENTS

There is a clear east–west divide when looking at Mormonism as a percentage of church adherents. As might be expected, 90 per cent of churchgoers in Utah are Mormons. Just to the north in Idaho the percentage is 53, while to the west and east, in Nevada 23 per cent are Mormons, while in Wyoming the figure is 21 per cent. In Arizona, Montana, Washington and Oregon, Mormons make up more than 7 per cent of their populations.

MORMONS AS A PERCENT OF ALL CHURCH ADHERENTS, 1990

- 90
- 40
- 15
- 7
- 3
- 0.7
- 0.1

PROTESTANTS IN THE USA; CATHOLICS IN THE USA

PROTESTANTS IN THE USA

Enshrined in the constitution of the United States is freedom of religion and as a result there is a multitude of different faiths. Being a country that has been populated entirely by immigrants it is only natural that different groups have brought their own religions with them, and this is reflected in their distribution. The traditional Protestant heartland is the so-called "Bible Belt" of the south, where the Southern Baptist Convention continues to reign supreme. Another state with a particularly high percentage of Protestantism is Utah, which is the home state and world headquarters of Mormonism.

CATHOLICS AS A PERCENT OF TOTAL POPULATION, BY STATE, 1990

63
28
21
14
7
2

CATHOLICS IN THE USA

During the time of the Thirteen Colonies, Roman Catholicism in the US was a tiny minority faith. Today just over a quarter of the American population is Catholic. The main source of Roman Catholics in the United States was the huge number of European immigrants during the 19th and early 20th centuries from countries such as Ireland, Southern Germany, Italy, Poland and eastern Europe. Modern Catholic immigrants tend to come from the Philippines and Latin America, particularly Mexico. As is to be expected, percentages are very high in the northeast, the point of arrival for European immigrants, and in New Mexico, the entry point for Latin Americans.

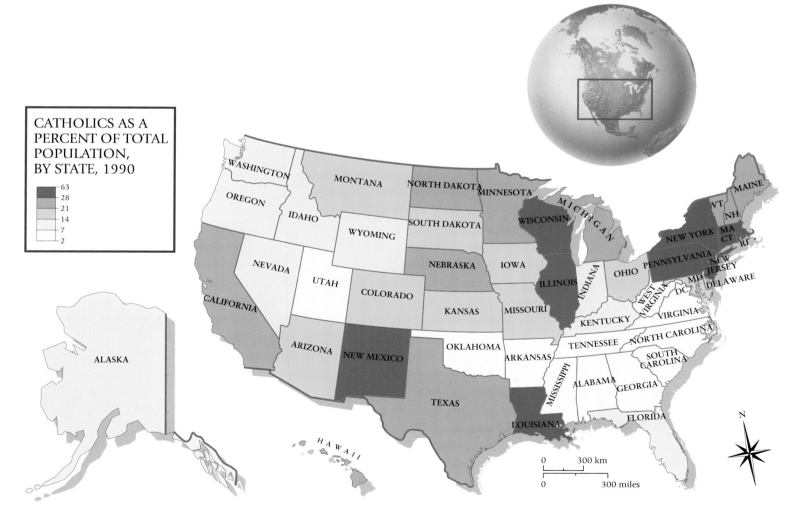

CATHOLICS AS A PERCENT OF TOTAL POPULATION, BY STATE, 1990

63
28
21
14
7
2

HOLINESS; PENTECOSTALISM

HOLINESS

The Church of the Nazarene is a Protestant Christian church in the Wesleyan–Holiness tradition. The American Holiness Movement began in the 1840s and 50s as an endeavour to preserve and propagate John Wesley's teaching on entire sanctification and Christian perfection. The Church of the Nazarene's interests include higher education and missions. They have eight universities in the United States and others worldwide. Total membership in the United States is 640,000.

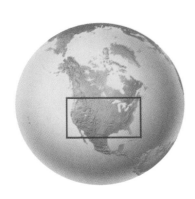

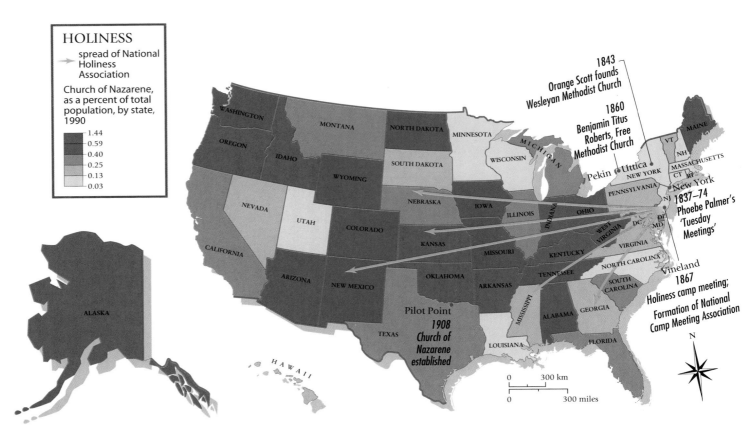

HOLINESS

→ spread of National Holiness Association

Church of Nazarene, as a percent of total population, by state, 1990

- 1.44
- 0.59
- 0.40
- 0.25
- 0.13
- 0.03

1843 Orange Scott founds Wesleyan Methodist Church

1860 Benjamin Titus Roberts, Free Methodist Church

New York *1837–74* Phoebe Palmer's 'Tuesday Meetings'

Vineland *1867* Holiness camp meeting; Formation of National Camp Meeting Association

Pilot Point *1908* Church of Nazarene established

PENTECOSTALISM

This is a movement within Evangelical Christianity that places special emphasis on the direct personal experience of God through the baptism of the Holy Spirit, as shown in the Biblical account of the Day of Pentecost. Most Pentecostalists believe that one must be saved by believing in Jesus as Lord and Saviour for the forgiveness of sins and to be made acceptable to God.

Pentecostalists also believe that the Bible has definite authority in matters of faith. Receiving of the Holy Spirit is necessary for salvation and includes 'speaking in tongues'.

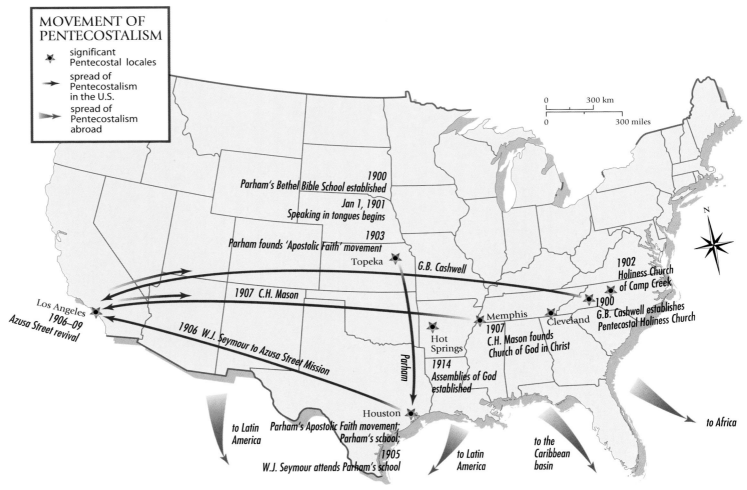

MOVEMENT OF PENTECOSTALISM

✷ significant Pentecostal locales

→ spread of Pentecostalism in the U.S.

→ spread of Pentecostalism abroad

1900 Parham's Bethel Bible School established

Jan 1, 1901 Speaking in tongues begins

1903 Parham founds 'Apostolic Faith' movement

Topeka

G.B. Cashwell

1907 C.H. Mason

Los Angeles *1906–09* Azusa Street revival

1906 W.J. Seymour to Azusa Street Mission

Memphis

Hot Springs

1907 C.H. Mason founds Church of God in Christ

Cleveland

1902 Holiness Church of Camp Creek

1900 G.B. Cashwell establishes Pentecostal Holiness Church

1914 Assemblies of God established

Houston

Parham's Apostolic Faith movement; Parham's school;

1905 W.J. Seymour attends Parham's school

to Latin America

to Latin America

to the Caribbean basin

to Africa

UNIFICATION CHURCH; COMMUNITARIANISM

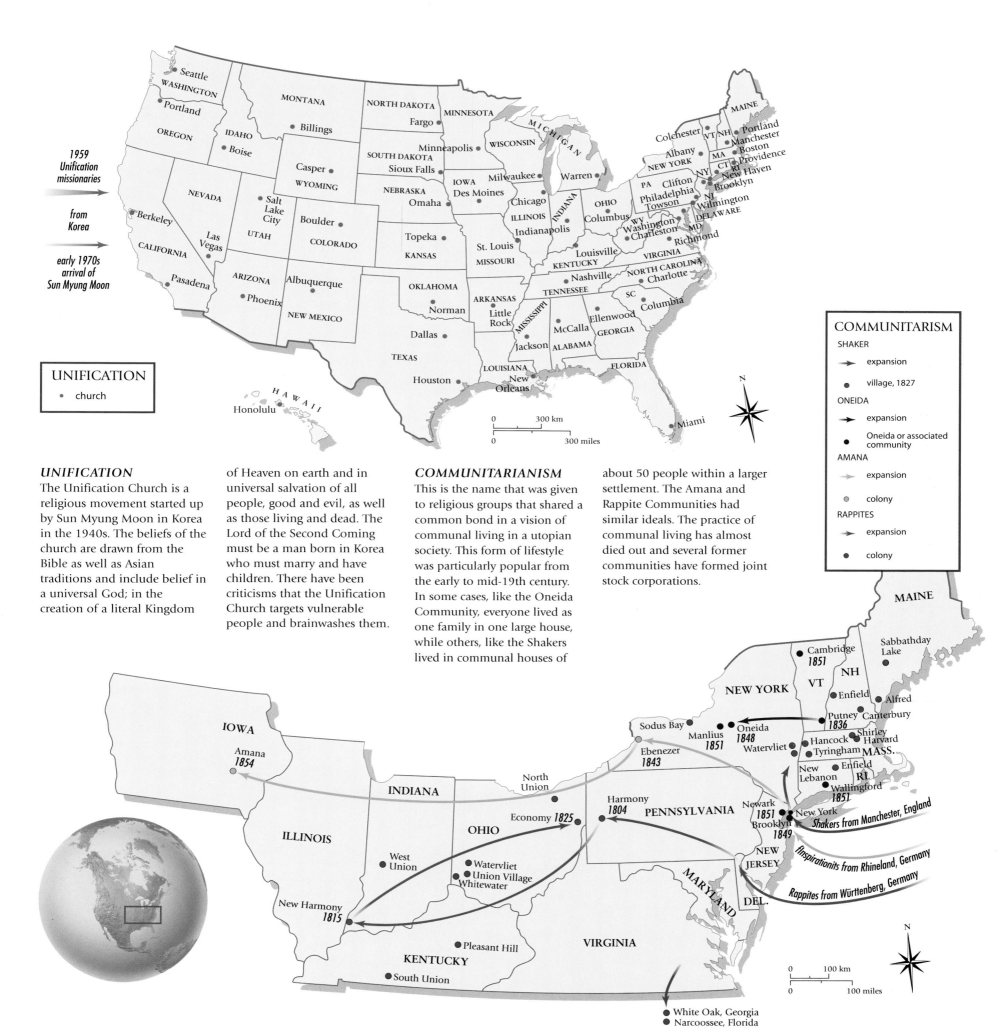

1959
Unification
missionaries

from
Korea

early 1970s
arrival of
Sun Myung Moon

UNIFICATION

- church

UNIFICATION

The Unification Church is a religious movement started up by Sun Myung Moon in Korea in the 1940s. The beliefs of the church are drawn from the Bible as well as Asian traditions and include belief in a universal God; in the creation of a literal Kingdom of Heaven on earth and in universal salvation of all people, good and evil, as well as those living and dead. The Lord of the Second Coming must be a man born in Korea who must marry and have children. There have been criticisms that the Unification Church targets vulnerable people and brainwashes them.

COMMUNITARIANISM

This is the name that was given to religious groups that shared a common bond in a vision of communal living in a utopian society. This form of lifestyle was particularly popular from the early to mid-19th century. In some cases, like the Oneida Community, everyone lived as one family in one large house, while others, like the Shakers lived in communal houses of about 50 people within a larger settlement. The Amana and Rappite Communities had similar ideals. The practice of communal living has almost died out and several former communities have formed joint stock corporations.

COMMUNITARISM

SHAKER
- → expansion
- ● village, 1827

ONEIDA
- → expansion
- ● Oneida or associated community

AMANA
- → expansion
- ● colony

RAPPITES
- → expansion
- ● colony

SOUTHERN BAPTIST CONVENTION

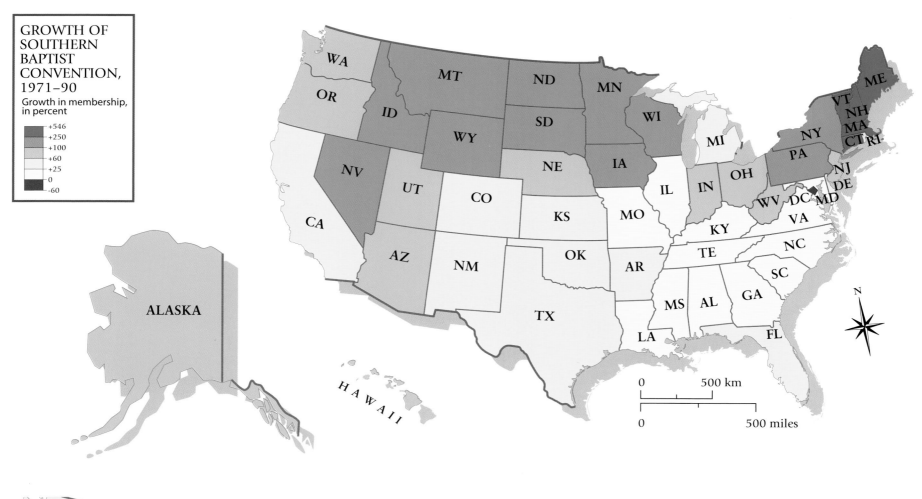

GROWTH OF SOUTHERN BAPTIST CONVENTION, 1971–90

Growth in membership, in percent

- +546
- +250
- +100
- +60
- +25
- 0
- -60

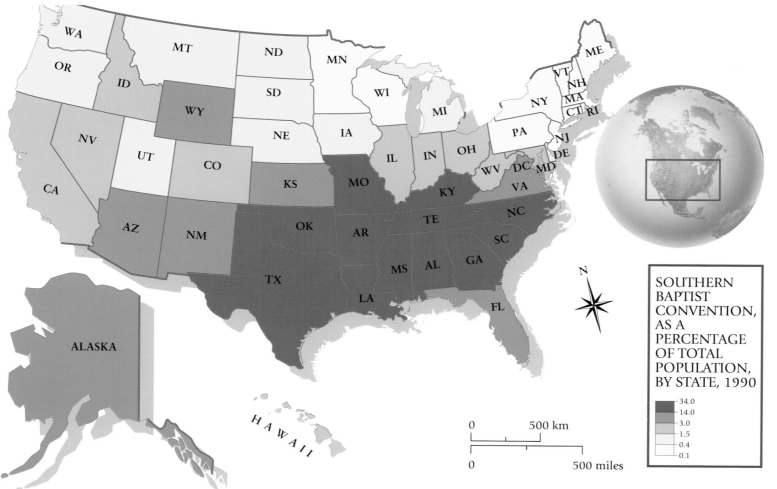

SOUTHERN BAPTIST CONVENTION AS PERCENTAGE OF POPULATION BY STATE 1971–1990

The Southern Baptist Convention (SBC) is the largest Baptist group in the world and the largest Protestant denomination in the United States. With a national membership of some 16 million, the SBC is able to exercise considerable influence in the state and national political scene, which it often uses to control the content of educational material in schools. In recent years the SBC has grown from its regional roots to become a major force in American and international Christianity. This growth has been significant in the more northerly states of the Union.

SOUTHERN BAPTIST CONVENTION, AS A PERCENTAGE OF TOTAL POPULATION, BY STATE, 1990

- 34.0
- 14.0
- 3.0
- 1.5
- 0.4
- 0.1

CHRISTIANITY IN AFRICA

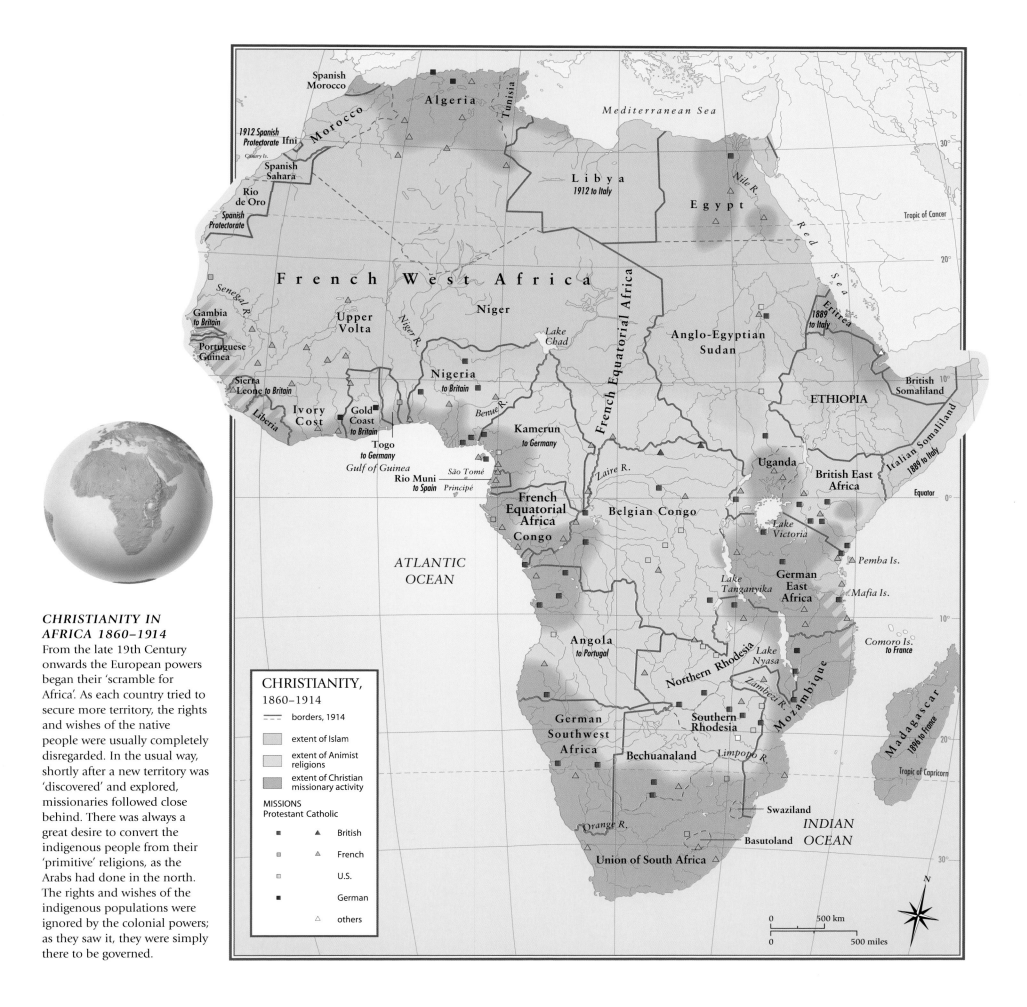

CHRISTIANITY IN AFRICA 1860–1914

From the late 19th Century onwards the European powers began their 'scramble for Africa'. As each country tried to secure more territory, the rights and wishes of the native people were usually completely disregarded. In the usual way, shortly after a new territory was 'discovered' and explored, missionaries followed close behind. There was always a great desire to convert the indigenous people from their 'primitive' religions, as the Arabs had done in the north. The rights and wishes of the indigenous populations were ignored by the colonial powers; as they saw it, they were simply there to be governed.

CHRISTIANITY, 1860–1914

- - - - borders, 1914

   extent of Islam

   extent of Animist religions

   extent of Christian missionary activity

MISSIONS

Protestant	Catholic	
■	▲	British
▣	△	French
▢		U.S.
■		German
	△	others

Map labels:

Spanish Morocco · Algeria · Tunisia · Mediterranean Sea · 1912 Spanish Protectorate Ifni · Morocco · Canary Is. · Spanish Sahara · Libya 1912 to Italy · Egypt · Nile R. · Red Sea · Tropic of Cancer · Rio de Oro · Spanish Protectorate · French West Africa · Senegal R. · Gambia to Britain · Upper Volta · Niger R. · Niger · Lake Chad · French Equatorial Africa · Anglo-Egyptian Sudan · Eritrea 1889 to Italy · Portuguese Guinea · Sierra Leone to Britain · Nigeria to Britain · Benue R. · ETHIOPIA · British Somaliland · Liberia · Ivory Coast · Gold Coast to Britain · Kamerun to Germany · Togo to Germany · Gulf of Guinea · Rio Muni to Spain · São Tomé · Príncipe · Zaire R. · Uganda · British East Africa · Italian Somaliland 1889 to Italy · Equator · ATLANTIC OCEAN · French Equatorial Africa Congo · Belgian Congo · Lake Victoria · German East Africa · Pemba Is. · Lake Tanganyika · Mafia Is. · Angola to Portugal · Comoro Is. to France · Northern Rhodesia · Lake Nyasa · Zambezi R. · Mozambique · Madagascar 1896 to France · German Southwest Africa · Southern Rhodesia · Bechuanaland · Limpopo R. · Swaziland · INDIAN OCEAN · Tropic of Capricorn · Orange R. · Basutoland · Union of South Africa

0 500 km · 0 500 miles

CHRISTIANS IN THE WORLD 2007

CHRISTIANITY IN THE WORLD 2007

Christianity is the world's biggest religion. It is estimated that 33 per cent of the world's population, or 2.1 billion profess to be Christians. They come from many sects and denominations, but the unifying factor is that all believe in the divinity of Jesus Christ and that he died for the sins of the world and then rose from the dead. The world's second religion is Islam. This comes some way behind Christianity with 1.3 billion members, making up 21 per cent of the world's population. Many Muslims claim that although Christians are more numerous, there are more practicing Muslims than practicing Christians in the world.

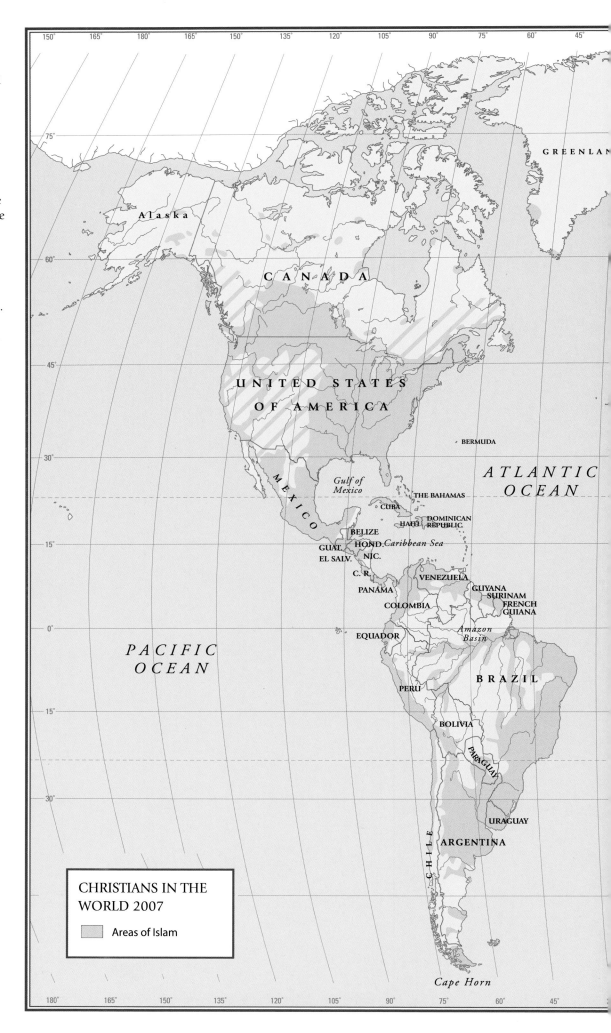

CHRISTIANS IN THE WORLD 2007

Areas of Islam

JERUSALEM TODAY

JERUSALEM TODAY

Christians, Muslims and Jews all consider Jerusalem to be a holy place. To members of the Jewish faith the holiest place in the world is the Western Wall of the ruined temple that remained standing after the temple was destroyed by the Romans in AD 70. It is seen as a symbol that God remained with them despite great hardships. To Muslims Jerusalem is the holy site where Muhammad ascended to Heaven to meet God and to Christians it is the place where Christ was crucified and three days later rose from the dead.

JERUSALEM TODAY

Key religious areas

- Christian
- Muslim
- Jewish

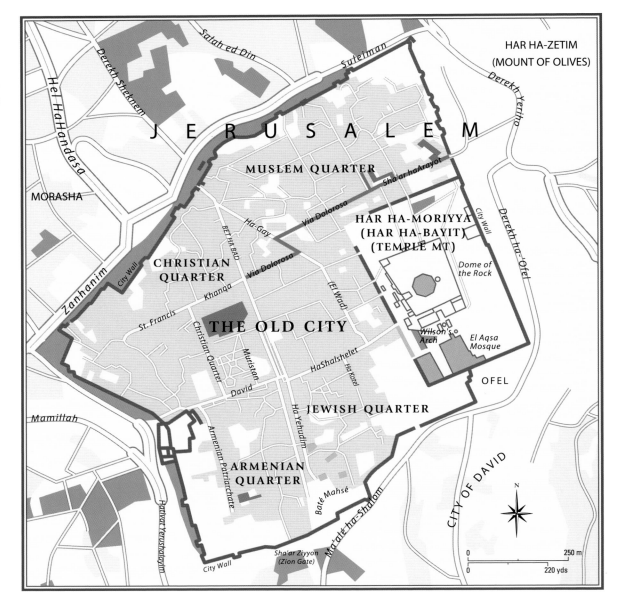

PART 6

ISLAM

The Holy Book of Islam is the Qur'an, a collection of revelations made to Muhammad by God but initiated by the Angel Gabriel. The basic teachings of this religious book state that there is one God, omnipotent and omniscient, who created everything that exists. All men must submit themselves totally to the will of God. All those who rebel against God's prophets will be punished in this world and the hereafter. After death the good go to heaven or paradise while the evil are punished. At the end of time and the end of the world there will be a resurrection of all bodies and a universal judgement will take place.

There are five pillars of Islam. The first of these is a profession of faith: there is no God but God and Muhammad is his Prophet.

The second pillar is prayer whether du'a', a personal spontaneous prayer; or the salat, a set ritual of five daily prayers. The third is the pilgrimage, or hajj, to Mecca while the fourth is fasting in the month of Ramadan, when Muslims must abstain from food, drink, and sex between sunrise and sunset. The final pillar is the zakat, a financial 'tax', originally alms, paid by Muslims to the community or state.

226 – 632

ARABIA BEFORE THE MUSLIM CONQUESTS

ARABIA BEFORE THE MUSLIM CONQUESTS

Before the Muslim conquest in the mid-7th century much of the Middle East was ruled by the Sassanid Empire. This empire lasted from 226 to 651, but when it eventually lost a 14-year struggle to the Muslims, its demise was rapid. At its height the Empire's territory included all of present-day Iran, Iraq, Armenia, Afghanistan, eastern Turkey and parts of India, Syria, Pakistan and central Asia. By the time of Muhammad's death in 632, large areas of Arabia had been converted to the new Islamic faith. Following his death and with the formation of the Islamic caliphate, Islam spread rapidly.

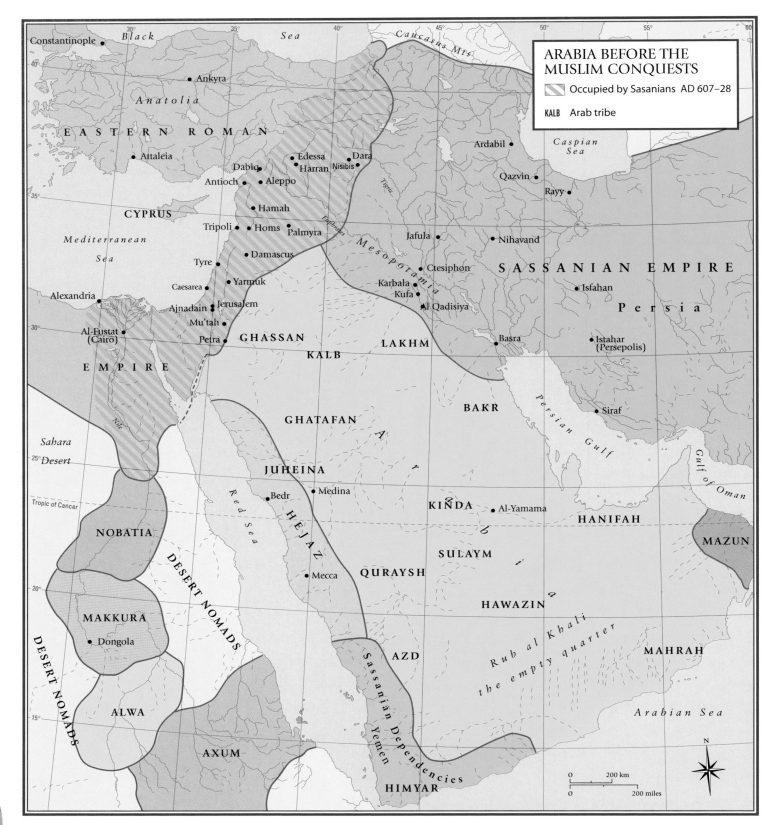

ARABIA BEFORE THE
MUSLIM CONQUESTS
Occupied by Sasanians AD 607–28
KALB Arab tribe

MUHAMMAD'S MISSIONS AND CAMPAIGNS

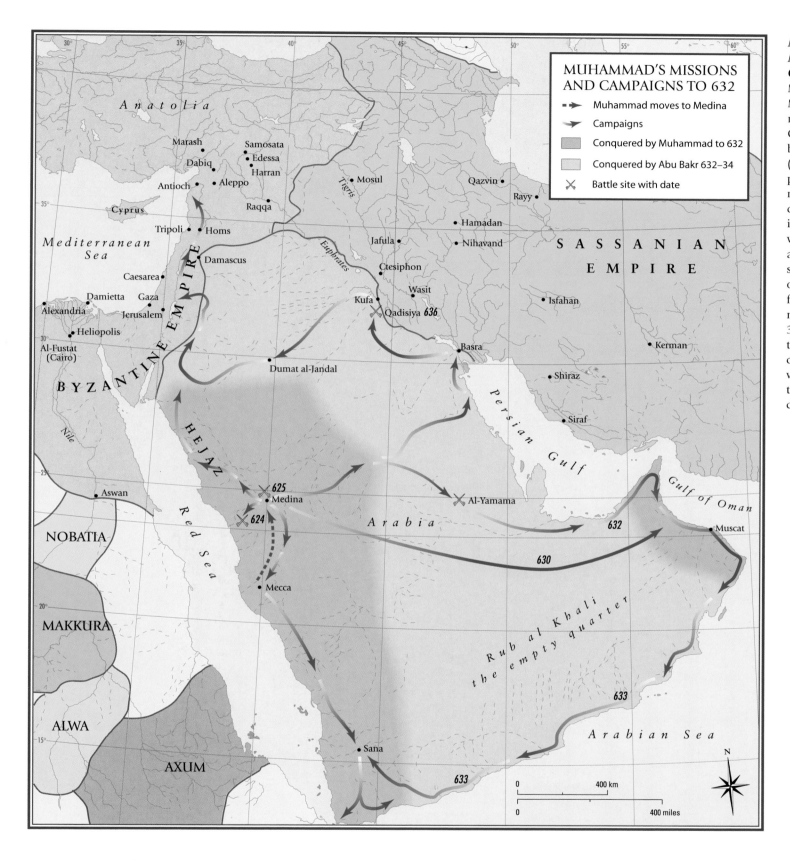

Muhammad's home was in Mecca. He had received a number of revelations from God, which he wrote in what became the Holy Koran (Qur'an). When he began preaching about these revelations, local opposition caused him to flee to Medina in 622. Medina and Mecca were at war with each other and in 624 Muhammad led some 300 warriors in a raid on a Meccan caravan. The following year the Meccans marched on Medina with 3000 men, but failed to take the town. After a number of campaigns the whole of Arabia was converted to Islam by the time of Muhammad's death in 632.

EXPANSION OF ISLAM TO 750

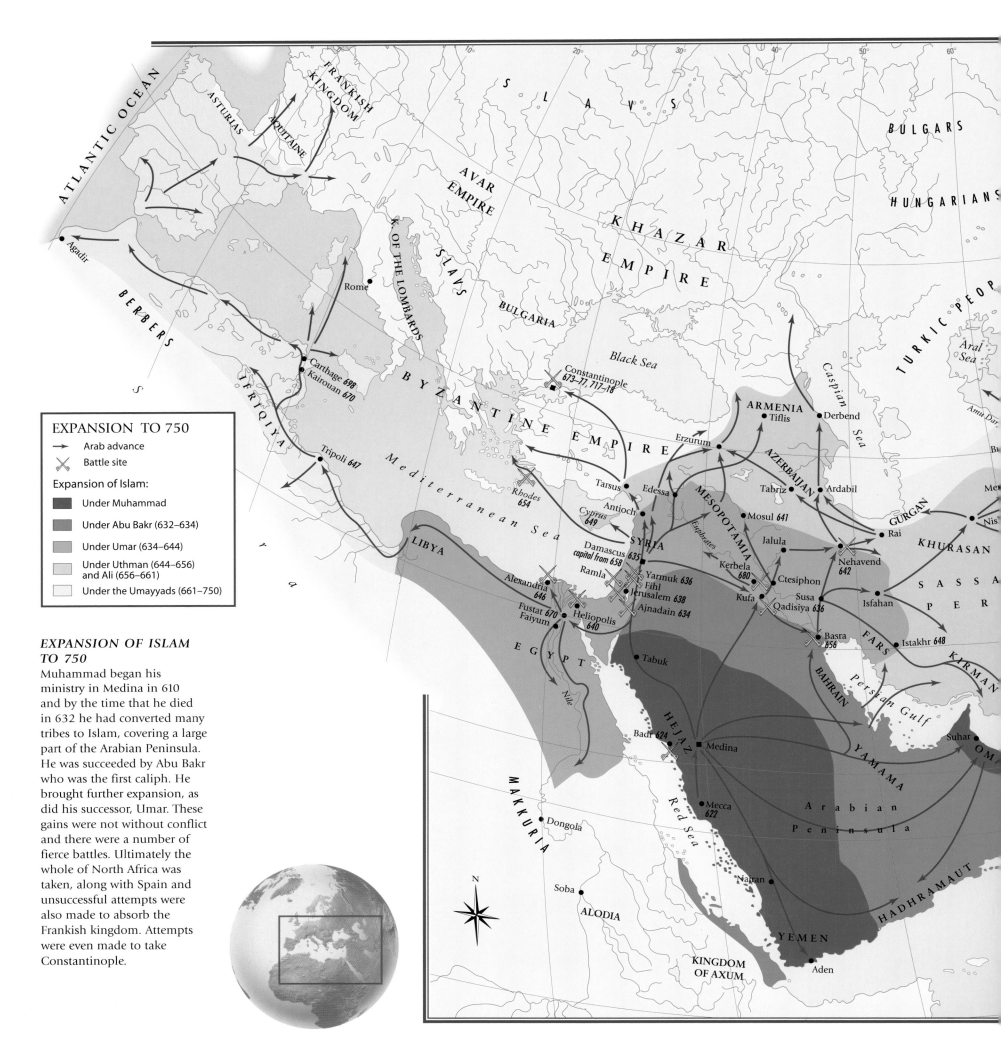

EXPANSION TO 750

→ Arab advance

✕ Battle site

Expansion of Islam:

Under Muhammad

Under Abu Bakr (632–634)

Under Umar (634–644)

Under Uthman (644–656)
and Ali (656–661)

Under the Umayyads (661–750)

EXPANSION OF ISLAM TO 750

Muhammad began his ministry in Medina in 610 and by the time that he died in 632 he had converted many tribes to Islam, covering a large part of the Arabian Peninsula. He was succeeded by Abu Bakr who was the first caliph. He brought further expansion, as did his successor, Umar. These gains were not without conflict and there were a number of fierce battles. Ultimately the whole of North Africa was taken, along with Spain and unsuccessful attempts were also made to absorb the Frankish kingdom. Attempts were even made to take Constantinople.

MUSLIM SPAIN; CHRISTIAN RECONQUEST

MUSLIM SPAIN C. 1030

The 7th century had seen Muslim forces invade and conquer the Iberian peninsula, driving out the Visigoths. The conquest was completed within two years in 713 and it must be remembered that this was only 81 years since the death of the prophet Muhammad. In 719 Cordoba became the residence of the Arab governors of al-Andalus and in 755 the Umayyad Dynasty was installed, firmly establishing Muslim society and culture in Spain. The period around 930 was the 'golden age', but by 1030 Muslim Spain was beginning to break up and Christians were gaining ground from the north.

THE CHRISTIAN RECONQUEST

In Spain, a Christian Reconquista commenced in the tiny northern Christian kingdoms of Leon, Aragon, Navarre and the county of Barcelona. By 1275, only Granada remained in Muslim hands. The Catholic monarchs, Isabella of Castile and Ferdinand II of Aragon captured Granada in 1492, and in a burst of intolerance expelled Jews and converted Muslims, the Moriscos. The Muslims had lived in Spain for 700 years and the Jews for 1000. Any remaining Muslims or Jews were forcibly converted to Christianity by the Spanish Inquisition.

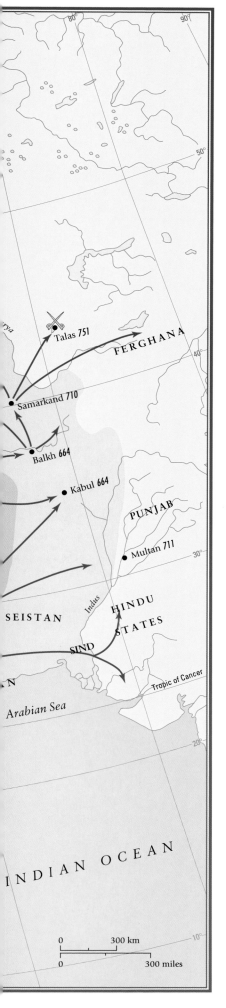

MUSLIM SPAIN, c. 1030

- Christian states
- Caliphate of Cordoba to 1031
- Murcia Islamic (or Party) kingdoms after 1031
- ⚓ archdiocese
- ✡ important Jewish community

POPULATION
- Christian
- mostly Berber and converts
- mostly Arabic

THE CHRISTIAN RECONQUEST

DATE OF RECONQUEST
- 1080
- 1130
- 1210
- 1250
- 1275
- Muslim domination
- ⚓ archdiocese

MILITARY ORDERS
- Hospital
- Santiago
- Caltrava
- Alcántra
- Avis
- Cristo
- Montesa

C. 850

THE ABBASID EMPIRE

THE ABBASID EMPIRE
The Abbasid Empire was the
second of the two Sunni
dynasties of the Arab Empire.
It seized power in 750 and
shifted the capital from
Damascus to Baghdad, where
it flourished for two centuries,
before going into a decline
following a rise in power of
the Turkish army that the
Abbasids themselves had
created. At its height it
controlled vast areas, but vast
areas are notoriously difficult
to control and there were a
number of incursions from the
east. The empire slowly
crumbled away until it finally
collapsed in 1258 when
Hulagu Khan, the Mongol
conqueror, sacked Baghdad.

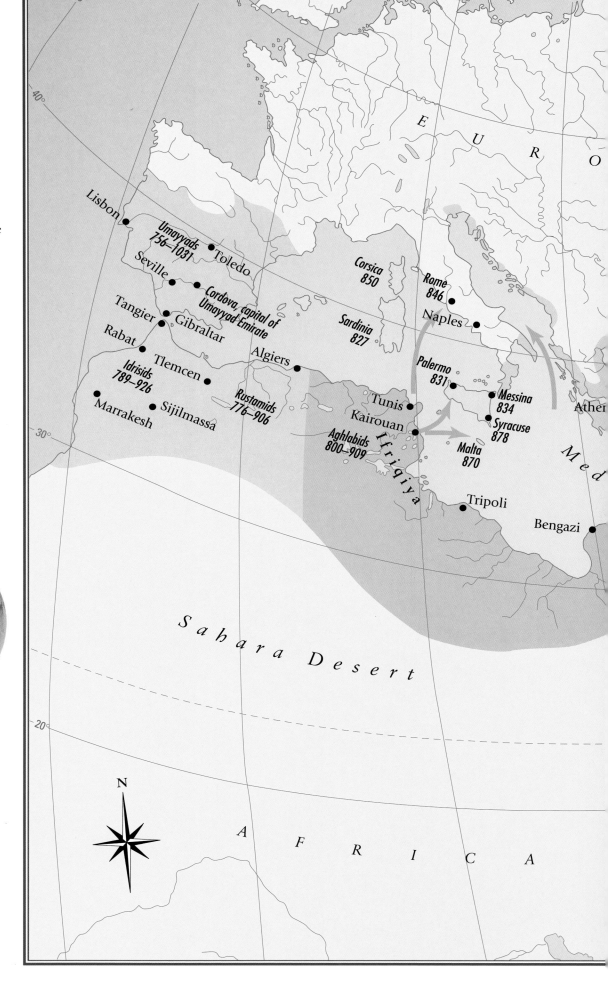

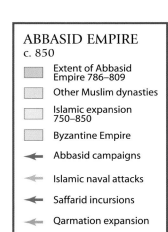

ABBASID EMPIRE
c. 850

Extent of Abbasid
Empire 786–809

Other Muslim dynasties

Islamic expansion
750–850

Byzantine Empire

Abbasid campaigns

Islamic naval attacks

Saffarid incursions

Qarmation expansion

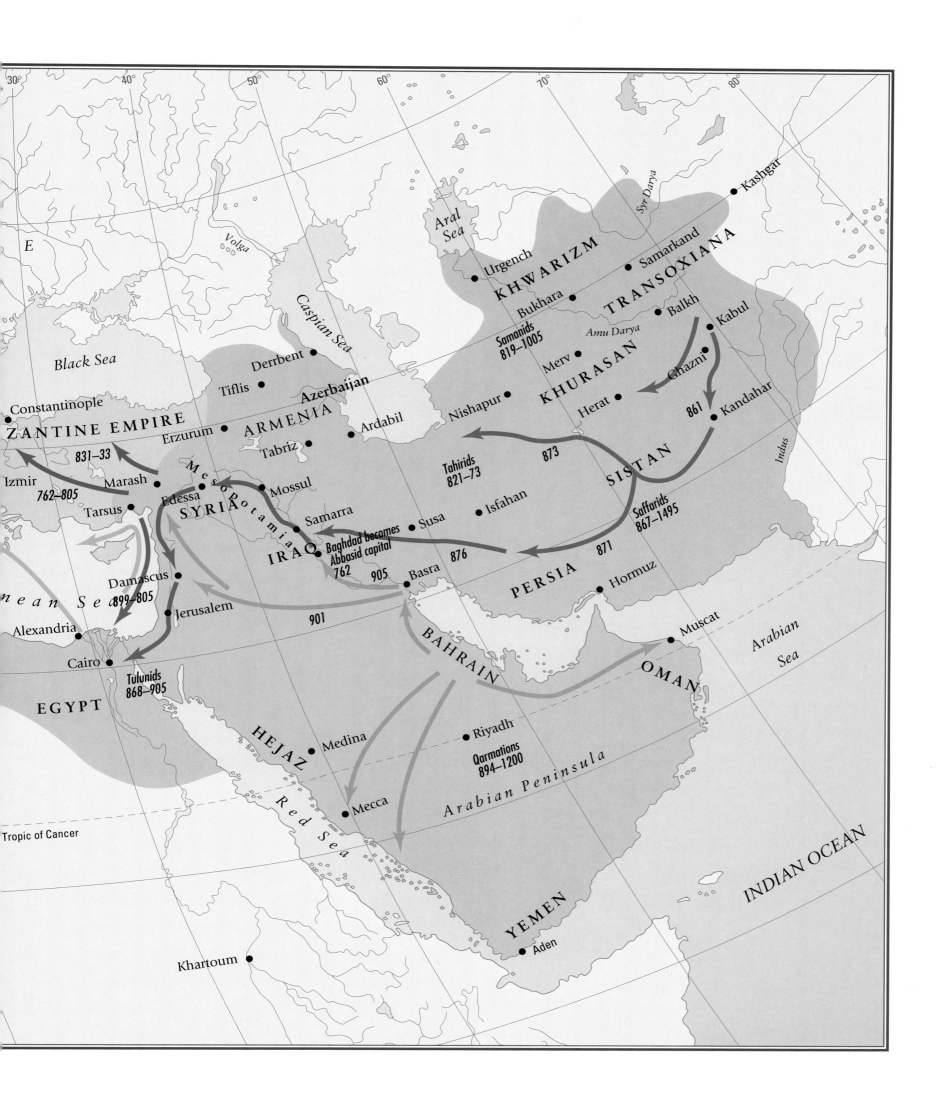

Aral
Sea

Volga

Syr Darya

Kashgar

Urgench

KHWARIZM

Samarkand

TRANSOXIANA

Bukhara

Balkh

Kabul

Caspian Sea

Samanids
819–1005

Amu Darya

Merv

KHURASAN

Ghazni

Derrbent

Black Sea

Tiflis

Azerbaijan

ARMENIA

Nishapur

Herat

861

Kandahar

Constantinople

ZANTINE EMPIRE

Erzurum

Ardabil

873

Tabriz

Tahirids
821–73

SISTAN

Indus

831–33

Mossul

Isfahan

Saffarids
867–1495

Izmir

Marash

Meso

Edessa

Samarra

Susa

potamia

SYRIA

762–805

Tarsus

IRAQ

Baghdad becomes
Abbasid capital
762

876

871

899–805

Damascus

905

Basra

PERSIA

Hormuz

Jerusalem

901

Muscat

*Arabian
Sea*

Alexandria

nean Sea

Cairo

BAHRAIN

OMAN

Tulunids
868–905

EGYPT

HEJAZ

Medina

Riyadh

Qarmations
894–1200

INDIAN OCEAN

Red Sea

Mecca

Arabian Peninsula

Tropic of Cancer

Khartoum

YEMEN

Aden

REGIMES IN THE 10TH AND 11TH CENTURIES

POST-IMPERIAL SUCCESSOR REGIMES LATE 10TH CENTURY

By the late 10th century the Abbasid Empire was already on the decline. At one time it had controlled huge swathes of the Middle East and although on paper it still controlled a large amount of territory, in practice much of its former power and control had been devolved to local groups such as the Samanids of Afghanistan and the Buyids from Persia.

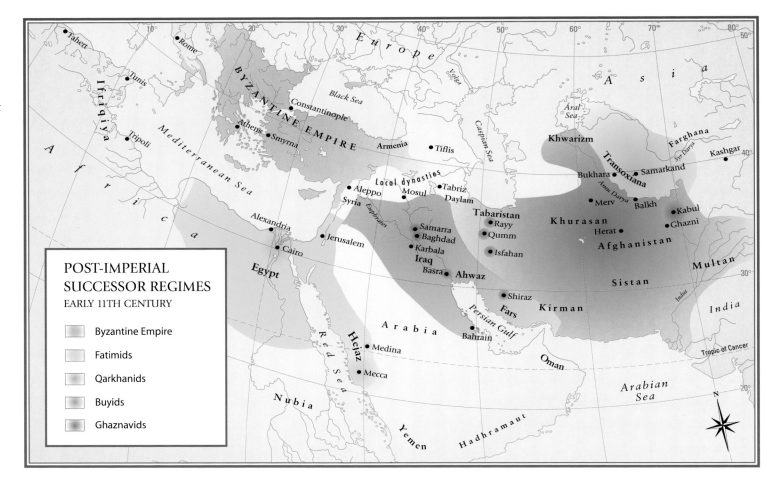

POST-IMPERIAL SUCCESSOR REGIMES
LATE 10TH CENTURY

— Abbasid Caliphate c. 900

Byzantine Empire

Fatimids

Hamadanids

Buyids

Samanids

Ghurids

POST IMPERIAL SUCCESSOR REGIMES EARLY 11TH CENTURY

Within a short time fortunes can change. Two military families arose from the Turkic Slave Guards of the Samanids and the result was the formation of the Ghaznivid Empire. This Empire pressed westward and pushed the Buyids in front as they went. The Empire moved north as far as the Aral Sea and south as far as the Arabian Sea. All the while these states were nominally part of the Abbasid Empire.

POST-IMPERIAL SUCCESSOR REGIMES
EARLY 11TH CENTURY

Byzantine Empire

Fatimids

Qarkhanids

Buyids

Ghaznavids

MUSLIMS IN THE NEAR EAST

MUSLIMS IN THE NEAR EAST 1127–1174

Imad ad-Din Zangi became Atabeg of Mosul in 1127 and of Aleppo the following year, uniting the two cities under his personal rule. He was a devoted enemy of crusader presence in Syria. After he was assassinated in 1146 his son, Nur ad-Din's dream was to unite all Muslim territory between the Euphrates and the Nile to make a common front against the Crusaders. In 1154 he captured Damascus, which brought the whole of Syria under his control. In 1174 he died before he could invade Egypt. After Saladin married Nur ad-Din's widow he fulfilled his predecessor's dream by unifying all Muslim territory in 1185.

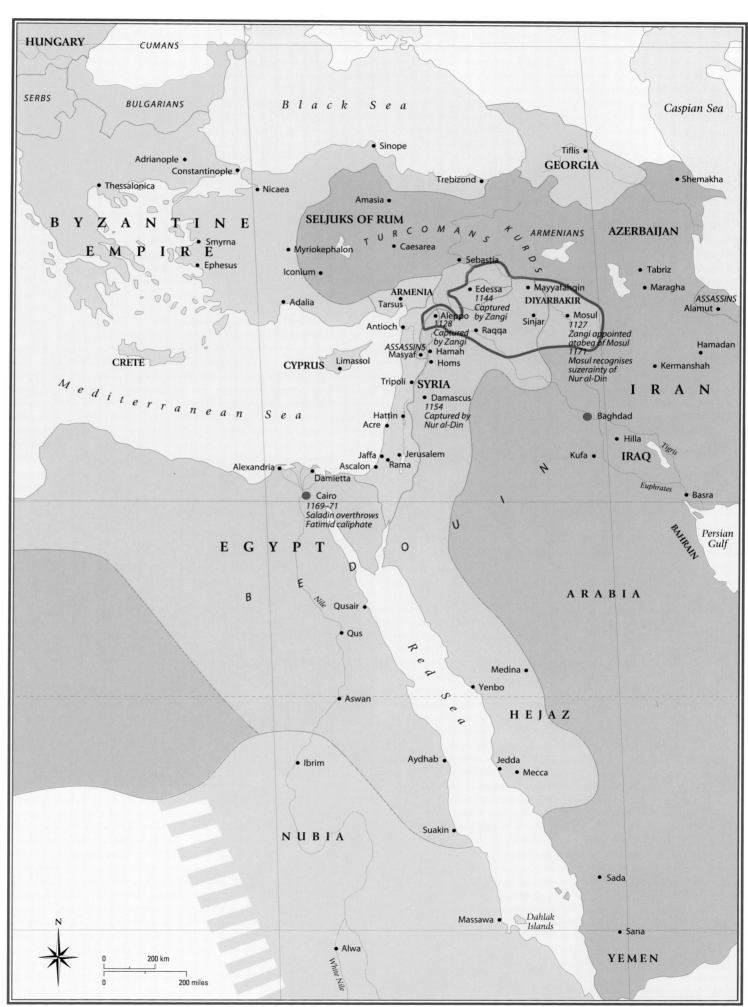

MUSLIMS IN THE NEAR EAST 1127–74

- Zangi territory c.1174
- Nur al-Din territory c.1174
- Other Muslim territory
- Christian territory
- Seat of Abbasid caliphate
- Seat of Fatimid caliphate

MAMELUKE RECONQUEST OF THE CRUSADER LANDS

MAMLUK RECONQUEST OF THE CRUSADER LANDS

After the First Crusade in 1099 a series of Christian Kingdoms was created. At first the Muslims had little concern for these little kingdoms, but as the 12th century progressed the notion of jihad once again began to surface and their increasingly united Mamluk neighbours began to win back territory. The Mamluks were originally slave-soldiers who had converted to Islam. Over the course of time they became very powerful, especially after they had been reorganised by leaders such as Saladin. Jerusalem fell to Saladin in 1187 and by the 13th century the former Crusader territories were little more than a coastal strip. By 1291 Muslim re-conquest was complete.

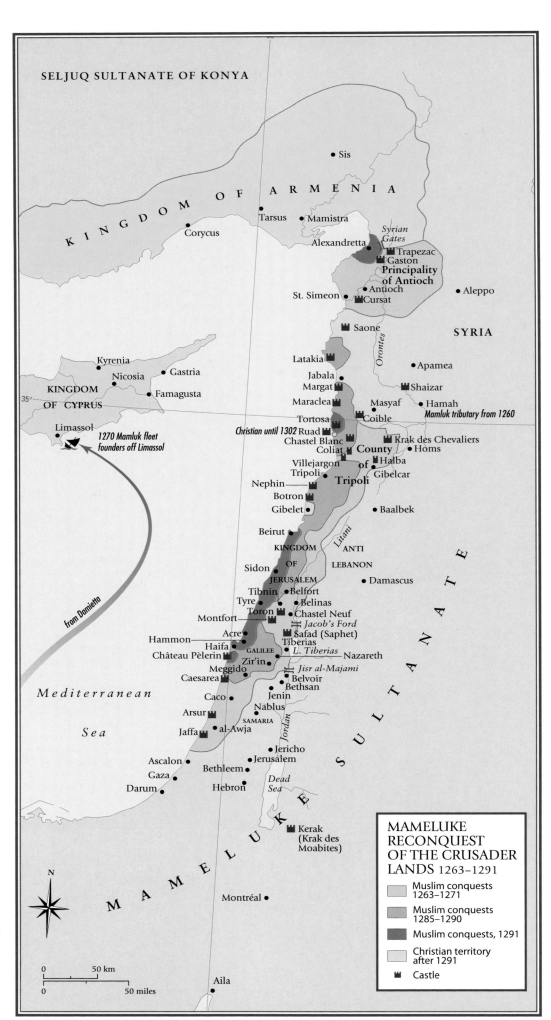

SUFI ORDERS
1145–1389 (RIGHT)

Sufi is a name given to a movement of Muslim mystics in and around the 12th to 14th centuries. Sufism exercised a tremendous influence, partly through mystical poetry and partly through the formation of religious brotherhoods. These brotherhoods grew out of the practice of disciples studying under a mystical guide or 'saint' to achieve direct communication with God. Some of these brotherhoods had a significant missionary impact.

MAMELUKE RECONQUEST OF THE CRUSADER LANDS 1263–1291

- Muslim conquests 1263–1271
- Muslim conquests 1285–1290
- Muslim conquests, 1291
- Christian territory after 1291
- Castle

SUFI ORDERS

ORDER	FOUNDING SAINT	SITE LOCATION
Suhrawardiya	Shihab al-din Abu Hafs Umar (1145–1234)	Baghdad
Rifaiya	Ahmad ibn Ali al-Rifai (1106–82)	Umm Abida
Qadiriya	Abd al-Qadir al-Jifani (1077–1106)	Baghdad
Shadhiliya	Abu Madyan Shuaib (1126–97)	Tiemcan
	Abul Hasan Ali al-Shadhili (1196–1258) Pupil of a pupil of Abu Madyan who gave his name to the Order	
Badawiya	Ahmad al-Badawi (1199–1276)	Tanta
Kubrawiya	Najm al-din Kubra (1145–1221)	Khiva
Yasawiya	Ahmad ibn Ibrahim ibn Ali of Yasi (later known as Turkestan) (d. 1166)	Turkestan
Mawalawiya	Jalal al-din Rumi (1207–73)	Konya
Naqshbandiyya	Muhammad Baha al-din al-Naqshbandi (1318–89) Abd al-Khaliq al-Ghujdawani (d. 1220) is regarded as the first organizer of the Order	Bukhara
Chishtiya	Muin al-din Hasan Chishti (1142–1236)	Ajmere

SUFI ORDERS 1145–1389

- ●   Shrine of founding saint of most important Orders
-   Egyptian and north African tradition derived from Iraqi tradition
-   Iranian and central Asian traditions from al-Junaid and al-Bistami
-   Iraqi tradition from al-Junaid

RIFAIYA   Major Order in development of institutional Sufism. All subsequent Orders trace their lineage back to one or more of these Orders. Located where they first developed, although by 1500 they had spread widely beyond these regions except for Mawlawiya, Qadiriya, and Chishtiya

Alwaiya   Other Orders of importance in 1500, located where they were most prominent

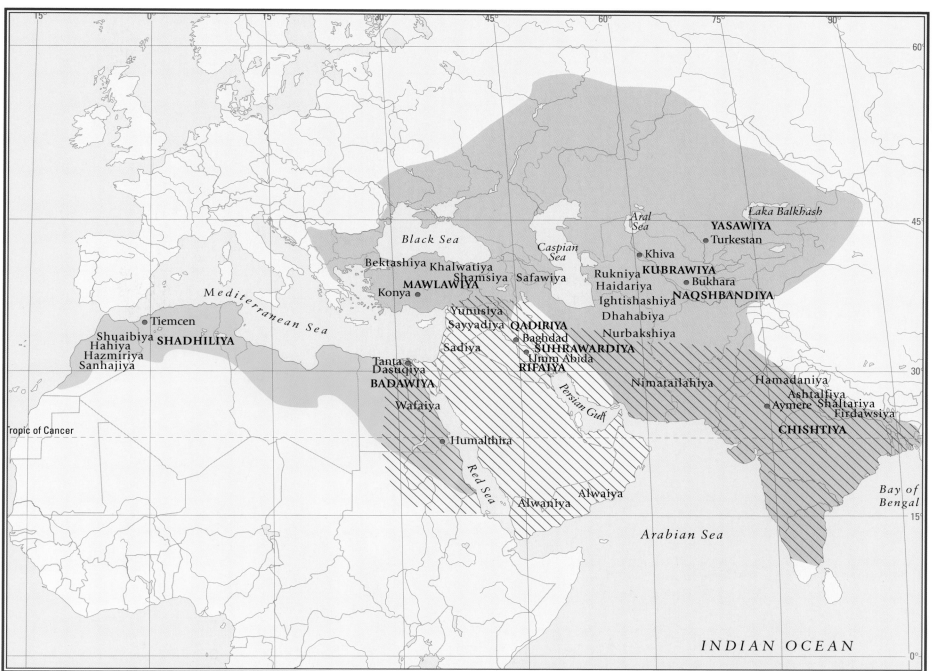

1500 TRADE ROUTES

TRADE ROUTES TO 1500
Historically the Arabs have always been traders. Since the beginning of time their caravan routes crossed the territories of the Middle East, but the spread of Islam enabled new markets and trade routes to develop throughout Persia and into India. The Arabs also began trading down the west coast of Africa and as time went on their ships began to venture far out into the Arabian Sea and even to Indonesia and China. The perils of these long journeys were great, but the merchants felt that the rich rewards at the end of such a voyage far outweighed the risks involved.

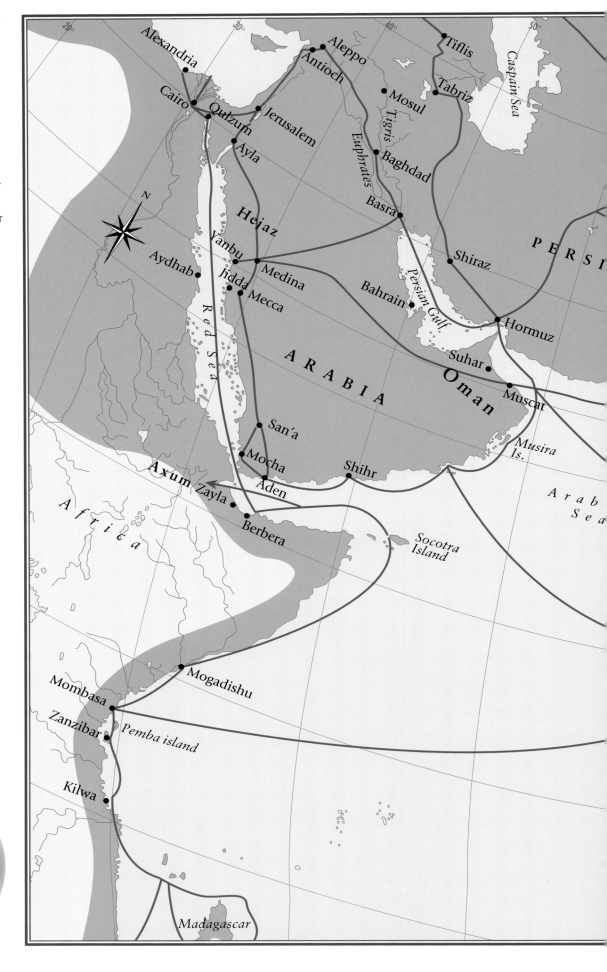

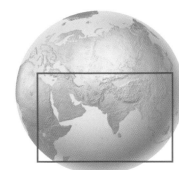

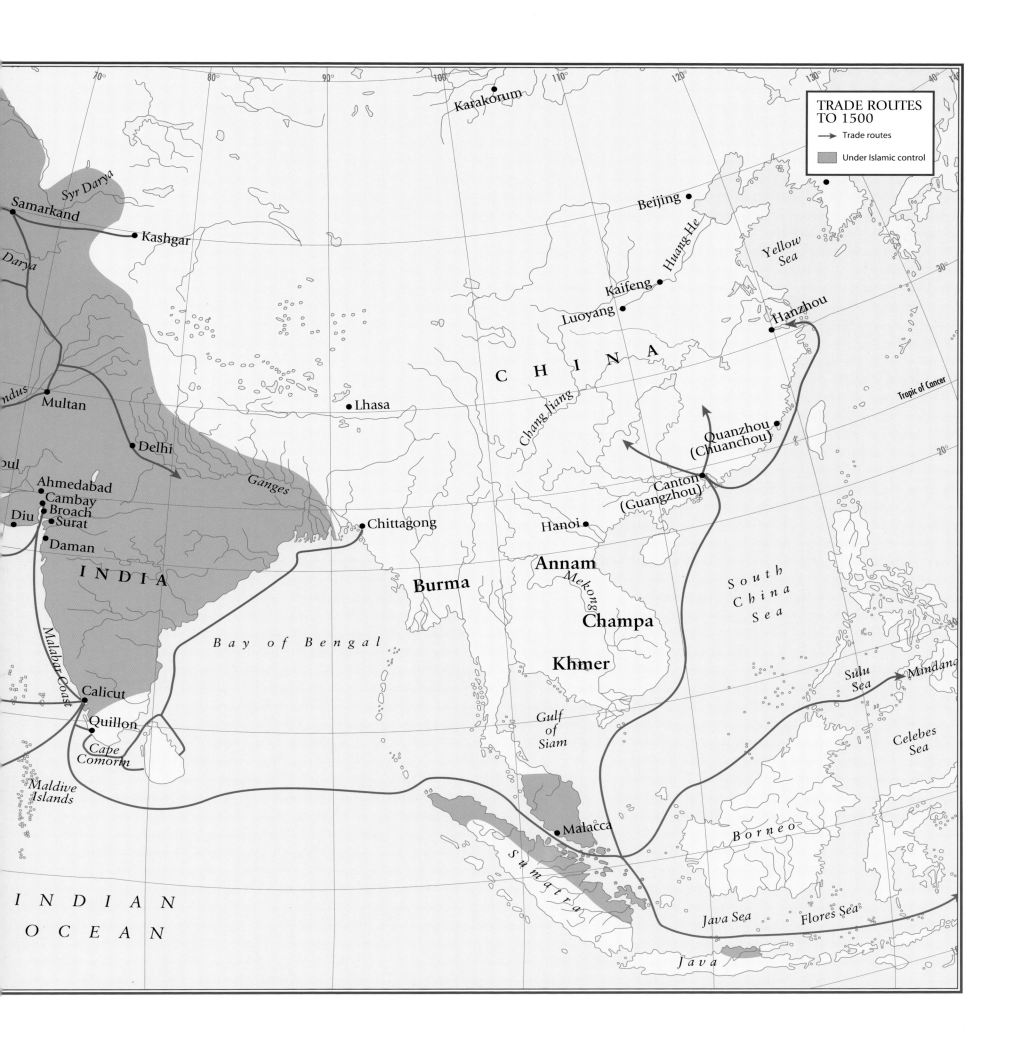

SPREAD OF ISLAM IN AFRICA TO c. 1500

Map labels

Tangier
Algiers
Tunis
ZIYANIDS
Fez
Tlemcen
Marrakesh
WATTASIDS
HAFSIDS
Tripoli
Mediterranean Sea
Awijila
Siwa
Cairo
Asyut
MAMLUKS
Qusair
Medina
Tropic of Cancer
Murzuq
Ghat
Kufra
Nile R.
Selima
Red Sea
Mecca
Walata
Timbuktu
Tekedda
Agadès
NUBIA
Suakin
SONGHAY
Gao
AIR
Central Sudan
Massawa
Western Sudan
DARFUR
Soba
Jenne
Sokoto
Zinder
KANEM
Lake Chad
SOBA c.1499 fell to Islam
Gondar
Aden
SONINKÉ
Ouagadougou
HAUSA STATES
Kano
BORNU
Ngazargamu
Abeche
El Fasher
ETHIOPIA
MALI
NUPE
WADAI
ADAL
Zaila
Berbera
Bidderi
Massenia
BAGIRMI
Fashoda
Harar
SOMALI
IFE
OYO
Niger R.
Benue R.
AGAU
fort built by Portuguese to aid the defense of Christian Ethiopia
OROMO
AKAN STATES
YORUBA
BENIN
Lagos
Benin
IGBO
NILOTES
MALINKE
Elmina
1492 Portuguese
Gulf of Guinea
Calabar
DUALA
Mogadishu
Brava
Equator
Lake Victoria
Lamu
Pate
VILI
BIGO
Malindi
Zaïre R.
Mbanza Congo
Mombasa
Pemba Is.
CONGO
Lake Tanganyika
Zanzibar
Mafia Is.
NDONGO
Kilwa Kivinje
Lindi
OVIMBUNDU
Lake Nyasa
Comoro Is.
Zambezi R.
Mozambique
TONGA
SHONA
Quelimane
MADAGASCAR
TONGA
Sofala
Tropic of Capricorn
Orange R.
INDIAN OCEAN
ATLANTIC OCEAN
N

SPREAD OF ISLAM TO c. 1500

extent of Islam at the death of Muhammad, 632

extent of Islam at the death of Uthman, 650

extent of Islam at the end of the Umayyad dynasty, 750

extent of Islam, 1250

extent of Islam, 1500

Christian state, 1500

Animist religions, 1500

areas of Africa's Jewish settlers, 1492–96

→ Christian crusades, 1096–1570s

• centres of Islamic learning

— pilgrimage route developing, 15–16th century

→ Jihad (Holy War) of Ahmad Gran, 1531–43

→ Ottoman aid to Jihad

DARFUR states, c. 1500

OROMO major tribe

— trans-Sahara trade routes

0   500 km
0   500 miles

SPREAD OF ISLAM TO c. 1500

Following the death of Muhammad in 632 the spread of Islam was rapid. Egypt was conquered in 640 and by 652 the whole of North Africa as far as Western Tunisia and most of the Sahara. There was then a southward movement down as far as Lake Chad. In the early days the spread of Islam in North Africa had been military, but as time passed it became peaceful and was based on the spread of trade and intermarriage. Islam also spread through Islamic education along developing trade routes down the west coast of Africa and across the Sahara.

SUNNI MUSLIMS; SHI'A MUSLIMS

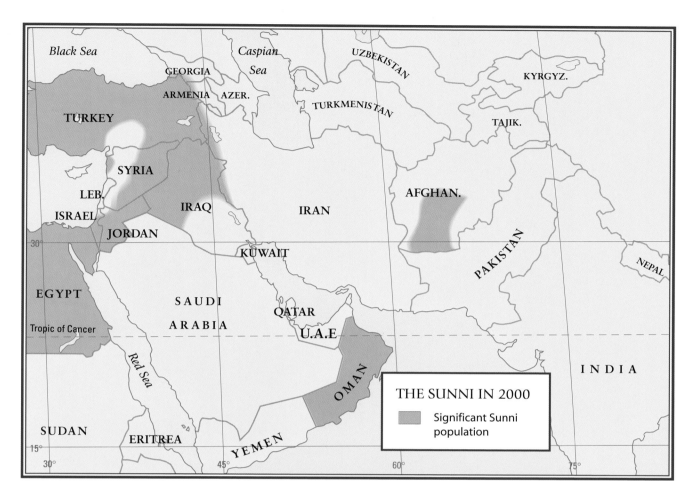

THE SUNNI IN 2000

Significant Sunni population

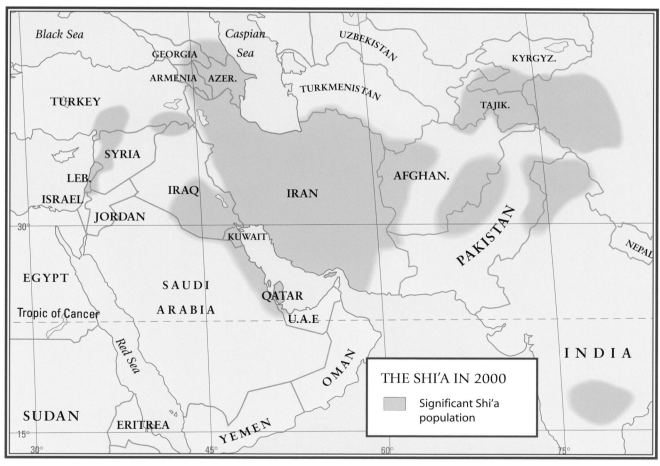

THE SHI'A IN 2000

Significant Shi'a population

THE SUNNI IN 2000
THE SHI'A IN 2000

The Shi'a and the Sunni are the world's two major Islamic groups. Their split occurred in the years following the death of the Prophet Muhammad in 632. In simple terms Shi'as believe that Muhammad's succession should have passed down through his direct descendents, while Sunnis accept that it is appropriate for the succession to pass down through 'rightly guided prophets', chosen by consensus.

Today Sunni Muslims are the larger sect and they comprise 85 per cent of the world's Muslims. Although Shi'as make up only 15 per cent, this distribution is not spread evenly throughout the world. In Iran 90 per cent of the population are Shi'a and in Iraq the figure is around 65 per cent. This group suffered particularly from persecution under the regime of Saddam Hussein and this has resulted in a serious backlash against the Sunnis that has been supported by Shi'as from Iran.

Al-Qaeda is a radical Sunni group. Its aims include the establishment of Islamic states throughout the world and the overthrow of 'un-Islamic' regimes. Some groups linked to al-Qaeda have advocated the persecution of the Shi'a as heretics and these groups have been held responsible for violent attacks and suicide bombings at a number of Shi'a gatherings.

CONQUEST AND DOMINIONS OF TIMUR

1328 – 1566

THE CONQUEST AND DOMINIONS OF TIMUR (TAMERLANE)

Timur, or Tamerlane, was a 14th century warlord whose home was near Samarkand in present-day Uzbekistan. He founded the Timurid Empire in 1370 and the Timurid Dynasty, which lasted in some form until 1857. Timur was of Turkic/Mongol origin, but had been brought up in the Persian culture. During the course of many campaigns he extended his empire until it covered much of western and central Asia. His biggest wars were against Muslim states, but he also conducted other campaigns, particularly against the Khanate of the Golden Horde to the north, which fragmented after the war. In 1398 Timur's army invaded the Sultanate of Delhi. The city was sacked and according to Timur's memoirs, 100,000 prisoners were beheaded, 10,000 in one hour. Damascus and Baghdad were also sacked and destroyed and millions were slaughtered. Timur died in 1404 or 1405 while planning an expedition against China.

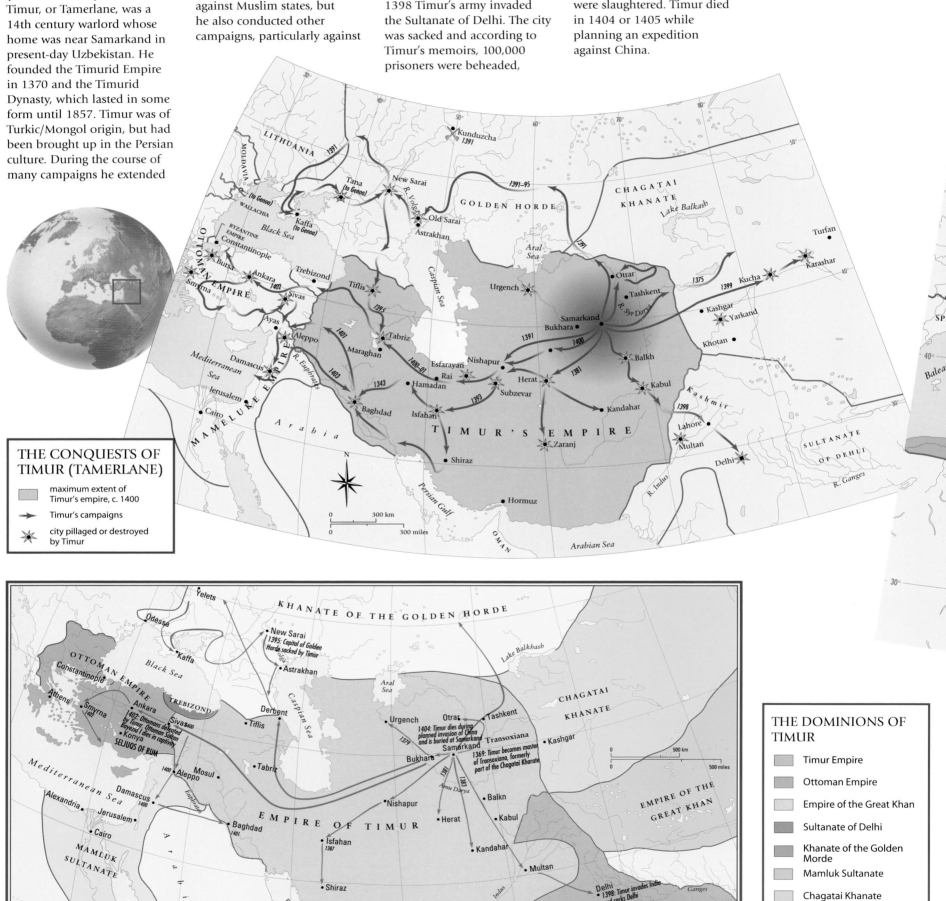

THE CONQUESTS OF TIMUR (TAMERLANE)

- ▨ maximum extent of Timur's empire, c. 1400
- → Timur's campaigns
- ✴ city pillaged or destroyed by Timur

THE DOMINIONS OF TIMUR

- ▨ Timur Empire
- ▨ Ottoman Empire
- ▨ Empire of the Great Khan
- ▨ Sultanate of Delhi
- ▨ Khanate of the Golden Morde
- ▨ Mamluk Sultanate
- ▨ Chagatai Khanate
- ↳ Major attacks and campaigns

EXPANSION OF THE OTTOMAN EMPIRE

EXPANSION OF THE OTTOMAN EMPIRE
The Ottoman Empire came into being in what is now Turkey. Initially there was a conglomeration of small states that spent most of their time fighting each other. Byzantine rule was in terminal decline

and Osman I seized his chance and moved in. Considerable territorial gains were made in the years that followed and in 1453 Constantinople was captured by the 21-year-old Mehmed II. This led to a long period of conquest and expansion, particularly

under the rule of Suleiman the Magnificent. Following Suleiman's death in 1566 territorial gains were few.

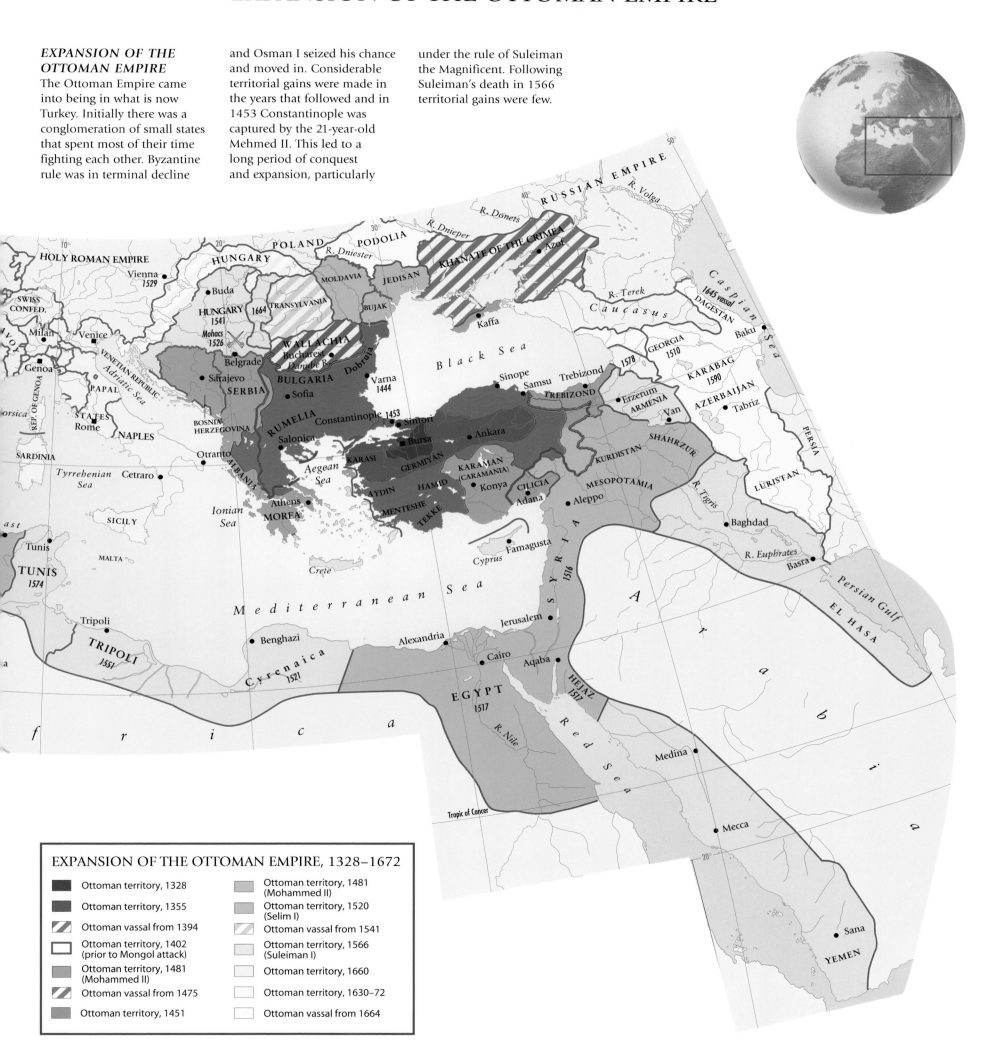

EXPANSION OF THE OTTOMAN EMPIRE, 1328–1672

- Ottoman territory, 1328
- Ottoman territory, 1355
- Ottoman vassal from 1394
- Ottoman territory, 1402 (prior to Mongol attack)
- Ottoman territory, 1481 (Mohammed II)
- Ottoman vassal from 1475
- Ottoman territory, 1451
- Ottoman territory, 1481 (Mohammed II)
- Ottoman territory, 1520 (Selim I)
- Ottoman vassal from 1541
- Ottoman territory, 1566 (Suleiman I)
- Ottoman territory, 1660
- Ottoman territory, 1630–72
- Ottoman vassal from 1664

THE SELJUQ ERA

THE SELJUQ ERA

→	Major Seljuq campaign
	Seljuq sultinate at its maximum extent, c. 1090
	Byzantine Empire, c. 1095
	Territory lost to Byzantine Empire and crusader states, 1097–99
⬭	Extent of the Khwarizm Shahdom, c. 1220

THE SELJUQ ERA

The Seljuqs were a Sunni Muslim dynasty that ruled parts of Central Asia and the Middle East from the 11th to 14th Centuries. The Seljuq dynasty were descendants of the Central Asian Turkic Oghuz tribe, and with their conquest of Baghdad in 1055, they were soon able to gain control of present-day Iraq, Iran and Syria. Expansion to the west was soon achieved, with their victory over the Byzantine Empire at the Battle of Manzikert in 1071 opening up Anatolia to Turkic settlement. At its height in 1090, the Seljuq Empire stretched from Anatolia to the Punjab. However, despite these early successes, the Seljuq's did not retain their hegemony in the region for very long. By the time of the First Crusade in 1095 Palestine had already been lost to the Fatimids, who came from Egypt and belonged to the rival Shia Muslim dynasty. Although the Empire lasted for a further 200 years, it was deprived of any significant power through much of the the thirteenth century, and early in the 14th century it effectively came to an end.

MUSLIM INDIA

Arab traders had brought a small Muslim population to India from earliest times, but there was no Muslim rule until the 12th century when Muhammad of Ghur's cavalry smashed the Hindu Rajputs at Tarori near Delhi. The Muslims stayed to the north of the country and the south remained largely Hindu. The Sultanate of Delhi eventually defeated two Mongol invasions in 1304 and 1306, exacted tribute, and seized Gujerat, Malwa and the Deccan. The end came in 1398 when the Mongol warlord Timur invaded Delhi. Many Hindus lived in the city and according to Timur's memoirs, 10,000 were beheaded in one hour.

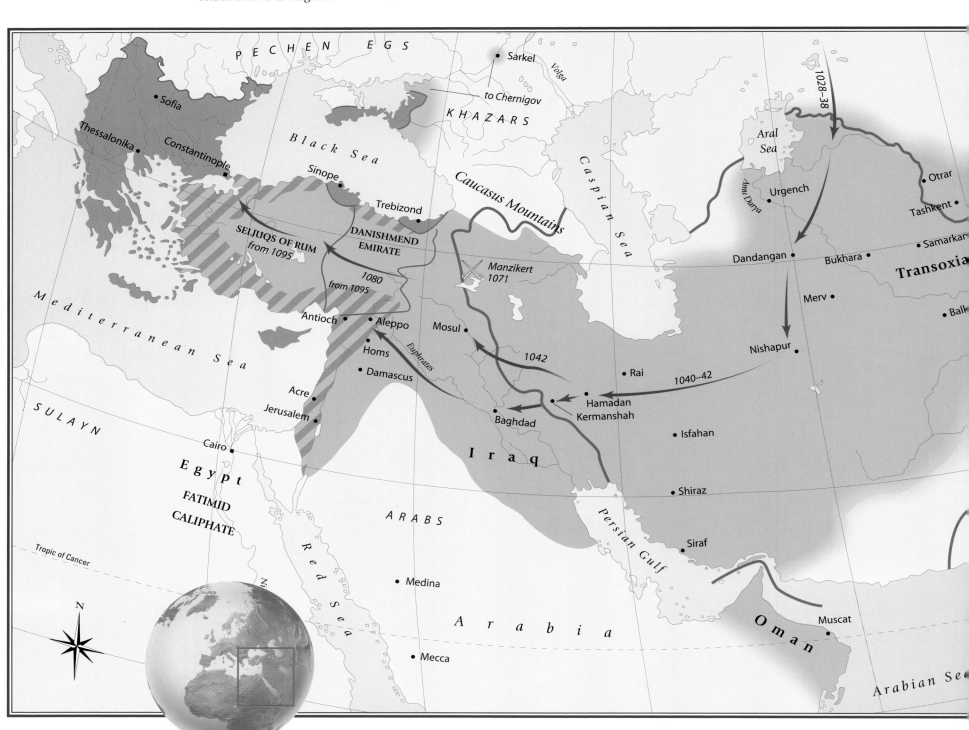

MUSLIM INDIA

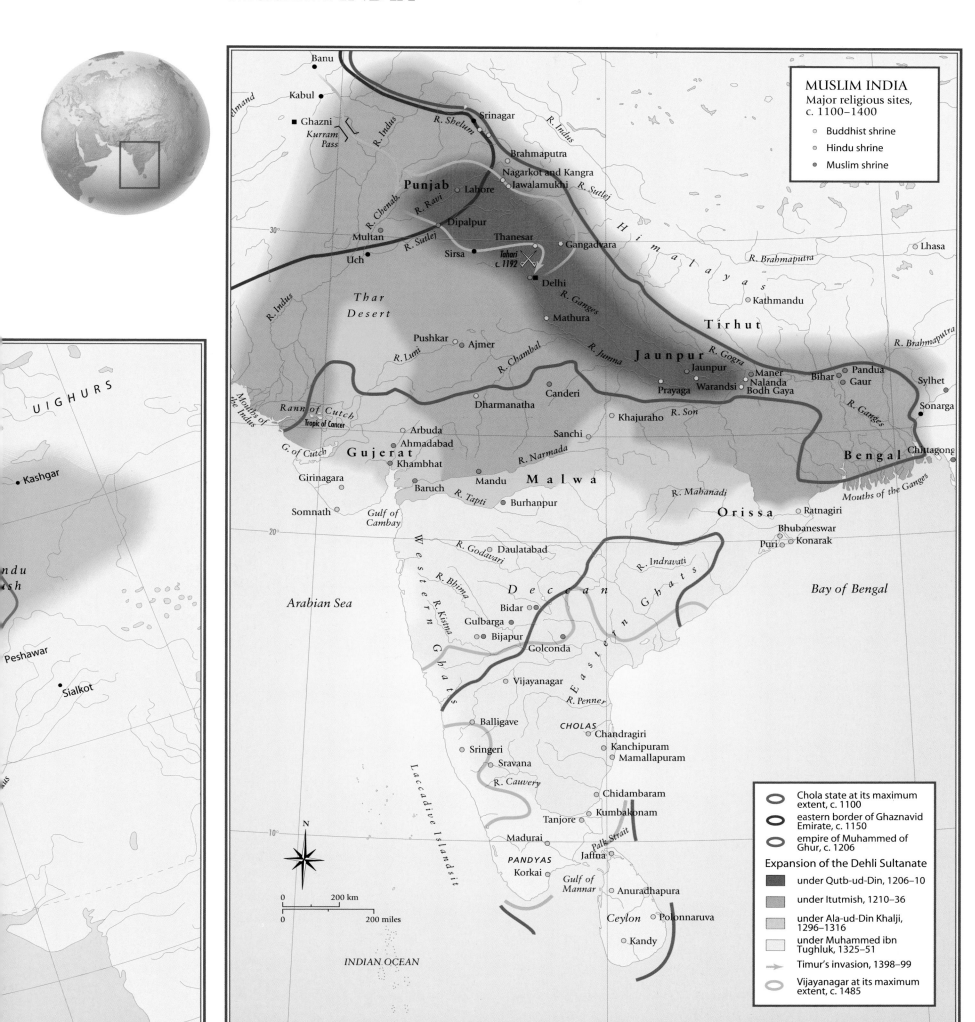

Banu

Kabul

■ Ghazni

Kurram Pass

R. Shelum · Srinagar

R. Indus

R. Sutlej

Brahmaputra

Nagarkot and Kangra

Jawalamukhi

Punjab · Lahore

R. Chenab.

R. Ravi

Dipalpur

Multan

R. Sutlej

Uch

Sirsa · Thanesar · Gangadvara

Tahari c. 1192 ⚔

■ Delhi

R. Ganges

Mathura

Thar Desert

Pushkar · Ajmer

R. Luni

R. Chambal

R. Jumna

Jaunpur

Canderi

Dharmanatha

Khajuraho

R. Son

Prayaga · Warandsi · Nalanda · Bodh Gaya

Jaunpur · Maner

Bihar · Pandua · Gaur

Sylhet

Sonarga

Mouths of the Indus

Gujerat

Rann of Cutch

Tropic of Cancer

Arbuda

Ahmadabad

Khambhat

R. Narmada

Sanchi

G. of Cutch

Girinagara

Baruch · Mandu · **Malwa**

R. Tapti · Burhanpur

R. Mahanadi

Orissa

Somnath

Gulf of Cambay

Ratnagiri

Bhubaneswar

Puri · Konarak

Arabian Sea

R. Godavari · Daulatabad

R. Bhima

R. Krishna · Bidar

Gulbarga

Bijapur

Golconda

Western Ghats

R. Indravati

Deccan

Eastern Ghats

Bay of Bengal

Vijayanagar

R. Penner

Balligave

CHOLAS

Chandragiri

Kanchipuram

Mamallapuram

Sringeri

Sravana

R. Cauvery

Chidambaram

Tanjore · Kumbakonam

Madurai

Jaffna

PANDYAS

Korkai

Palk Strait

Gulf of Mannar

Anuradhapura

Laccadive Islands

Ceylon · Polonnaruva

Kandy

N

0   200 km

0   200 miles

INDIAN OCEAN

Kathmandu

Himalayas

Tirhut

R. Brahmaputra

Lhasa

R. Brahmaputra

R. Gogra

R. Ganges

Chittagong

Mouths of the Ganges

Bengal

Inset (left)

UIGHURS

· Kashgar

...ndu ...sh

· Peshawar

· Sialkot

Legend

MUSLIM INDIA
Major religious sites,
c. 1100–1400

○ Buddhist shrine
○ Hindu shrine
○ Muslim shrine

⬭ Chola state at its maximum extent, c. 1100
⬭ eastern border of Ghaznavid Emirate, c. 1150
⬭ empire of Muhammed of Ghur, c. 1206

Expansion of the Dehli Sultanate

◼ under Qutb-ud-Din, 1206–10
◼ under Itutmish, 1210–36
◼ under Ala-ud-Din Khalji, 1296–1316
◻ under Muhammed ibn Tughluk, 1325–51
→ Timur's invasion, 1398–99
⬭ Vijayanagar at its maximum extent, c. 1485

19TH CENTURY – 2007   MUSLIM MIGRATION TO THE USA

LATE 19TH AND EARLY 20TH CENTURY MUSLIM MIGRATION TO THE USA

The USA has traditionally acted as a magnet for those seeking a better life and Muslims have always been a part of this. Columbus made use of Muslim navigational

expertise and it is certain that many of the African slaves were originally Muslim. Voluntary emigration of Muslims began in the late 19th century, initially from the Middle East, settling mainly in Michigan and Idaho. Muslims from India tended to settle in California. Later Muslim groups arrived who were fleeing from the Bolshevik Revolution in Russia. All of these groups were in relatively small in numbers.

ISLAM IN THE WORLD 2007

As a result of migration and general population movement, it is now possible to find Islamic groups just about anywhere in the world. Somewhere over a fifth of the world's population are Muslim, but the major concentrations of population have not altered for many years. The map gives a very good indication of these areas, but since it is based on density of population, many areas that are regarded as predominately Islamic are not shaded because the population of those areas is so small.

LATE 19TH AND EARLY 20TH CENTURIES

- Area of Islam
- → Migration

MUSLIM MIGRATION TO THE USA AFTER WORLD WAR II

Since World War II and particularly in the last 30 years, substantial numbers of Muslims have migrated from developing countries to the USA. Many of these migrants have gone to study, while others have gone seeking better job opportunities. Often the original intention was to return, but most have stayed. Islam is now said to be the fastest growing religion in North America. Due to the Islamic emphasis on equality and brotherhood, it has a considerable appeal to groups who were historically oppressed.

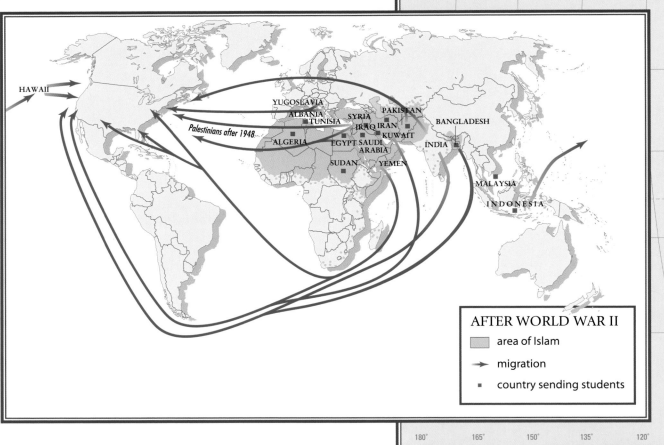

AFTER WORLD WAR II

- area of Islam
- → migration
- ▪ country sending students

MUSLIMS IN THE WORLD

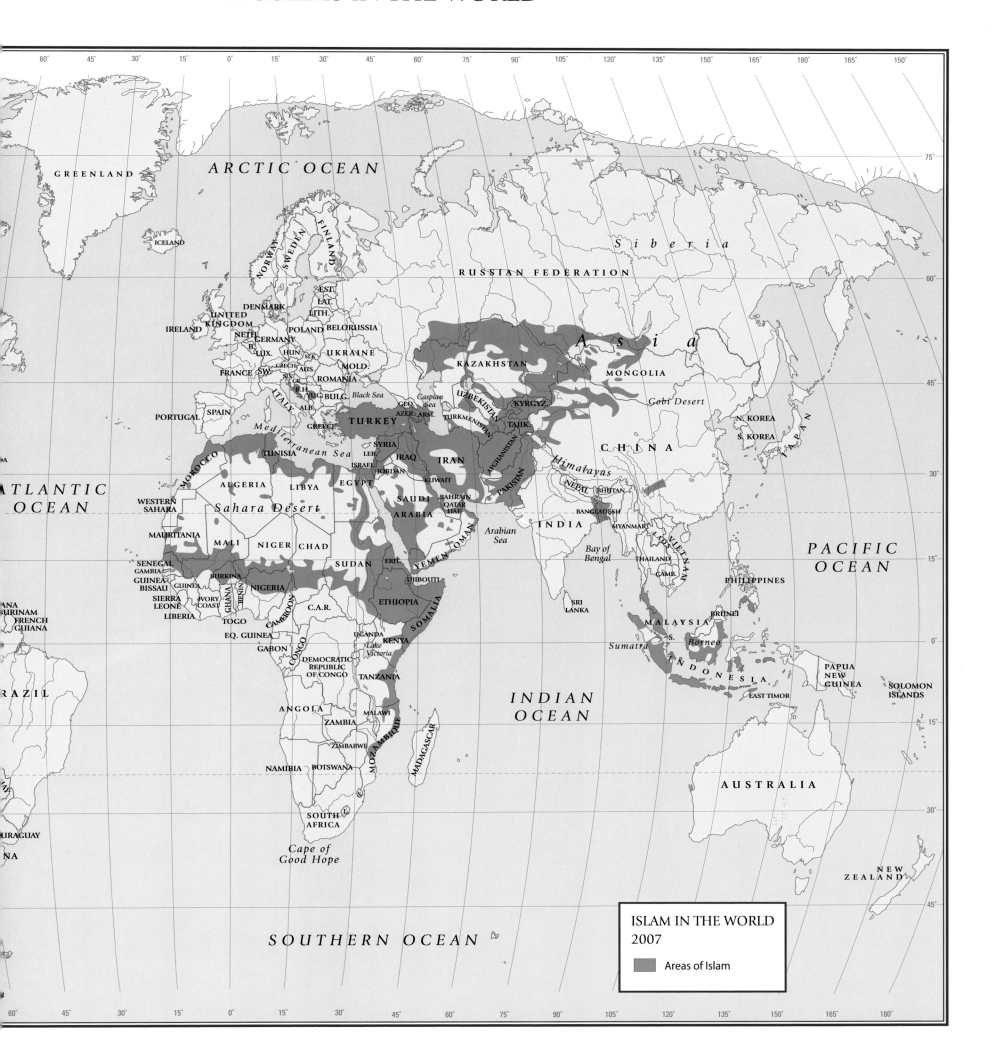

ISLAM IN THE WORLD
2007

Areas of Islam

MUSLIM MIGRATION INTO THE EUROPEAN UNION

1957 – 2004

MUSLIM MIGRATION INTO THE EUROPEAN UNION

There has been a significant amount of Muslim immigration to EU countries, mainly from people seeking better job opportunities. Large numbers have come to the UK from Commonwealth countries such as India and Pakistan. The Netherlands also received large numbers from their former East Indian colonies and France received large numbers from her former North African colonies. Other countries have received immigrants from closer to home. Large numbers of Turks moved to Germany, the Netherlands and Denmark, and Italy and Spain have both accepted large numbers from North Africa.

MUSLIM MIGRATION INTO THE EUROPEAN UNION

- Signature of the Treaty of Rome, 1957
- EEC member added 1973
- EEC member added 1986
- Became part of the EEC after unification of Germany, 1990
- EEC member added 1995
- EEC membership approved May 2004
- Membership pending
- Directions and the sources of immigration

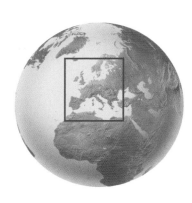

MECCA CITY

MECCA CITY

Mecca is of inestimable importance to all Muslims everywhere. Its most sacred place is the Ka'bah mosque. According to Moslim tradition, this was built by Abraham on the first place that was created on Earth. All Muslims, wherever they are in the world, pray five times a day always turning to face the direction of the Ka'bah in Mecca. For those who can afford it, a pilgrimage to Mecca is required as one of the Five Pillars of Faith. Every year about three million gather for the major pilgrimage or Hajj. Only Muslims are permitted to take part in these rites and rituals.

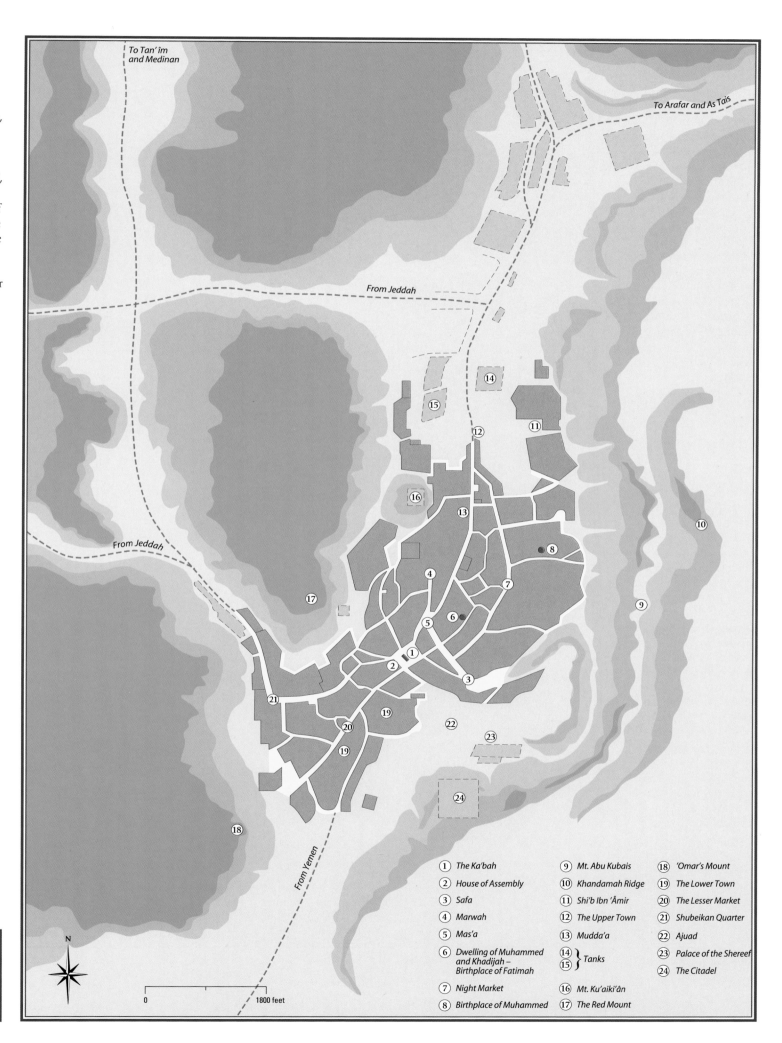

MECCA CITY

● Important sites

▨ Built-up areas

① The Ka'bah	⑨ Mt. Abu Kubais	⑱ 'Omar's Mount
② House of Assembly	⑩ Khandamah Ridge	⑲ The Lower Town
③ Safa	⑪ Shi'b Ibn 'Âmir	⑳ The Lesser Market
④ Marwah	⑫ The Upper Town	㉑ Shubeikan Quarter
⑤ Mas'a	⑬ Mudda'a	㉒ Ajuad
⑥ Dwelling of Muhammed and Khadijah – Birthplace of Fatimah	⑭ ⑮ } Tanks	㉓ Palace of the Shereef
⑦ Night Market	⑯ Mt. Ku'aiki'ân	㉔ The Citadel
⑧ Birthplace of Muhammed	⑰ The Red Mount	

NATION OF ISLAM; MOSQUES BY STATE

NATION OF ISLAM

The Nation of Islam is the oldest Black Nationalist organisation in the USA. It was founded in Detroit by Wallace Fard Muhammad, whom the Nation of Islam believe to be the long awaited Messiah of the Christians and the Mahdi of both Sunni and Shi'a Muslims. One of Fard's disciples was Elijah Muhammad, who toured the country setting up mosques, which he numbered in order of his arrival in any given place. The one in the Harlem district of New York was the seventh and is still called Temple Number 7. Today there are mosques in more than 30 states.

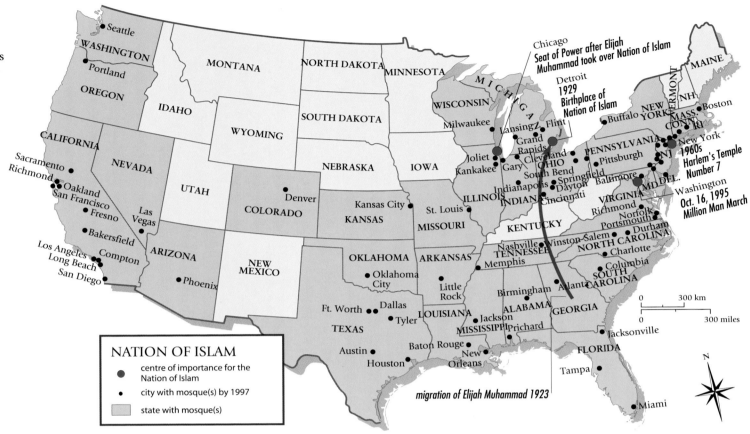

NATION OF ISLAM
- ● centre of importance for the Nation of Islam
- • city with mosque(s) by 1997
- state with mosque(s)

migration of Elijah Muhammad 1923

ISLAM MOSQUES BY STATE 2000

There are just over 1200 mosques in the United States and California has the greatest number of any state. Most American mosques are fairly small; America's largest mosque is near Washington DC and has a weekly attendance of only about 3000. Latest estimates put the number of American Muslims at around 2 million. Up to a third of these are African-Americans who have converted to Islam. The remainder are foreign-born and most have immigrated since 1990. Whether a mosque follows the Shi'a or Sunni traditions depends largely on the composition of the local Muslim immigrant populations.

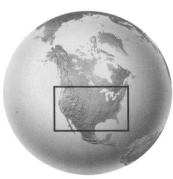

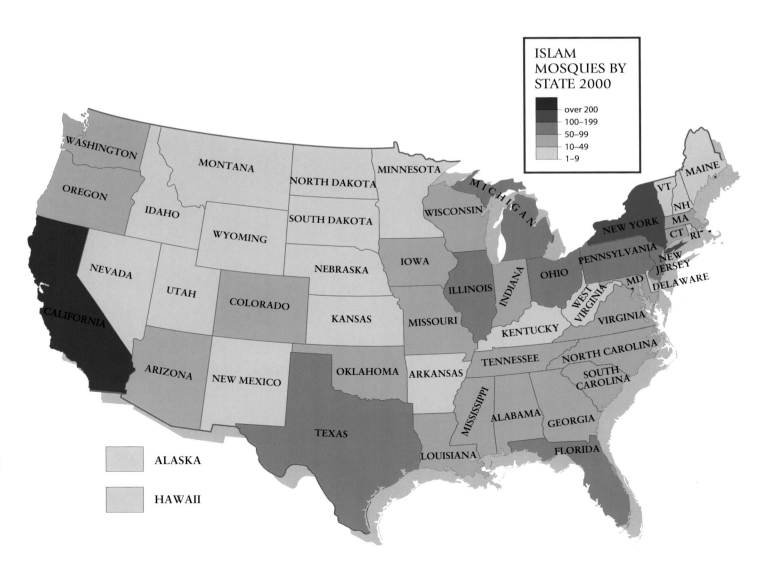

ISLAM MOSQUES BY STATE 2000
- over 200
- 100–199
- 50–99
- 10–49
- 1–9

ALASKA

HAWAII

PART 7

RELIGIONS OF THE FAR EAST

Apart from Buddhism, the three major religions indigenous to the Far East are Confucianism, Taoism and Shinto. The Religions have often interacted with one another, and with Buddhism, to create the philosophical, moral and spiritual landscape of the region.

Confucianism is a philosophy or worldview concerned with humanism, which was developed by the 6th Century BC Chinese thinker and social philosopher Confucius. Thinking and study are at the heart of Confucianism, as Confucius was more interested in promoting free thought than a systematic doctrine. Confucianism doesn't talk about an afterlife and neglects many spiritual questions discussed by other faiths, leading many people to argue that it is not actually a religion.

Taoism was a tradition of philosophy and religion originating during fourth century BC China. The Tao, or Way, attempts to deal with a world torn apart by social and political changes. Only through inaction, known as 'wu wei', just being, not thinking of ideologies nor facts, and by emptying oneself, can unity with the Way and its power be achieved. There is much more emphasis on the spiritual in Taoism than there is in Confucianism.

Unlike most other religions, Shinto has no real founder, no written scriptures, no body of religious law, and only a very loosely-organised priesthood. Shinto, which was formalised in the 8th century, involves the worship of Kami, or spirits. Some Kami are related to specific areas, while others are related to natural objects or processes of nature.

SHINTOISM IN JAPAN

SHINTOISM IN JAPAN
600–1500

Shintoism is the native religion of Japan and was once its state religion. After World War II Shinto lost its status as the state religion of Japan. Many of the old Shinto traditions have been dropped and most of those that remain no longer have any religious significance. For around a thousand years Shinto happily existed in combination with Buddhism, but in 1868 this practice was banned. Shinto became the official religion and the Emperor was worshipped as a god. Shintoism and patriotism became intertwined and became more pronounced as time progressed.

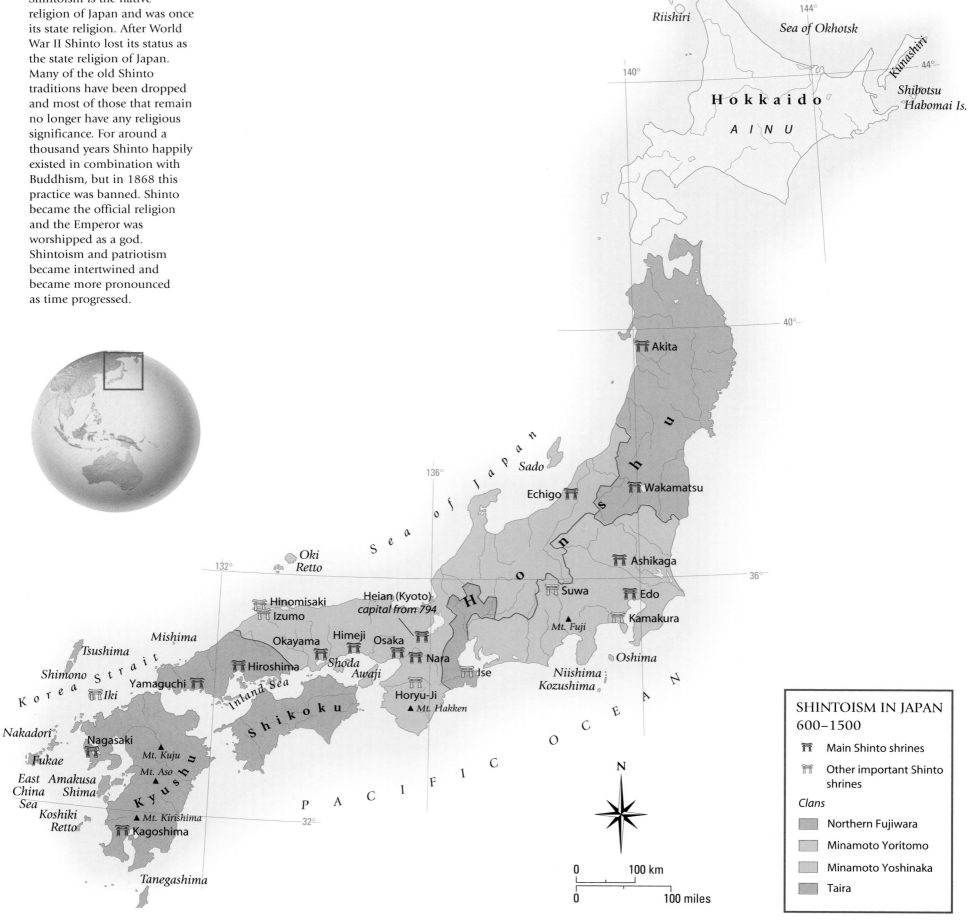

SHINTOISM IN JAPAN
600–1500

⛩ Main Shinto shrines

⛩ Other important Shinto shrines

Clans

Northern Fujiwara

Minamoto Yoritomo

Minamoto Yoshinaka

Taira

FOUR SHINTO SHRINES

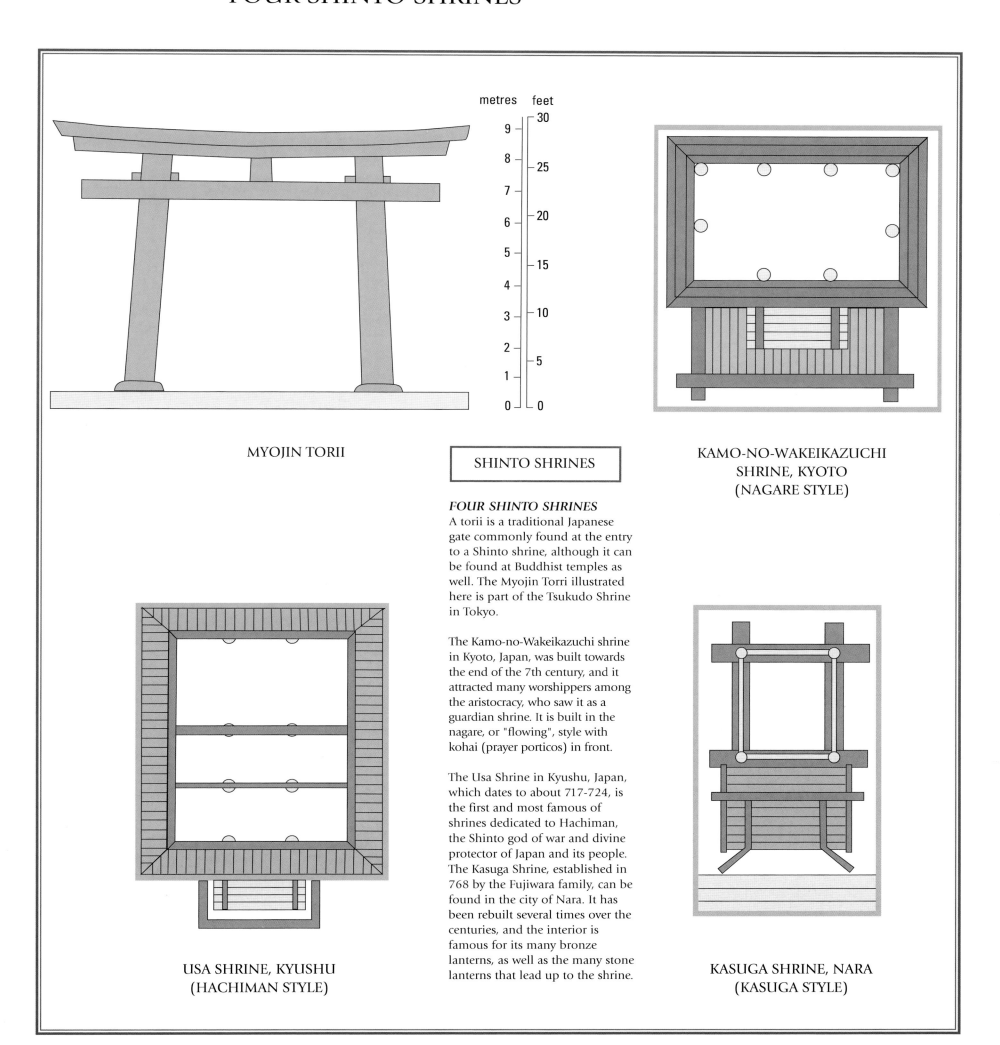

MYOJIN TORII

SHINTO SHRINES

KAMO-NO-WAKEIKAZUCHI
SHRINE, KYOTO
(NAGARE STYLE)

FOUR SHINTO SHRINES

A torii is a traditional Japanese gate commonly found at the entry to a Shinto shrine, although it can be found at Buddhist temples as well. The Myojin Torri illustrated here is part of the Tsukudo Shrine in Tokyo.

The Kamo-no-Wakeikazuchi shrine in Kyoto, Japan, was built towards the end of the 7th century, and it attracted many worshippers among the aristocracy, who saw it as a guardian shrine. It is built in the nagare, or "flowing", style with kohai (prayer porticos) in front.

The Usa Shrine in Kyushu, Japan, which dates to about 717-724, is the first and most famous of shrines dedicated to Hachiman, the Shinto god of war and divine protector of Japan and its people. The Kasuga Shrine, established in 768 by the Fujiwara family, can be found in the city of Nara. It has been rebuilt several times over the centuries, and the interior is famous for its many bronze lanterns, as well as the many stone lanterns that lead up to the shrine.

USA SHRINE, KYUSHU
(HACHIMAN STYLE)

KASUGA SHRINE, NARA
(KASUGA STYLE)

600 BC – 550 BC   TAOISM IN CHINA

TAOISM IN CHINA
Taoism is believed to have been started by Lao Tzu in around 600 BC. The belief is that life has two sides, a dark side, the yin and a light side, the yang. Every person has characteristics of both yin and yang and Chinese doctors believe that most illnesses are caused by an imbalance of the two. There are now some 20 million followers of Taoism worldwide and although there are a great number of Taoist temples in mainland China, the religion is now primarily centred in Taiwan where the Heavenly Masters Sect moved after the Communist takeover of the mainland in 1949.

TAOISM IN CHINA

🛕 Important Taoist Temples

▲ Traditionally important Taoist hills/mountains

➡ Heavenly Masters Sect HQ retreat to Taiwan in 1949

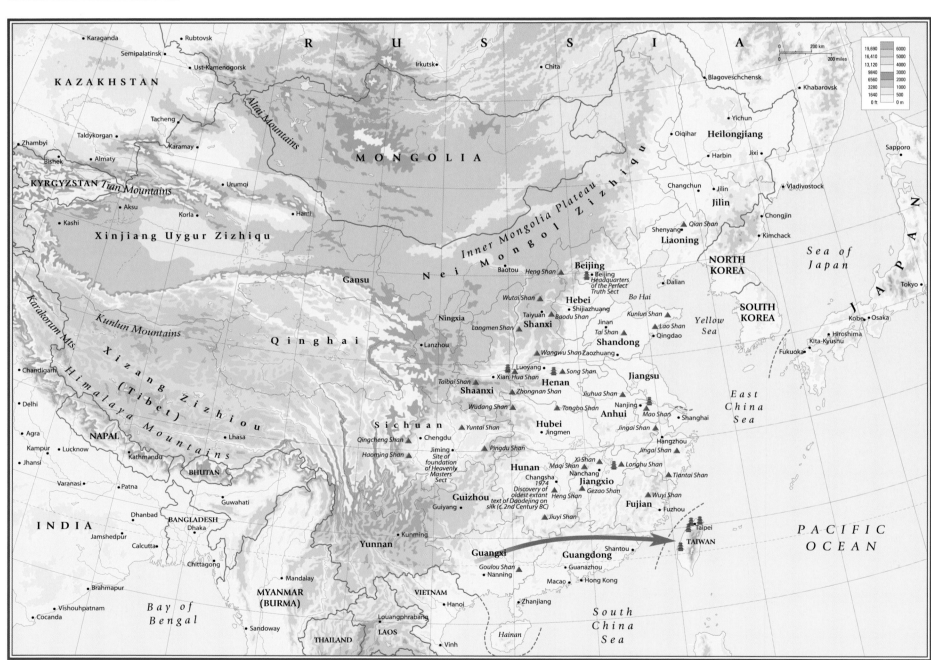

CONFUCIUS IN CHINA; CONFUCIAN TEMPLE

CONFUCIANISM IN CHINA 550 BC

Confucius (Kong Fuzi) lived between 551 and 479 BC. Details of his early life are scanty and there are many legends about him. Some say that he was an important civil servant in the justice ministry, while others say that he held a more humble position. According to tradition, Confucius decided to set out a long journey, or series of journeys around the fragmented provinces of north-east China. During this time he gave advice to the provincial rulers and accumulated a small band of students. In his later life he returned to Lu, where he spent his time teaching.

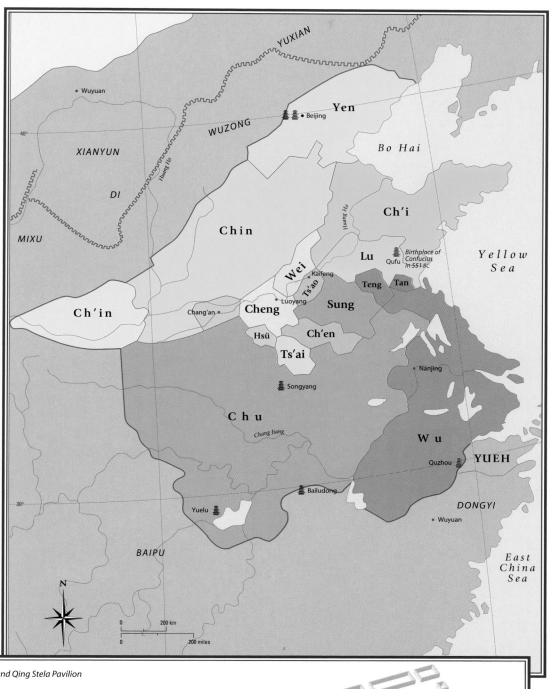

CONFUCIUS IN CHINA 550 BC

- 🏯 Confucian Temple
- 🏯 Confucian academy
- • Capitals of China from 4th Century BC
- — Zhou China border
- ⊔⊓ Wall of China
- ▨ States with Confucian influence
- *MIXU* Barbarian tribe

CONFUCIAN TEMPLE (*BELOW*)

The oldest and largest temple is found in Confucius's home town, the present-day Qufu in Shandong province. The front portal of the temple (16) is called the Lingxing Gate. Most Confucian temples have three inner courtyards, sometimes two, although the temple at Qufu has nine. The main building, the Hall of Great Perfection (2), is situated in an inner courtyard and is reached through the Gate of Perfection (5). This housed the Confucius Ancestral Tablet and those of other important masters and sages. In front of the Hall was the Apricot Platform where Confucius is said to have lectured students in the arts and classics.

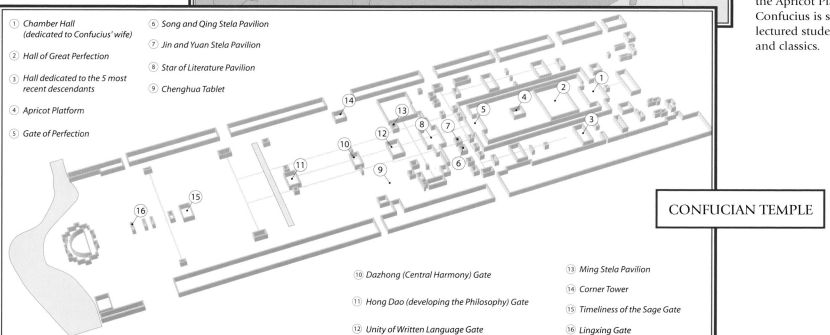

1. Chamber Hall (dedicated to Confucius' wife)
2. Hall of Great Perfection
3. Hall dedicated to the 5 most recent descendants
4. Apricot Platform
5. Gate of Perfection
6. Song and Qing Stela Pavilion
7. Jin and Yuan Stela Pavilion
8. Star of Literature Pavilion
9. Chenghua Tablet
10. Dazhong (Central Harmony) Gate
11. Hong Dao (developing the Philosophy) Gate
12. Unity of Written Language Gate
13. Ming Stela Pavilion
14. Corner Tower
15. Timeliness of the Sage Gate
16. Lingxing Gate

CONFUCIAN TEMPLE

CHINA UNDER THE MANCHU DYNASTY

1644 – 1840

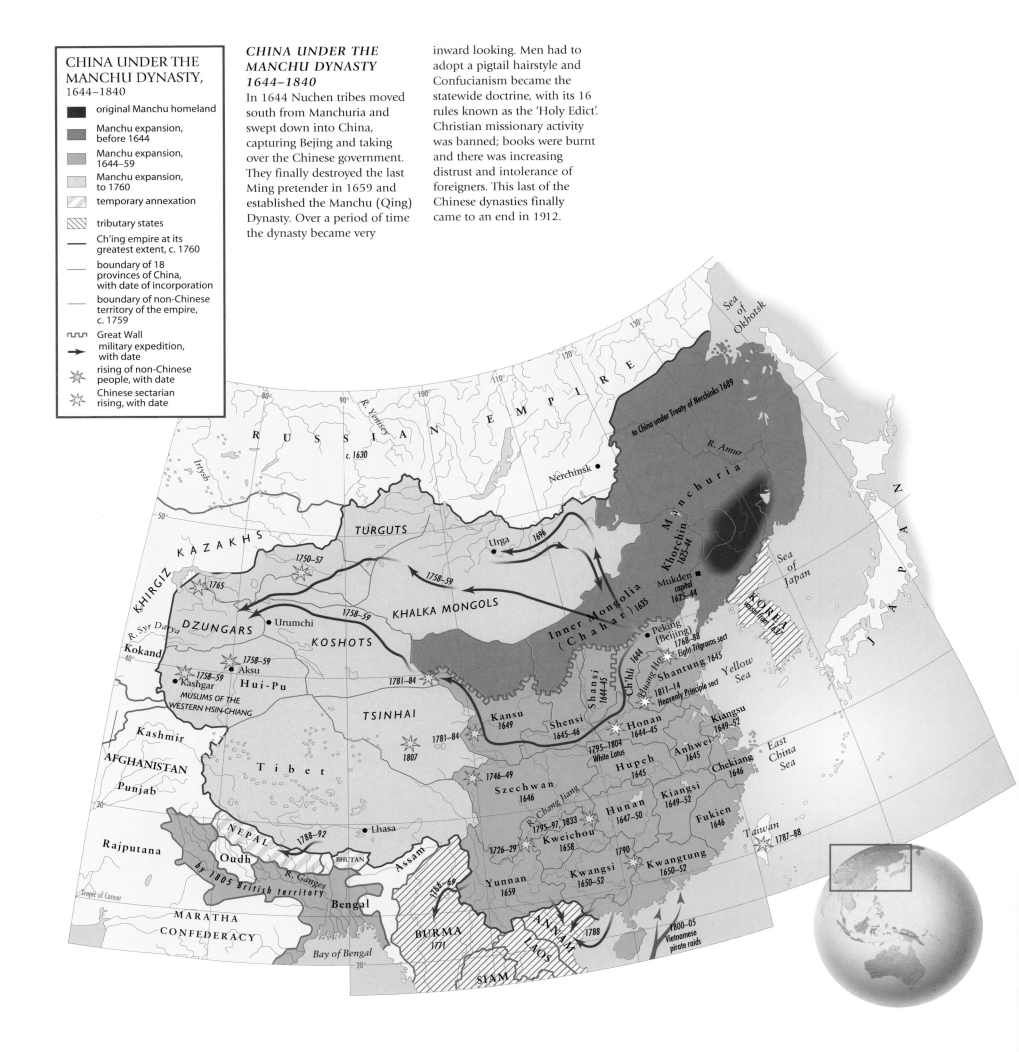

CHINA UNDER THE MANCHU DYNASTY, 1644–1840

- ■ original Manchu homeland
- ▨ Manchu expansion, before 1644
- ▨ Manchu expansion, 1644–59
- ▨ Manchu expansion, to 1760
- ▨ temporary annexation
- ▨ tributary states
- ── Ch'ing empire at its greatest extent, c. 1760
- ── boundary of 18 provinces of China, with date of incorporation
- ── boundary of non-Chinese territory of the empire, c. 1759
- ᘓᘓ Great Wall
- ➤ military expedition, with date
- ✹ rising of non-Chinese people, with date
- ✹ Chinese sectarian rising, with date

CHINA UNDER THE MANCHU DYNASTY 1644–1840

In 1644 Nuchen tribes moved south from Manchuria and swept down into China, capturing Bejing and taking over the Chinese government. They finally destroyed the last Ming pretender in 1659 and established the Manchu (Qing) Dynasty. Over a period of time the dynasty became very inward looking. Men had to adopt a pigtail hairstyle and Confucianism became the statewide doctrine, with its 16 rules known as the 'Holy Edict'. Christian missionary activity was banned; books were burnt and there was increasing distrust and intolerance of foreigners. This last of the Chinese dynasties finally came to an end in 1912.

PART 8

OTHER RELIGIONS

*I*n this section we have included a survey of the world's indigenous religions – those that are localised by nature – as well as three of the most well-known modern religions: Baha'ism, Scientology and Rastafarianism.

The world's indigenous religions are concentrated in northern Russia, Siberia, parts of North America (among the Inuit and Native Americans), sub-Saharan Africa, parts of South America and Australasia. What unites most of these areas is their remoteness from western civilisation, which helps to explain the survival of these ancient, local belief systems. Today, about six per cent of the world's population follow these indigenous religions.

The Baha'i is a worldwide religion founded by Bahá'u'lláh in 19th-century Persia (Iran). Baha'i teachings claim the unity of all religions and the unity of humankind. Baha'i views existing religions as aspects of God's divine plan, and practitioners strive for an end to class, racial and religious divisions.

Scientology is a system of beliefs and practices that emerged in the second half of the 20th century that focus on the development of the spirit. It has been a controversial belief system since its inception, with allegations of abuse, exploitation and harassment levelled at it, all of which it vehemently refutes.

Rastafarianism, which accepts Haile Selassie I, the former Emperor of Ethiopia, as its God, emerged among the working class of Jamaica in the early 1930s and promotes the superiority of African culture and civilisation and extols freedom from all types of slavery – physical, spiritual and psychological.

GLOBAL INDIGENOUS RELIGIONS

***INDIGENOUS
RELIGIONS 2007***

Indigenous religions are spread
throughout the world. They are
the religions that existed in
regions before colonial settlers
established their own religious
practices. These indigenous
religions are practised by about
6 per cent of the world's
population, but any one locality
membership is usually small or
is scattered over a very large
area. In many cases the present
concentrations exist for the
simple reason that there have
been few colonists. One
example is Central Australia,
where the Aboriginals have
developed a lifestyle that suits
a harsh environment that is
unendurable for the settlers.
A further example is the
religion of the Inuit people
of the Arctic, which believes
in the spirituality of natural
phenomena such as animals
and weather.

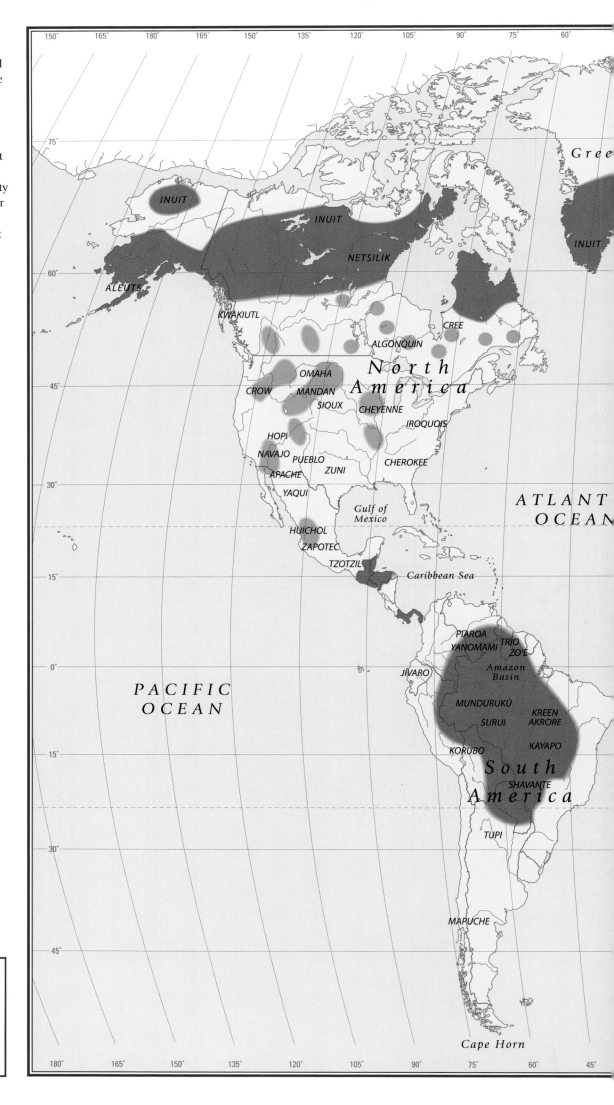

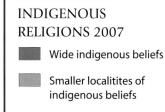

INDIGENOUS
RELIGIONS 2007

Wide indigenous beliefs

Smaller localitites of
indigenous beliefs

LAST 40,000 YEARS ABORIGINAL RELIGIONS; RELIGIONS OF THE PACIFIC

AUSTRALIAN ABORIGINAL RELIGIONS

Before colonisation in January 1788 there were between 250,000 and 500,000 Aborigines living throughout Australia. They spoke some 250 different languages, but their one unifying factor was their lifestyle based on Dreamtime beliefs. For thousands of years this lifestyle and their cultural practices remained virtually unchanged. With no written history, we must rely on archaeological evidence, but migration appears to have originally come from the north. There are a number of sacred sites. Uluru is a 600-metre-high monolith in the centre of the Australian desert and is the most sacred site in Aboriginal tradition. It is surrounded by ancestral sites associated with the Dreamtime era.

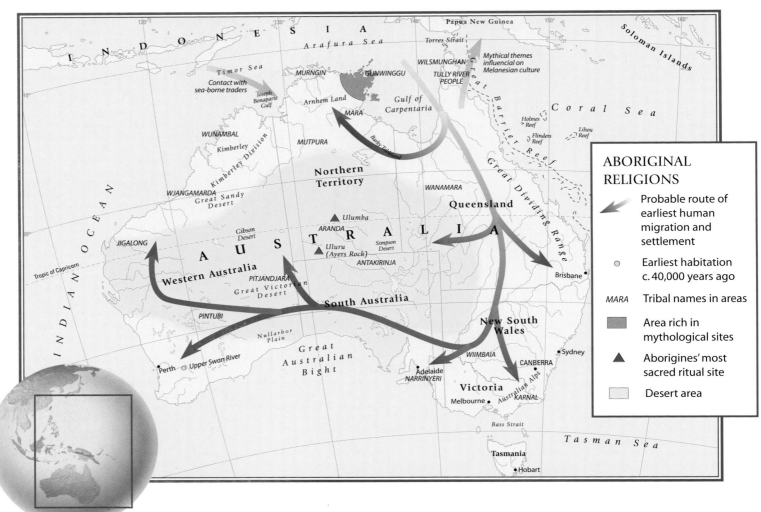

ABORIGINAL RELIGIONS

→ Probable route of earliest human migration and settlement

○ Earliest habitation c. 40,000 years ago

MARA Tribal names in areas

▨ Area rich in mythological sites

▲ Aborigines' most sacred ritual site

▢ Desert area

RELIGIONS OF THE PACIFIC C. 2000

The Polynesians were great seafarers and masters of navigation and their religion and myths strongly reflected the importance of nature and the sea. They believed that all things in nature, including humans, contained a sacred and supernatural power called *mana*. This could be good or evil and individuals, objects and animals contained varying amounts. Mana was sacred and ordinary people were not even allowed to touch the shadow of a great chief. Protestant and Catholic missionaries began to arrive in the South Pacific in the late 1700s. Today most of the islanders are Christian, following a wide variety of denominations.

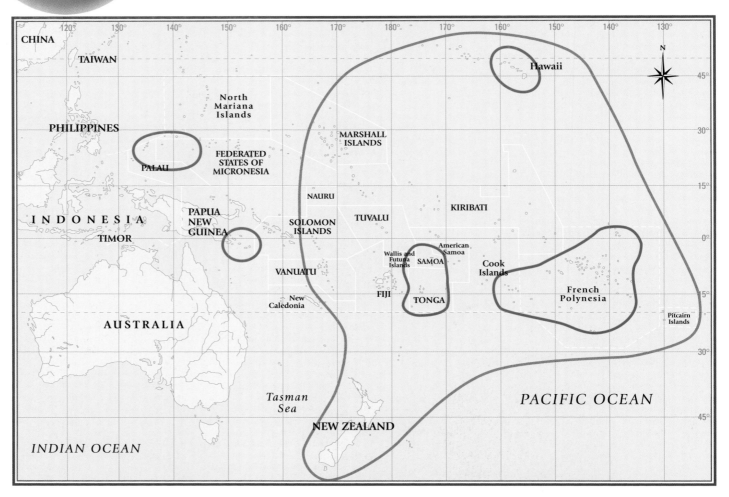

RELIGIONS OF THE PACIFIC c. 2000

⬭ Extent of Polynesian religions

⬭ Areas with temples or altars

AFRICAN HEALING CULTS AND SACRED KINGSHIPS

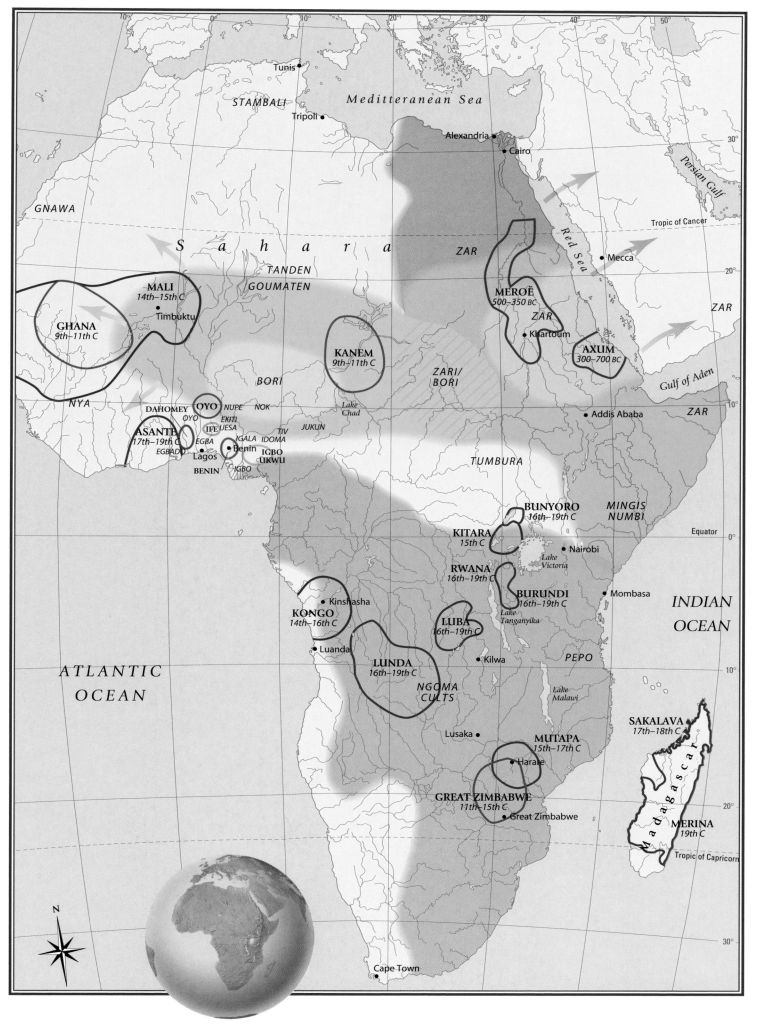

AFRICAN HEALING CULTS AND SACRED KINGSHIPS

From the beginning of time, it was always the extended family that provided social services. Older female relatives would act as midwives and there would always be a fund of experience and information to deal with various illnesses. Various healing cults grew up in Africa, such as the Zar Cult in north-eastern Africa. This was a ceremony conducted only by women and it was required to pacify evil spirits and cleanse women from afflictions caused by demons. Various periods also saw the growth of sacred kingships in different parts of Africa, where the chieftain was always regarded as a God.

AFRICAN HEALING CULTS AND SACRED KINGSHIPS

Healing Cults

■ Ngoma cults

□ Bori cult 1400

▨ Bori cults 15th–16th centuries

▨ Zar cult 1800

▨ Zar cult 1820s

▨ Zar cult 1850s

← Spread of Bori cult

← Spread of Zar cult

Sacred Kingships: approximate extent with dates

○ Pre-800

○ 9th–13th centuries

○ 14th–15th centuries

○ 16th–19th centuries

Nigeria and Benin: centre with political influence

○ Igbo Ukwu, 9th century

○ Ife, 15th century

○ Oyo, 15th–19th centuries

○ Benin, 15th–19th centuries

○ Dahomey, 18th–19th centuries

ZAR Peoples

INDIGENOUS RELIGIONS IN NORTH AMERICA BEFORE EUROPEAN SETTLEMENT

INDIGENOUS RELIGIONS IN NORTH AMERICA

Long before the arrival of European settlers, the diverse peoples of North America had developed their own languages and religions. They also developed distinctive lifestyles largely according to their environment. A common thread runs through each religion. There will be some form of spirit who must be worshipped or appeased. If things go badly wrong, such as a famine or an epidemic of illness, this will generally be because the deity is angry for some reason. Priests or medicine men played an important part in each religion, maintaining the welfare of the tribe and the individual through intercessions with good spirits.

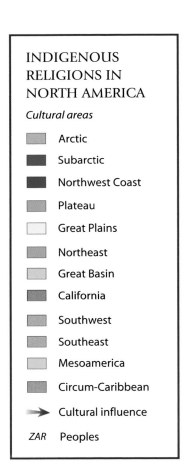

INDIGENOUS RELIGIONS IN NORTH AMERICA

Cultural areas

- Arctic
- Subarctic
- Northwest Coast
- Plateau
- Great Plains
- Northeast
- Great Basin
- California
- Southwest
- Southeast
- Mesoamerica
- Circum-Caribbean
- → Cultural influence
- ZAR Peoples

SCIENTOLOGY MISSIONS AND CHURCHES IN THE USA 2000

SCIENTOLOGY MISSIONS AND CHURCHES IN THE USA

Scientology was founded in the 1950s. It holds that an individual is basically an immortal spiritual being that has a body and a mind. Each individual is adversely affected by forgotten decisions left over from past trauma and stored mental energies. Scientology training and counselling aims to eliminate these adverse effects and to allow devotees to regain native spiritual abilities that have been lost over the course of many lifetimes. Many refer to the Church of Scientology as an unscrupulous cult that victimises its members. Although in the U.S. the first Church of Scientology was in New Jersey, today most are in California. In addition to churches there a number of missions. Missions are small churches that deliver basic services, but being small are unable to deliver the complete range. Once they can, they become churches.

BAHA'ISM IN THE WORLD

BAHA'ISM IN THE WORLD

The Baha'i faith is a religion that was founded in 19th century Persia and was established in America by Ibrahim George Kheiralla in 1894. There are now some six million members in more than 200 countries around the world. The latest estimated number of members in the US is 140,000, which is up from around 75,000 at the end of the 1970s. These numbers have been boosted partly by a recruitment drive among African Americans and partly by the number of Iranians that moved to the West Coast following persecution by Iran's hardline Shi'a government.

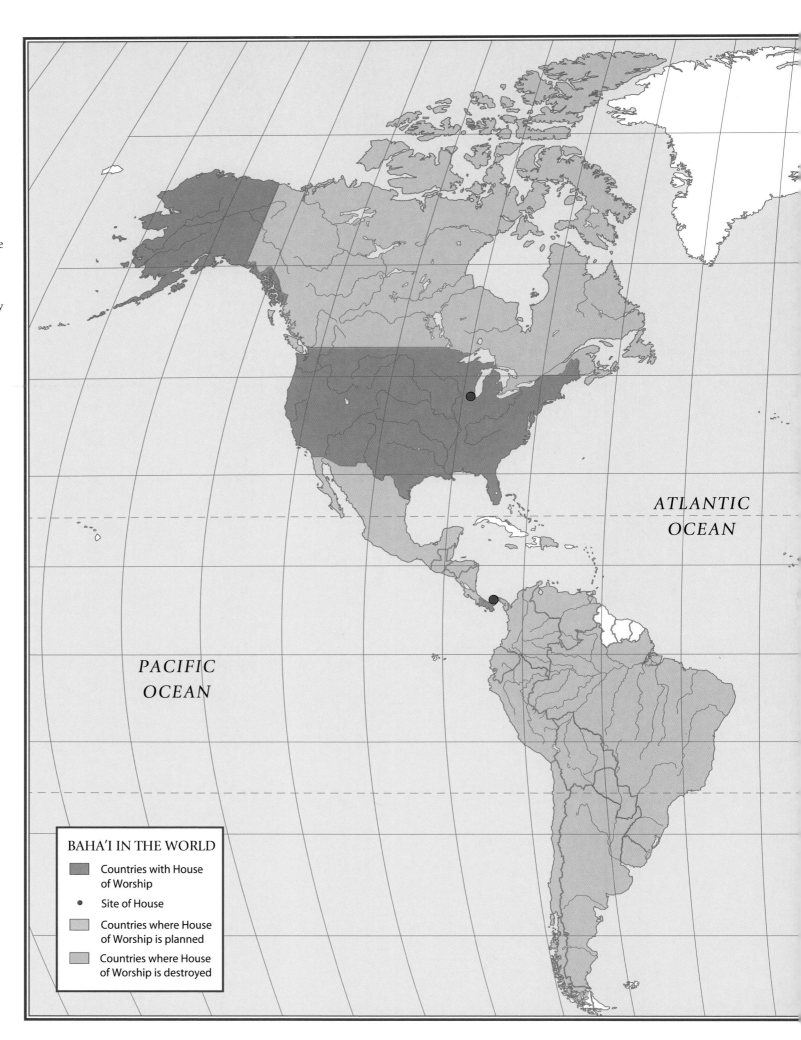

ATLANTIC
OCEAN

PACIFIC
OCEAN

BAHA'I IN THE WORLD

- Countries with House of Worship
- Site of House
- Countries where House of Worship is planned
- Countries where House of Worship is destroyed

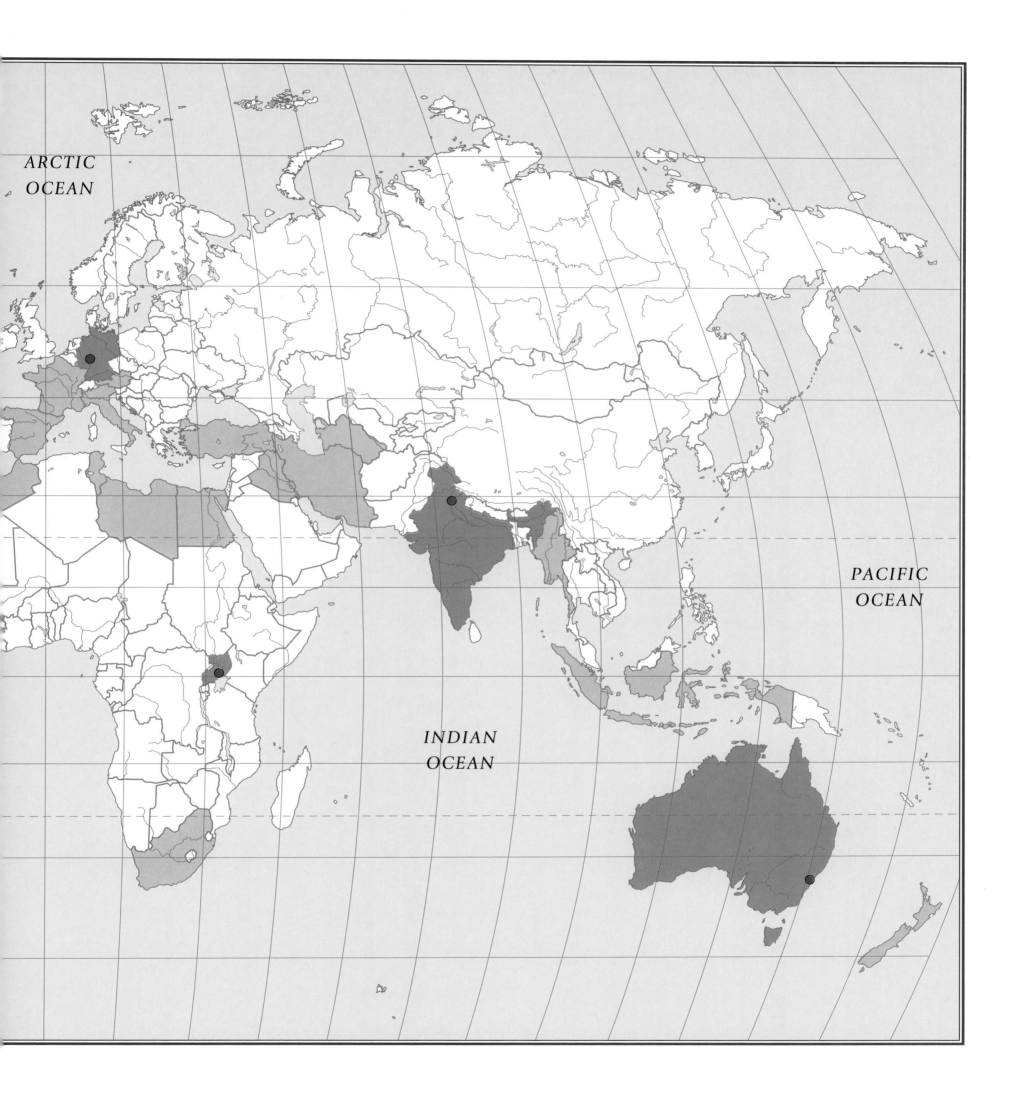

ARCTIC
OCEAN

PACIFIC
OCEAN

INDIAN
OCEAN

RASTAFARARIANISM

1930 – 1975

The Rastafarian movement
began in the early 1930s among
working class people in Jamaica.
The religion accepts as God
Haile Selassie I, the former
Emperor of Ethiopia, whose
original name was Ras Tafari
Makonnen. The movement has
spread throughout much of the
world, largely through interest
generated by reggae music.
Between five and ten per cent of
Jamaicans identify themselves
as Rastafarians and by the mid-
1970s there were around a
million Rastafarians worldwide.
Features of Rastafarianism
include dreadlocked hair, the
smoking of cannabis and the
wearing of hats coloured red,
yellow, green (the colours of the
Ethiopian flag) and black (to
symbolise pan-African unity).

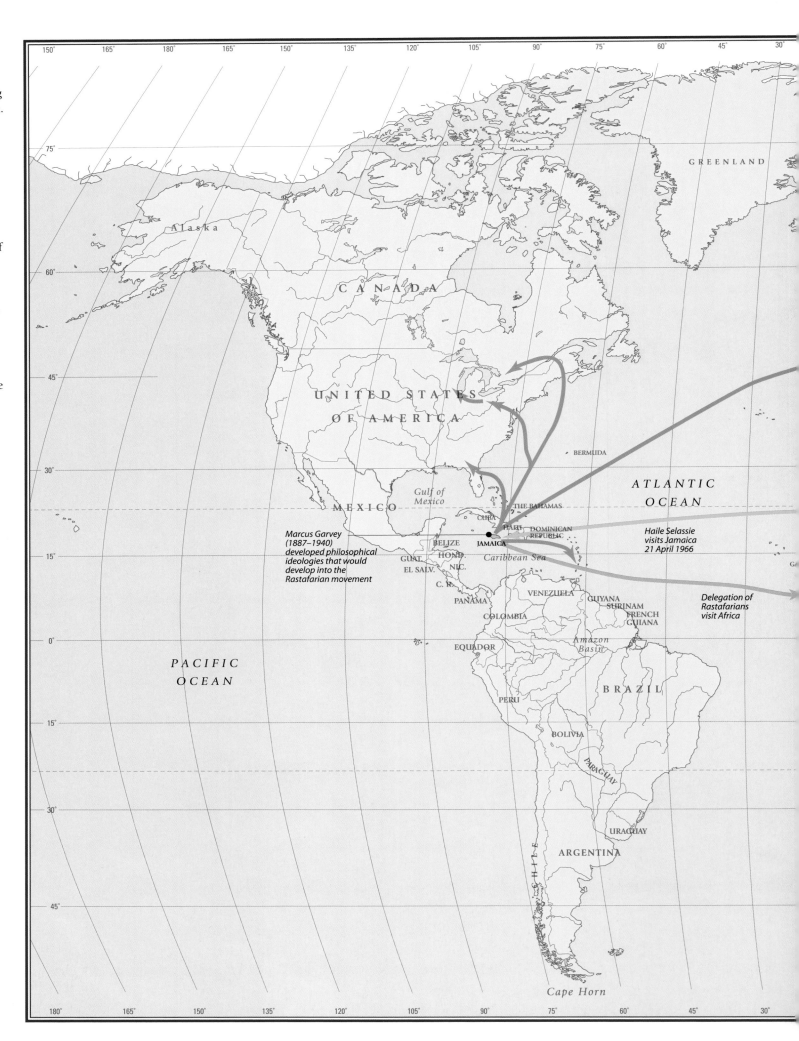

Marcus Garvey
(1887–1940)
developed philosophical
ideologies that would
develop into the
Rastafarian movement

Haile Selassie
visits Jamaica
21 April 1966

Delegation of
Rastafarians
visit Africa

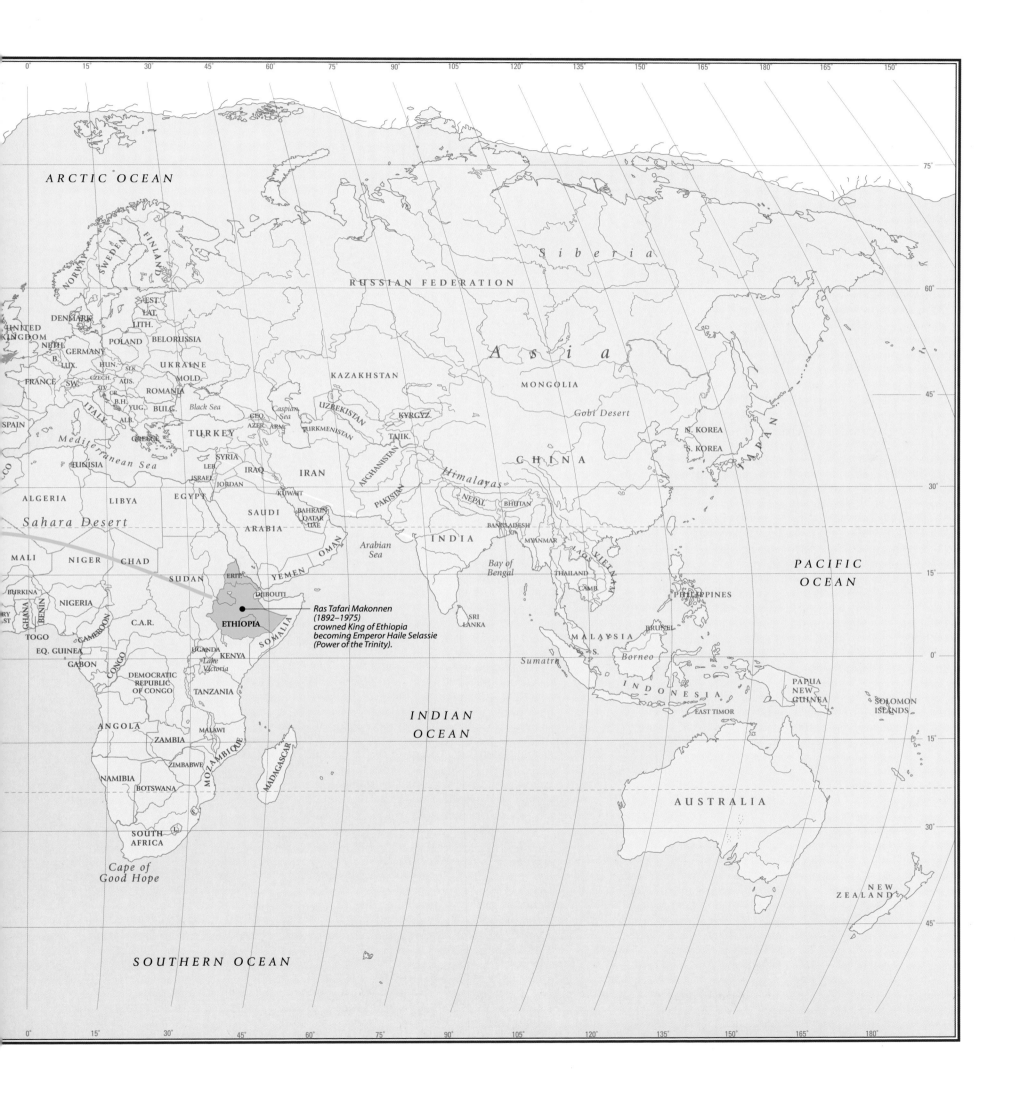

Ras Tafari Makonnen
(1892–1975)
crowned King of Ethiopia
becoming Emperor Haile Selassie
(Power of the Trinity).

MAPS AND RECONSTRUCTIONS